Modern Buddhism

Also by Geshe Kelsang Gyatso

Meaningful to Behold
Clear Light of Bliss
Heart of Wisdom
Universal Compassion
Joyful Path of Good Fortune
Guide to Dakini Land
The Bodhisattva Vow
Heart Jewel
Great Treasury of Merit
Introduction to Buddhism
Understanding the Mind
Tantric Grounds and Paths
Ocean of Nectar
Essence of Vajrayana
Living Meaningfully, Dying Joyfully
Eight Steps to Happiness
Transform Your Life
The New Meditation Handbook
How to Solve Our Human Problems
Mahamudra Tantra

Profits received by Tharpa Publications from
the sale of this book will be donated to the
NKT-IKBU International Temples Project
[Reg. Charity number 1015054 (England)]
A Buddhist Charity, Building for World Peace
www.kadampatemples.org

GESHE KELSANG GYATSO

Modern Buddhism

THE PATH OF COMPASSION
AND WISDOM

THARPA PUBLICATIONS
UK • US • CANADA
AUSTRALIA • HONG KONG

First published in 2011

The right of Geshe Kelsang Gyatso
to be identified as author of this work
has been asserted by him in accordance with
the Copyright, Designs, and Patents Act 1988.

Tharpa Publications UK Office   Tharpa Publications US Office
Conishead Priory   47 Sweeney Road
Ulverston, Cumbria   Glen Spey
LA12 9QQ, UK   NY 12737, USA

Tharpa Publications has offices around the world.
See page 391 for contact details.

Tharpa books are published in most major languages.
See page 391 for details.

© New Kadampa Tradition-International Kadampa Buddhist Union 2010

British Library Cataloguing in Publication Data
A catalogue record for this book is
available from the British Library.

ISBN 978-1906665-08-1 – hardback
ISBN 978-1906665-07-4 – paperback

Set in Palatino by Tharpa Publications.
Printed on Munken Pure 80 gsm acid-free paper
by CPI William Clowes, Beccles, NR34 7TL

Paper supplied from well-managed forests and other controlled
sources, and certified in accordance with the rules of the
Forest Stewardship Council.

Contents

Illustrations   viii

Preface   ix

PART ONE: SUTRA

Preliminary Explanation

What is Buddhism?   3

Buddhist Faith   7

Who are the Kadampas?   10

The Preciousness of Kadam Lamrim   20

The Path of a Person of Initial Scope

The Preciousness of our Human Life   25

What Does our Death Mean?   30

The Dangers of Lower Rebirth   32

Going for Refuge   35

What is Karma?   38

The Path of a Person of Middling Scope

What We Should Know   41

What We Should Abandon   56

What We Should Practise   58

What We Should Attain   61

The Path of a Person of Great Scope   63
The Supreme Good Heart – Bodhichitta   65
    Training in Affectionate Love   66
    Training in Cherishing Love   70
    Training in Wishing Love   77
    Training in Universal Compassion   79
    Training in Actual Bodhichitta   80
Training in the Path of Bodhichitta
    Training in the Six Perfections   83
    Training in Taking in Conjunction with the
       Practice of the Six Perfections   87
    Training in Giving in Conjunction with the
       Practice of the Six Perfections   92
Training in Ultimate Bodhichitta   97
    What is Emptiness?   98
    The Emptiness of our Body   100
    The Emptiness of our Mind   109
    The Emptiness of our I   110
    The Emptiness of the Eight Extremes   116
    Conventional and Ultimate Truths   121
    The Union of the Two Truths   127
    The Practice of Emptiness in our Daily Activities   132
    A Simple Training in Ultimate Bodhichitta   135
Examination of our Lamrim practice   141

PART TWO: TANTRA
The Preciousness of Tantra   145
The Tantra of Generation Stage   153
The Tantra of Completion Stage
    The Central Channel   159
    The Indestructible Drop   161
    The Indestructible Wind and Mind   162

How to Meditate on the Central Channel 165
How to Meditate on the Indestructible Drop 166
How to Meditate on the Indestructible Wind and Mind 167
The Completion Stage of Mahamudra 177
Great Bliss 181
The Practice of Heruka Body Mandala
The Lineage of these Instructions 193
What is the Heruka Body Mandala? 200
The Preliminary Practices 204
Training in the Generation Stage of Heruka
Body Mandala 223
Training in Completion Stage 234
The Instructions of Vajrayogini
The Yogas of Sleeping, Rising and Experiencing
Nectar 237
The Remaining Eight Yogas 243

Dedication 248

Appendix I – *Liberating Prayer* 249
Appendix II – *Prayers for Meditation* 251
Appendix III – An Explanation of Channels 261
Appendix IV – An Explanation of Inner Winds 267
Appendix V – *The Yoga of Buddha Heruka* 273
Appendix VI – *Blissful Journey* 291
Appendix VII – *Quick Path to Great Bliss* 315
Appendix VIII – The nada 363

Glossary 365
Bibliography 381
Study Programmes of Kadampa Buddhism 386
Tharpa Offices Worldwide 391
Index 393
Further Reading 419

Illustrations

Buddha Shakyamuni   2

Atisha   24

Je Tsongkhapa   64

Buddha of Compassion   96

Arya Tara   140

Wisdom Dharma Protector   144

Twelve-armed Heruka   152

Ghantapa   178

Guru Sumati Buddha Heruka   210

Buddha Vajradhara   218

Buddha Vajradharma   224

Venerable Vajrayogini   236

Mandala of Vajrayogini   244

Naropa   260

Tantric commitment objects: inner offering
     in kapala, vajra, bell, damaru, mala   274

Je Phabongkhapa   276

Kyabje Trijang Rinpoche   292

Preface

The instructions given in this book are scientific methods for improving our human nature and qualities through developing the capacity of our mind. In recent years our knowledge of modern technology has increased considerably, and as a result we have witnessed remarkable material progress, but there has not been a corresponding increase in human happiness. There is no less suffering in the world today, and there are no fewer problems. Indeed, it might be said that there are now more problems and greater dangers than ever before. This shows that the cause of happiness and the solution to our problems do not lie in knowledge of material things. Happiness and suffering are states of mind and so their main causes are not to be found outside the mind. If we want to be truly happy and free from suffering, we must learn how to control our mind.

When things go wrong in our life and we encounter difficult situations, we tend to regard the situation itself as our problem, but in reality whatever problems we experience come from the side of the mind. If we were to respond to difficult situations with a positive or peaceful mind they would not be problems for us; indeed, we may even come to regard them as challenges or opportunities for growth and development. Problems arise only if we respond to difficulties with a negative state of mind. Therefore, if we want to be free from problems, we must transform our mind.

Buddha taught that the mind has the power to create all pleasant and unpleasant objects. The world is the result of the karma, or actions, of the beings who inhabit it. A pure world is the result of pure actions and an impure world is the result of impure actions. Since all actions are created by mind, ultimately everything, including the world itself, is created by mind. There is no creator other than the mind.

Normally we say 'I created such and such', or 'He or she created such and such', but the actual creator of everything is the mind. We are like servants of our mind; whenever it wants to do something, we have to do it without any choice. Since beginningless time until now we have been under the control of our mind, without any freedom; but if we sincerely practise the instructions given in this book we can reverse this situation and gain control over our mind. Only then shall we have real freedom.

Through studying many Buddhist texts we may become a renowned scholar; but if we do not put Buddha's teachings into practice, our understanding of Buddhism will remain hollow, with no power to solve our own or others' problems. Expecting intellectual understanding of Buddhist texts alone to solve our problems is like a sick person hoping to cure his or her illness through merely reading medical instructions without actually taking the medicine. As Buddhist Master Shantideva says:

> We need to put Buddha's teachings, the Dharma, into
> practice
> Because nothing can be accomplished just by reading words.

A sick man will never be cured of his illness
Through merely reading medical instructions!

Each and every living being has the sincere wish to avoid all suffering and problems permanently. Normally we try to do this by using external methods, but no matter how successful we are from a worldly point of view – no matter how materially wealthy, powerful or highly respected we become – we shall never find permanent liberation from suffering and problems. In reality, all the problems we experience day to day come from our self-cherishing and self-grasping – misconceptions that exaggerate our own importance. However, because we do not understand this, we usually blame others for our problems, and this just makes them worse. From these two basic misconceptions arise all our other delusions, such as anger and attachment, causing us to experience endless problems.

I pray that everyone who reads this book may experience deep inner peace, or peace of mind, and accomplish the real meaning of human life. I particularly would like to encourage everyone to read specifically the chapter *Training in Ultimate Bodhichitta*. Through carefully reading and contemplating this chapter again and again with a positive mind, you will gain very profound knowledge, or wisdom, which will bring great meaning to your life.

Geshe Kelsang Gyatso

PART ONE:

Sutra

Buddha Shakyamuni

Preliminary Explanation

WHAT IS BUDDHISM?

Buddhism is the practice of Buddha's teachings, also called 'Dharma', which means 'protection'. By practising Buddha's teachings, living beings are permanently protected from suffering. The founder of Buddhism is Buddha Shakyamuni, who showed the manner of accomplishing the ultimate goal of living beings, the attainment of enlightenment, at Bodh Gaya in India in BC 589. At the request of the gods Indra and Brahma, Buddha then began to expound his profound teachings, or 'turned the Wheel of Dharma'. Buddha gave eighty-four thousand teachings, and from these precious teachings Buddhism developed in this world.

Today we can see many different forms of Buddhism, such as Zen and Theravada Buddhism. All these different aspects are practices of Buddha's teachings, and all are equally precious; they are just different presentations. In this book I shall explain about Buddhism according to the Kadampa tradition, which I have studied and practised. This explanation is not given for the purpose of intellectual understanding, but for gaining profound realizations through which we can solve our daily problems of delusions and accomplish the real meaning of our human life.

There are two stages to the practice of Buddha's teachings – the practices of Sutra and Tantra – both of which are explained in this book. Although the instructions presented here come from Buddha Shakyamuni, and Buddhist Masters such as Atisha, Je Tsongkhapa and our present Teachers, this book is called *Modern Buddhism* because its presentation of Dharma is designed especially for the people of the modern world. My intention in writing this book is to give the reader strong encouragement to develop and maintain compassion and wisdom. If everyone sincerely practises the path of compassion and wisdom all their problems will be solved and never arise again; I guarantee this.

We need to practise Buddha's teachings because there is no other real method to solve human problems. For example, because modern technology often causes more suffering and dangers, it cannot be a real method to solve human problems. Although we want to be happy all the time we do not know how to do this, and we are always destroying our own happiness by developing anger, negative views and negative intentions. We are always trying to escape from problems, even in our dreams, but we do not know how to liberate ourself from suffering and problems. Because we do not understand the real nature of things, we are always creating our own suffering and problems by performing inappropriate or non-virtuous actions.

The source of all our daily problems is our delusions such as attachment. Since beginningless time, because we have been so attached to the fulfilment of our own wishes, we have performed various kinds of non-virtuous actions – actions that harm others. As a result we continually experience various kinds of suffering and miserable conditions in life after life without end. When our wishes are not fulfilled we usually experience unpleasant feelings, such as unhappiness or depression; this is our own problem because we are so attached to the fulfilment of our wishes. When we lose a close friend we experience pain and unhappiness, but this is only because of our attachment to this friend. When we lose our possessions, position or reputation we experience unhappiness and depression because we are so attached to these things. If we had no attachment there would be no basis to experience these problems. Many people are engaged in fighting, criminal actions and even warfare; all these actions arise from their strong attachment to the fulfilment of their own wishes. In this way we can see that there is not a single problem experienced by living beings that does not come from their attachment. This proves that unless we control our attachment our problems will never cease.

The method for controlling our attachment and other delusions is the practice of Buddha's teachings. By practising Buddha's teachings on renunciation we can solve our daily problems that arise from attachment; by practising Buddha's teachings on universal compassion we can solve our daily problems that arise from anger; and by practising Buddha's teachings on the profound view of emptiness, ultimate truth, we can solve our daily problems that arise from ignorance. How to develop renunciation, universal compassion and the wisdom realizing emptiness will be explained in this book.

The root of attachment and of all our suffering is self-grasping ignorance, ignorance about the way things actually exist. Without relying upon Buddha's teachings we cannot recognize this ignorance; and without practising Buddha's teachings on emptiness we cannot abandon it. Thus we shall have no opportunity to attain liberation from suffering and problems. Through this explanation we can understand that, since all living beings, whether human or non-human, Buddhist or non-Buddhist, wish to be free from suffering and problems, they all need to practise Dharma. There is no other method to accomplish this aim.

We should understand that our problems do not exist outside of ourself, but are part of our mind that experiences unpleasant feelings. When our car, for example, has a problem we usually say 'I have a problem', but in reality it is the car's problem and not our problem. The car's problem is an outer problem, and our problem, which is our own unpleasant feeling, is an inner problem. These two problems are completely different. We need to solve the car's problem by repairing it, and we need to solve our own problem by controlling our attachment to the car. Even if we keep solving the car's problems, if we are unable to control our attachment to the car we shall continually experience new problems related to the car. It is the same with our house, our money, our relationships and so forth. Because of mistakenly believing that outer problems are their own problems, most people seek ultimate refuge in the wrong objects. As a result, their suffering and problems never end.

For as long as we are unable to control our delusions such as attachment, we shall have to experience suffering and problems continually, throughout this life and in life after life without end. Because we are bound tightly by the rope of attachment to samsara, the cycle of impure life, it is impossible for us to be free from suffering and problems unless we practise Dharma. Understanding this, we should develop and maintain the strong wish to abandon the root of suffering – attachment and self-grasping ignorance. This wish is called 'renunciation', and arises from our wisdom.

Buddha's teachings are scientific methods to solve the problems of all living beings permanently. By putting his teachings into practice we shall be able to control our attachment, and because of this we shall be permanently free from all our suffering and problems. From this alone we can understand how precious and important his teachings, the Dharma, are for everyone. As mentioned above, because all our problems come from attachment, and there is no method to control attachment other than Dharma, it is clear that only Dharma is the actual method to solve our daily problems.

BUDDHIST FAITH

For Buddhists, faith in Buddha Shakyamuni is their spiritual life; it is the root of all Dharma realizations. If we have deep faith in Buddha we shall naturally develop the strong wish to practise his teachings. With this wish we shall definitely apply effort in our Dharma practice, and with strong effort we shall accomplish permanent liberation from the suffering of this life and countless future lives.

The attainment of permanent liberation from suffering depends upon effort in our Dharma practice, which depends upon the strong wish to practise Dharma, which in turn depends upon deep faith in Buddha. Therefore we can understand that if we truly want to experience great benefit from our practice of Buddhism we need to develop and maintain deep faith in Buddha.

How do we develop and maintain this faith? First, we should know why we need to attain permanent liberation from suffering. It is not enough just to experience temporary liberation from a particular suffering; all living beings, including animals, experience temporary liberation from particular sufferings. Animals experience temporary liberation from human suffering, and humans experience temporary liberation from animal suffering. At the moment we may be free from physical suffering and mental pain, but this is only temporary. Later in this life and in our countless future lives we shall have to experience unbearable physical suffering and mental pain, again and again without end. In the cycle of impure life, samsara, no one has permanent liberation; everyone has to experience continually the sufferings of sickness, ageing, death and uncontrolled rebirth, in life after life without end.

Within this cycle of impure life there are various realms or impure worlds into which we can be reborn: the three lower realms – the animal, hungry ghost and hell realms – and the three higher realms – the god, demi-god and human realms. Of all impure worlds, hell is the worst; it is the world that appears to the very worst kind of mind. The world of an animal is less impure, and the world that appears to human beings is less impure than the world that appears to animals. However, there is suffering within every realm. When we take rebirth as a human being we have to experience human suffering, when we take rebirth as an animal we have to experience animal suffering, and when we take rebirth as a hell being we have to experience the suffering of a hell being. Through contemplating this we shall realize that just experiencing a temporary liberation from particular sufferings is not good enough; we definitely need to attain permanent liberation from the sufferings of this life and all our countless future lives.

How can we accomplish this? Only by putting Buddha's teachings into practice. This is because only Buddha's teachings are the actual methods to abandon our self-grasping ignorance, the source of all our suffering. In his teaching called *King of Concentration Sutra* Buddha says:

> A magician creates various things
> Such as horses, elephants and so forth.
> His creations do not actually exist;
> You should know all things in the same way.

This teaching alone has the power to liberate all living beings permanently from their suffering. Through practising and realizing this teaching, which is explained more fully in the chapter *Training in Ultimate Bodhichitta*, we can permanently eradicate the root of all our suffering, our self-grasping ignorance. When this happens we shall experience the supreme permanent peace of mind, known as 'nirvana', permanent liberation from suffering, which is our deepest wish and the real meaning of human life. This is the main purpose of Buddha's teachings.

Through understanding this we shall deeply appreciate the great kindness of Buddha to all living beings in giving profound methods to achieve permanent freedom from the cycle of suffering of sickness, ageing, death and rebirth. Even our mother does not have the compassion that wishes to liberate us from these sufferings; only Buddha has this compassion for all living beings without exception. Buddha is actually liberating us by revealing the wisdom path that leads us to the ultimate goal of human life. We should contemplate this point again and again until we develop deep faith in Buddha. This faith is the object of our meditation; we should transform our mind into faith in Buddha and maintain it single-pointedly for as long as possible. By continually practising this contemplation and meditation we shall maintain deep faith in Buddha day and night, throughout our life.

One of Buddha's main functions is to bestow mental peace upon each and every living being by giving blessings. By themselves living beings are unable to cultivate a peaceful mind; it is only through receiving Buddha's blessings upon their mental continuum that living beings, including even animals, can experience peace of mind. When their minds are peaceful and calm they are really happy; but if their minds are not peaceful they are not happy, even if their external conditions are perfect. This proves that happiness depends upon mental peace, and since this depends upon receiving Buddha's blessings, Buddha is therefore the source of all happiness. Understanding and contemplating this we should develop and maintain deep faith in Buddha, and generate the strong wish to practise his teachings in general and Kadam Lamrim in particular.

WHO ARE THE KADAMPAS?

'Ka' refers to Buddha's teachings and 'dam' refers to Atisha's instructions on Lamrim (the *Stages of the Path to Enlightenment*, also known as *Kadam Lamrim*). 'Kadam' therefore refers to the union of Buddha's teachings and Atisha's instructions, and sincere practitioners of Kadam Lamrim are called 'Kadampas'. There are two Kadampa traditions, the ancient and the new. Practitioners of the ancient Kadampa tradition appeared to emphasize the practice of Kadam Lamrim of Sutra more than the practice of Tantra. Later, Je Tsongkhapa and his disciples emphasized the practice of Kadam Lamrim of both Sutra and Tantra equally. This new tradition founded by Je Tsongkhapa is called the new Kadampa tradition.

Kadampas sincerely rely upon Buddha Shakyamuni because Buddha is the source of Kadam Lamrim; they sincerely rely upon Avalokiteshvara, the Buddha of Compassion, and upon the Wisdom Dharma Protector, indicating that their main practice is compassion and wisdom; and they sincerely rely upon Arya Tara because she promised Atisha that she would take special care of Kadampa practitioners in the future. For this reason, these four enlightened holy beings are called the 'Four Kadampa Guru Deities'.

The founder of the Kadampa tradition is the great Buddhist Master and scholar, Atisha. Atisha was born in AD 982 as a prince in East Bengal, India. His father's name was Kalyanashri (Glorious Virtue) and his mother's name was Prabhavarti Shrimati (Glorious Radiance). He was the second of three sons and when he was born he was given the name Chandragarbha (Moon Essence). The name Atisha, which means Peace, was given to him later by the Tibetan king Jangchub Ö because he was always calm and peaceful.

When he was still a child Chandragarbha's parents took him to visit a temple. All along the way thousands of people gathered to see if they could catch a glimpse of the prince. When he saw them Chandragarbha asked 'Who are these people?' and his parents replied 'They are all our subjects.' Compassion arose spontaneously in the prince's heart and he prayed 'May all these people enjoy good fortune as great as my own.' Whenever he met anyone the wish arose naturally in his mind, 'May this person find happiness and be free from suffering.'

Even as a small boy Chandragarbha received visions of Arya Tara, a female enlightened being. Sometimes, while he was on his mother's lap, blue upali flowers would fall from the sky and he would begin to speak, as if to the flowers. Yogis later explained to his mother that the blue flowers she had seen were a sign that Tara was appearing to her son and speaking to him.

When the prince was older his parents wanted to arrange a marriage for him, but Tara advised him 'If you become attached to your kingdom you will be like an elephant when he sinks into mud and cannot lift himself out again because he is so huge and heavy. Do not become attached to this life. Study and practise Dharma. You have been a Spiritual Guide in many of your previous lives and in this life also you will become a Spiritual Guide.' Inspired by these words Chandragarbha developed a very strong interest in studying and practising Dharma and he became determined to attain all the realizations of Buddha's teachings. He knew that to accomplish his aim he would need to find a fully qualified Spiritual Guide. At first he approached a famous Buddhist Teacher called Jetari, who lived nearby, and requested Dharma instructions on how to find release from samsara. Jetari gave him instructions on refuge and bodhichitta, and then told him that if he wanted to practise purely he should go to Nalanda and learn from the Spiritual Guide Bodhibhadra.

When he met Bodhibhadra the prince said 'I realize that samsara is meaningless and that only liberation and full enlightenment are really worthwhile. Please give Dharma instructions that will lead me quickly to the state beyond sorrow, nirvana.' Bodhibhadra gave him brief instructions on generating bodhichitta and then advised 'If you wish to practise Dharma purely you should seek the Spiritual Guide Vidyakokila.' Bodhibhadra knew that Vidyakokila was a great meditator who had gained a perfect realization of emptiness and was very skilful in teaching the stages of the profound path.

Vidyakokila gave Chandragarbha complete instructions on both the profound path and the vast path and then sent him to study with the Spiritual Guide Avadhutipa. Avadhutipa did not give guidance immediately but told the prince to go to Rahulagupta to receive instructions on *Hevajra* and *Heruka Tantras* and then to return to him to receive more detailed instructions on Tantra, or Secret Mantra. Rahulagupta gave Chandragarbha the secret name Janavajra (Indestructible Wisdom) and his first empowerment, which was into the practice of Hevajra. Then he told him to go home and obtain the consent of his parents.

Although the prince was not attached to worldly life it was still important for him to have his parents' permission to practise in the way he wished. Thus he returned to his parents and said 'If I practise Dharma purely, then, as Arya Tara has predicted, I shall be able to repay your kindness and the kindness of all living beings. If I can do this my human life will not have been wasted. Otherwise, even though I may spend all my time in a glorious palace, my life will be meaningless. Please give me your consent to leave the kingdom and dedicate my whole life to the practice of Dharma.' Chandragarbha's father was unhappy to hear this and wanted to prevent his son from giving up his prospects as future king, but his mother was delighted to hear that her son wished to dedicate his life to Dharma. She remembered that at his birth there had been marvellous signs, such as rainbows, and she remembered miracles like the blue upali flowers falling from the sky. She knew that her son was no ordinary prince and she gave her permission without hesitation. In time, the king also granted his son's wish.

Chandragarbha returned to Avadhutipa and for seven years he received instructions on Secret Mantra. He became so accomplished that on one occasion he developed pride, thinking 'Probably I know more about Secret Mantra than anyone else in the whole world.' That night in his dream Dakinis came and showed him rare scriptures that he had never seen before. They asked him 'What do these texts mean?', but he had no idea. When he awoke, his pride was gone.

Later, Chandragarbha began to think that he should imitate Avadhutipa's way of practising and strive as a layman to attain enlightenment quickly by practising Mahamudra depending upon an action mudra; but he received a vision of Heruka who told him that if he were to take ordination he would be able to help countless beings and spread Dharma far and wide. That night he dreamt that he was following a procession of monks in the presence of Buddha Shakyamuni, who was wondering why Chandragarbha had not yet taken ordination. When he awoke from his dream he resolved to become a monk. He received ordination from Shilarakshita, and was given the name Dhipamkara Shrijana.

From the Spiritual Guide Dharmarakshita, Dhipamkara Shrijana received extensive instructions on the *Seven Sets of Abhidharma* and the *Ocean of Great Explanation* – texts written from the point of view of the Vaibhashika system. In this way he mastered the Hinayana teachings.

Still not satisfied, Dhipamkara Shrijana went to receive detailed instructions at Bodh Gaya. One day he overheard a conversation between two ladies who were in fact emanations of Arya Tara. The younger asked the elder 'What is the principal method for attaining enlightenment quickly?' and the elder replied 'It is bodhichitta.' Hearing this, Dhipamkara Shrijana became determined to attain the precious bodhichitta. Later, while he was circumambulating the great stupa at Bodh Gaya, a statue of Buddha Shakyamuni spoke to him, saying 'If you wish to attain enlightenment quickly you must gain experience of compassion, love and the precious bodhichitta.' His desire to realize bodhichitta then became intense. He heard that the

Spiritual Guide Serlingpa, who was living far away in a place called Serling, in Sumatra, had attained a very special experience of bodhichitta and was able to give instructions on the *Perfection of Wisdom Sutras*.

It took Dhipamkara Shrijana thirteen months to sail to Sumatra. When he arrived there he offered Serlingpa a mandala and made his requests. Serlingpa told him that the instructions would take twelve years to transmit. Dhipamkara Shrijana stayed in Sumatra for twelve years and finally gained the precious realization of bodhichitta. Then he returned to India.

By relying upon his Spiritual Guides, Atisha gained special knowledge of the three sets of Buddha's teachings – the set of moral discipline, the set of discourses and the set of wisdom; and of the four classes of Tantra. He also mastered arts and sciences such as poetry, rhetoric and astrology, was an excellent physician, and was very skilled in crafts and technology.

Atisha also gained all the realizations of the three higher trainings: training in higher moral discipline, training in higher concentration and training in higher wisdom. Since all the stages of Sutra, such as the six perfections, the five paths, the ten grounds; and all the stages of Tantra, such as generation stage and completion stage, are included within the three higher trainings, Atisha therefore gained all the realizations of the stages of the path.

There are three types of higher moral discipline: the higher moral discipline of the Pratimoksha vows, or vows of individual liberation; the higher moral discipline of the Bodhisattva vow; and the higher moral discipline of the Tantric vows. The vows to abandon two hundred and fifty-three downfalls, undertaken by a fully ordained monk, are amongst the Pratimoksha vows. Atisha never broke any one of these. This shows that he possessed very strong mindfulness and very great conscientiousness. He also kept purely the Bodhisattva vow to avoid eighteen root downfalls and forty-six secondary downfalls, and he kept purely all his Tantric vows.

The attainments of higher concentration and higher wisdom are divided into common and uncommon. A common attainment is one that is gained by practitioners of both Sutra and Tantra, and an uncommon attainment is one that is gained only by practitioners of Tantra. By training in higher concentration Atisha gained the common concentration of tranquil abiding and, based on that, clairvoyance, miracle powers and the common virtues. He also attained uncommon concentrations such as the concentrations of generation stage and completion stage of Secret Mantra. By training in higher wisdom Atisha gained the common realization of emptiness, and the uncommon realizations of example clear light and meaning clear light of Secret Mantra.

Atisha mastered the teachings of both Hinayana and Mahayana and was held in respect by Teachers of both traditions. He was like a king, the crown ornament of Indian Buddhists, and was regarded as a second Buddha.

Before Atisha's time the thirty-seventh king of Tibet, Trisong Detsen (circa AD 754-97), had invited Padmasambhava, Shantarakshita and other Buddhist Teachers from India to Tibet, and through their influence pure Dharma had flourished; but some years later a Tibetan king called Lang Darma (circa AD 836) destroyed the pure Dharma in Tibet and abolished the Sangha. Until that time most of the kings had been religious, but it was a dark age in Tibet during Lang Darma's evil reign. About seventy years after his death Dharma began to flourish once again in the upper part of Tibet through the efforts of great Teachers such as the translator Rinchen Sangpo, and it also began to flourish in the lower part of Tibet through the efforts of a great Teacher called Gongpa Rabsel. Gradually, Dharma spread to central Tibet.

At that time there was no pure practice of the union of Sutra and Tantra. The two were thought to be contradictory, like fire and water. When people practised Sutra they abandoned Tantra, and when they practised Tantra they abandoned Sutra, including even the rules of the Vinaya. False teachers came from India wishing to procure some of Tibet's plentiful gold. Pretending to be Spiritual Guides and Yogis they introduced perversions such as black magic, creating apparitions, sexual practices and ritual murder. These malpractices became quite widespread.

A king called Yeshe Ö and his nephew Jangchub Ö, who lived in Ngari in western Tibet, were greatly concerned about what was happening to the Dharma in their country. The king wept when he thought of the purity of Dharma in former times compared with the impure Dharma now being practised. He was grieved to see how hardened and uncontrolled the minds of the people had become. He thought 'How wonderful it would be if pure Dharma were to flourish once again in Tibet to tame the minds of our people.' To fulfil this wish he sent Tibetans to India to learn Sanskrit and train in Dharma, but many of these people were unable to endure the hot climate. The few who survived learnt Sanskrit and trained very well in Dharma. Amongst them was the translator Rinchen Sangpo, who received many instructions and then returned to Tibet.

Since this plan had not met with much success Yeshe Ö decided to invite an authentic Teacher from India. He sent a group of Tibetans to India with a large quantity of gold, and gave them the task of seeking out the most qualified Spiritual

Guide in India. He advised them all to study Dharma and gain perfect knowledge of Sanskrit. These Tibetans suffered all the hardships of climate and travel in order to accomplish his wishes. Some of them became famous translators. They translated many scriptures and sent them to the king, to his great delight.

When these Tibetans returned to Tibet they informed Yeshe Ö, 'In India there are many very learned Buddhist Teachers, but the most distinguished and sublime of all is Dhipamkara Shrijana. We would like to invite him to Tibet, but he has thousands of disciples in India.' When Yeshe Ö heard the name 'Dhipamkara Shrijana' he was pleased, and became determined to invite this Master to Tibet. Since he had already used most of his gold and more was now needed to invite Dhipamkara Shrijana to Tibet, the king set off on an expedition to search for more gold. When he arrived at one of the borders a hostile non-Buddhist king captured him and threw him into prison. When the news reached Jangchub Ö he considered 'I am powerful enough to wage war on this king, but if I do so many people will suffer and I shall have to commit many harmful, destructive actions.' He decided to make an appeal for his uncle's release, but the king responded by saying 'I shall release your uncle only if you either become my subject or bring me a quantity of gold as heavy as your uncle's body.' With great difficulty Jangchub Ö managed to gather gold equal in weight to his uncle's body, less the weight of his head. Since the king demanded the extra amount, Jangchub Ö prepared to go in search of more gold, but before he set out he visited his uncle. He found Yeshe Ö physically weak but in a good state of mind. Jangchub Ö spoke through the bars of the prison 'Soon I shall be able to release you for I have managed to collect almost all the gold.' Yeshe Ö replied 'Please do not treat me as if I were important. You must not give the gold to this hostile king. Send it all to India and offer it to Dhipamkara Shrijana. This is my greatest wish. I shall give my life joyfully for the sake of restoring pure Dharma in Tibet. Please deliver this message to Dhipamkara Shrijana. Let him know that I have given my life to invite him to Tibet. Since he has compassion for the Tibetan people, when he receives this message he will accept our invitation.'

Jangchub Ö sent the translator Nagtso together with some companions to India with the gold. When they met Dhipamkara Shrijana they told him what was happening in Tibet and how the people wanted to invite a Spiritual Guide from India. They told him how much gold the king had sent as an offering and how many Tibetans had died for the sake of restoring pure Dharma. They told him how Yeshe Ö had sacrificed his life to bring him to Tibet. When they had made their request Dhipamkara Shrijana considered what they had said and accepted their invitation. Although he had many disciples in India and was working very hard there for the sake of Dharma, he knew that there was no pure Dharma in Tibet. He had also received a prediction from Arya Tara that if he were to go to Tibet he would benefit countless living beings. Compassion arose in his heart when he thought how many Tibetans had died in India, and he was especially moved by the sacrifice of Yeshe Ö.

Dhipamkara Shrijana had to make his way to Tibet in secret, for had his Indian disciples known that he was leaving India they would have prevented him. He said that he was making a pilgrimage to Nepal, but from Nepal he passed into Tibet. When his Indian disciples eventually realized that he was not going to return they protested that the Tibetans were thieves who had stolen their Spiritual Guide!

Since it was customary in those days, as it is today, to greet an honoured guest in style, Jangchub Ö sent an entourage of three hundred horsemen with many eminent Tibetans to the border to welcome Atisha and offer him a horse to ease the difficult journey to Ngari. Atisha rode at the centre of the three hundred horsemen, and by means of his miracle powers he sat one cubit above his horse's back. When they saw him, those who previously had no respect for him developed very strong faith, and everyone said that the second Buddha had arrived in Tibet.

When Atisha reached Ngari, Jangchub Ö requested him: 'O Compassionate Atisha, please give instructions to help the Tibetan people. Please give advice that everyone can follow. Please give us special instructions so that we can practise all the paths of Sutra and Tantra together.' To fulfil this wish Atisha composed and taught *Lamp for the Path to Enlightenment*, the first text written on the stages of the path, Lamrim. He gave these instructions first in Ngari and then in central Tibet. Many disciples who heard these teachings developed great wisdom.

THE PRECIOUSNESS OF KADAM LAMRIM

Atisha wrote the original Kadam Lamrim based on *Ornament of Clear Realization* by Buddha Maitreya, which is a commentary to the *Perfection of Wisdom Sutras* that Buddha Shakyamuni taught on Massed Vultures Mountain in Rajagriha, India. Later, Je Tsongkhapa wrote his extensive, middling and condensed Kadam Lamrim texts as commentaries to Atisha's Kadam Lamrim instructions, and through this the precious Buddhadharma of Kadam Lamrim flourished in many countries in the East and now in the West. The Kadam Lamrim instructions, the union of Buddha's teachings and Atisha's special instructions, are presented in three stages: the instructions on the stages of the path of a person of initial scope; the instructions on the stages of the path of a person of middling scope; and the instructions on the stages of the path of a person of great scope.

All Buddha's teachings, both Sutra and Tantra, are included within these three instructions. Buddha's teachings are the supreme medicine that permanently cures both physical sickness and the sickness of delusions. Just as doctors give different medicine for different sicknesses, so Buddha gave different Dharma medicine according to people's different capacities. He gave simple teachings to those of initial scope, profound teachings to those of middling scope, and very profound teachings to those of great scope. In practice, all these teachings are part of Kadam Lamrim, which is the main body of Buddha's teachings; there is not a single teaching of Buddha that is not included within Kadam Lamrim. For this reason, Je Tsongkhapa said that when we listen to the entire Lamrim we are listening to all Buddha's teachings and when we practise the entire Lamrim we are practising all Buddha's teachings. Kadam Lamrim is the condensation of all Buddha's teachings; it is very practical and suitable for everyone and its presentation is superior to other instructions.

Through gaining experience of Lamrim we shall understand that none of Buddha's teachings are contradictory, we shall put all Buddha's teachings into practice, we shall easily realize Buddha's ultimate view and intention, and we shall become free from all mistaken views and intentions. Everyone, both Buddhist and non-Buddhist, needs permanent liberation from suffering, and pure and everlasting happiness. This wish will be fulfilled through Lamrim practice; therefore it is the real wishfulfilling jewel.

In general, all Buddha's teachings, the Dharma, are very precious, but Kadam Dharma or Lamrim is a very special Buddhadharma that is suitable for everyone without exception. The great Master Dromtonpa said: 'Kadam Dharma is like a mala made of gold.' Just as everyone, even those who do not use a mala (or prayer beads), would be happy to accept a gift of a gold mala because it is made of gold, in a similar way, everyone, even non-Buddhists, can receive benefit from Kadam Dharma. This is because there is no difference between Kadam Dharma and people's everyday experiences. Even without studying or listening to Dharma, some people often come to similar conclusions as those explained in Kadam Dharma teachings through looking at newspapers or television and understanding the world situation. This is because Kadam Dharma accords with people's daily experience; it cannot be separated from daily life. Everyone needs it to make their lives happy and meaningful, to solve temporarily their human problems, and to enable them ultimately to find pure and ever-lasting happiness through controlling their anger, attachment, jealousy, and especially ignorance.

In this spiritually degenerate time there are five impurities that are increasing throughout the world: (1) our environment is becoming increasingly impure because of pollution; (2) our water, air and food are becoming increasingly impure, also because of pollution; (3) our body is becoming increasingly impure because sickness and disease are now more prevalent; (4) our mind is becoming increasingly impure because our delusions are getting stronger and stronger; and (5) our actions are becoming increasingly impure because we have no control over our delusions.

Because of these five impurities, suffering, problems and dangers are increasing everywhere. However, through Lamrim practice we can transform our experience of all these impurities into the spiritual path that leads us to the pure and everlasting happiness of liberation and enlightenment. We can use all the difficulties that we see in the world as spiritual teachings that encourage us to develop renunciation, the wish to liberate ourself from the cycle of impure life; compassion, the wish that others may be liberated permanently from the cycle of impure life; and the wisdom that realizes that all these impurities are the results of our non-virtuous actions. In this way, through Lamrim practice we can transform all adverse conditions into opportunities for developing realizations of the spiritual path that will bring us pure and everlasting happiness.

Whenever Lamrim practitioners experience difficulties and suffering they think: 'Countless other living beings experience greater suffering and difficulties than I do', and in this way they develop or increase their compassion for all living beings, which leads them quickly to the supreme happiness of enlightenment. Kadam Lamrim is the supreme medicine that can permanently cure all the sufferings of sickness, ageing, death and rebirth; it is the scientific method to improve our human nature and qualities, and to solve our daily problems. Kadam Lamrim is the great mirror of Dharma in which we can see the way things really are; and through which we can see what we should know, what we should abandon, what we should practise and what we should attain. And it is only by using this mirror that we can see the great kindness of all living beings.

Atisha

The Path of a Person of Initial Scope

In this context, a 'person of initial scope' refers to someone who has an initial capacity for developing spiritual understanding and realizations.

THE PRECIOUSNESS OF OUR HUMAN LIFE

The purpose of understanding the preciousness of our human life is to encourage ourself to take the real meaning of our human life and not to waste it in meaningless activities. Our human life is very precious and meaningful, but only if we use it to attain permanent liberation and the supreme happiness of enlightenment. We should encourage ourself to accomplish the real meaning of our human life through understanding and contemplating the following explanation.

Many people believe that material development is the real meaning of human life, but we can see that no matter how much material development there is in the world it never reduces human suffering and problems. Instead, it often causes suffering and problems to increase; therefore it is not the real meaning of human life. We should know that at present we have reached the human world for just a brief moment from our former lives, and we have the opportunity to attain the supreme happiness of enlightenment through practising Dharma. This is our extraordinary good fortune. When we attain enlightenment we shall have fulfilled our own wishes, and we can fulfil the wishes of all other living beings; we shall have liberated ourself permanently from the sufferings of this life and countless future lives, and we can directly benefit each and every living being every day. The attainment of enlightenment is therefore the real meaning of human life.

Enlightenment is the inner light of wisdom that is permanently free from all mistaken appearance, and whose function is to bestow mental peace upon each and every living being every day. Right now we have obtained a human rebirth and have the opportunity to attain enlightenment through Dharma practice, so if we waste this precious opportunity in meaningless activities there is no greater loss and no greater foolishness. This is because in future such a precious opportunity will be extremely hard to find. In one Sutra Buddha illustrates this by giving the following analogy. He asks his disciples: 'Suppose there existed a vast and deep ocean the size of this world, and on its surface there floated a golden yoke, and at the bottom of the ocean there lived a blind turtle who surfaced only once in every one hundred thousand years. How often would that turtle raise its head through the middle of the yoke?' His disciple, Ananda, answers that, indeed, it would be extremely rare.

In this context, the vast and deep ocean refers to samsara – the cycle of impure life that we have experienced since beginningless time, continually in life after life without end – the golden yoke refers to Buddhadharma, and the blind turtle refers to us. Although we are not physically a turtle, mentally we are not much different; and although our physical eyes may not be blind, our wisdom eyes are. For most of our countless previous lives we have remained at the bottom of the ocean of samsara, in the three lower realms – the animal, hungry ghost and hell realms – surfacing only once in every one hundred thousand years or so as a human being. Even when we briefly reach the upper realm of samsara's ocean as a human being, it is extremely rare to meet the golden yoke of Buddhadharma: the ocean of samsara is extremely vast, the golden yoke of Buddhadharma does not remain in one place but moves from place to place, and our wisdom eyes are always blind. For these reasons, Buddha says that in the future, even if we obtain a human rebirth, it will be extremely rare to meet Buddhadharma again; meeting Kadam Dharma is even more rare than this. We can see that the great majority of human beings in the world, even though they have briefly reached the upper realm of samsara as human beings, have not met Buddhadharma. This is because their wisdom eyes have not opened.

What does 'meeting Buddhadharma' mean? It means entering into Buddhism by sincerely seeking refuge in Buddha, Dharma and Sangha, and thus having the opportunity to enter and make progress on the path to enlightenment. If we do not meet Buddhadharma we have no opportunity to do this, and therefore we have no opportunity to accomplish the pure and everlasting happiness of enlightenment, the real meaning of human life. In conclusion, we should think:

At present I have briefly reached the human world and have the opportunity to attain permanent liberation from suffering and the supreme happiness of enlightenment through putting Dharma into practice. If I waste this precious opportunity in meaningless activities there is no greater loss and no greater foolishness.

With this thought we make the strong determination to practise the Dharma of Buddha's teachings on renunciation, universal
compassion and the profound view of emptiness now, while we
have the opportunity. We then meditate on this determination
again and again. We should practise this contemplation and
meditation every day in many sessions, and in this way encourage ourself to take the real meaning of our human life.

We should ask ourself what we consider to be most
important – what do we wish for, strive for, or daydream
about? For some people it is material possessions, such as a
large house with all the latest luxuries, a fast car or a well-paid
job. For others it is reputation, good looks, power, excitement
or adventure. Many try to find the meaning of their life in
relationships with their family and circle of friends. All these
things can make us superficially happy for a short while but
they will also cause us much worry and suffering. They will
never give us the real happiness that all of us, in our hearts,
long for. Since we cannot take them with us when we die, if
we have made them the principal meaning of our life they will
eventually let us down. As an end in themselves worldly attainments are hollow; they are not the real meaning of human life.

With our human life we can attain the supreme permanent
peace of mind, known as 'nirvana', and enlightenment by
putting Dharma into practice. Since these attainments are
non-deceptive and ultimate states of happiness they are the
real meaning of human life. However, because our desire for
worldly enjoyment is so strong, we have little or no interest
in Dharma practice. From a spiritual point of view, this lack
of interest in Dharma practice is a type of laziness called the
'laziness of attachment'. For as long as we have this laziness,
the door to liberation will be closed to us, and consequently we
shall continue to experience misery and suffering in this life and

in countless future lives. The way to overcome this laziness, the main obstacle to our Dharma practice, is to meditate on death.

We need to contemplate and meditate on our death again and again until we gain a deep realization of death. Although on an intellectual level we all know that eventually we are going to die, our awareness of death remains superficial. Since our intellectual knowledge of death does not touch our hearts, each and every day we continue to think 'I shall not die today, I shall not die today.' Even on the day of our death, we are still thinking about what we shall do tomorrow or next week. This mind that thinks every day 'I shall not die today' is deceptive – it leads us in the wrong direction and causes our human life to become empty. On the other hand, through meditating on death we shall gradually replace the deceptive thought 'I shall not die today' with the non-deceptive thought 'I may die today.' The mind that spontaneously thinks each and every day 'I may die today' is the realization of death. It is this realization that directly eliminates our laziness of attachment and opens the door to the spiritual path.

In general, we may die today or we may not die today – we do not know. However, if we think each day 'I may not die today', this thought will deceive us because it comes from our ignorance; whereas if instead we think each day 'I may die today', this thought will not deceive us because it comes from our wisdom. This beneficial thought will prevent our laziness of attachment, and will encourage us to prepare for the welfare of our countless future lives or to put great effort into entering the path to liberation and enlightenment. In this way, we shall make our present human life meaningful. Until now we have wasted our countless former lives without any meaning; we have brought nothing with us from our former lives except delusions and suffering.

WHAT DOES OUR DEATH MEAN?

Our death is the permanent separation of our body and mind. We may experience many temporary separations of our body and mind, but these are not our death. For example, when those who have completed their training in the practice known as 'transference of consciousness' engage in meditation, their mind separates from their body. Their body remains where they are meditating, and their mind goes to a Pure Land and then returns to their body. At night, during dreams, our body remains in bed but our mind goes to various places of the dream world and then returns to our body. These separations of our body and mind are not our death because they are only temporary.

At death our mind separates from our body permanently. Our body remains at the place of this life but our mind goes to various places of our future lives, like a bird leaving one nest and flying to another. This clearly shows the existence of our countless future lives, and that the nature and function of our body and mind are very different. Our body is a visual form that possesses colour and shape, but our mind is a formless continuum that always lacks colour and shape. The nature of our mind is empty like space, and its function is to perceive or understand objects. Through this we can understand that our brain is not our mind. The brain is simply a part of our body that, for example, can be photographed, whereas our mind cannot.

We may not be happy to hear about our death, but contemplating and meditating on death is very important for the effectiveness of our Dharma practice. This is because it prevents the main obstacle to our Dharma practice – the laziness of attachment to the things of this life – and it encourages us to practise pure Dharma right now. If we do this we shall accomplish the real meaning of human life before our death.

HOW TO MEDITATE ON DEATH

First we engage in the following contemplation:

I shall definitely die. There is no way to prevent my body from finally decaying. Day by day, moment by moment, my life is slipping away. I have no idea when I shall die; the time of death is completely uncertain. Many young people die before their parents, some die the moment they are born – there is no certainty in this world. Furthermore, there are so many causes of untimely death. The lives of many strong and healthy people are destroyed by accidents. There is no guarantee that I shall not die today.

Having repeatedly contemplated these points, we mentally repeat over and over again 'I may die today, I may die today', and concentrate on the feeling it evokes. We transform our mind into this feeling 'I may die today' and remain on it single-pointedly for as long as possible. We should practise this meditation repeatedly until we spontaneously believe each and every day 'I may die today'. Eventually we shall come to a conclusion: 'Since I shall soon have to depart from this world, there is no sense in my becoming attached to the things of this life. Instead, from now on I will devote my whole life to practising Dharma purely and sincerely.' We then maintain this determination day and night.

During the meditation break, without laziness we should apply effort to our Dharma practice. Realizing that worldly pleasures are deceptive, and that they distract us from using our life in a meaningful way, we should abandon attachment to them. In this way, we can eliminate the main obstacle to pure Dharma practice.

THE DANGERS OF LOWER REBIRTH

The purpose of this explanation is to encourage us to prepare protection from the dangers of lower rebirth. If we do not do this now, while we have a human life with its freedoms and endowments and we have the opportunity to do so, it will be too late once we have taken any of the three lower rebirths; and it will be extremely difficult to obtain such a precious human life again. It is said to be easier for human beings to attain enlightenment than it is for beings such as animals to attain a precious human rebirth. Understanding this will encourage us to abandon non-virtue, to practise virtue and to seek refuge in Buddha, Dharma and Sangha (the supreme spiritual friends); this is our actual protection.

Performing non-virtuous actions is the main cause of taking lower rebirth, whereas practising virtue and seeking refuge in Buddha, Dharma and Sangha are the main causes of taking a precious human rebirth – a rebirth in which we have the opportunity to attain permanent liberation from all suffering. Heavy non-virtuous actions are the main cause of rebirth as a hell being, middling non-virtuous actions are the main cause of rebirth as a hungry ghost, and lesser non-virtuous actions are the main cause of rebirth as an animal. There are many examples given in Buddhist scriptures of how non-virtuous actions lead to rebirth in the three lower realms.

There was once a hunter whose wife came from a family of animal farmers. After he died he took rebirth as a cow belonging to his wife's family. A butcher then bought this cow, slaughtered it and sold the meat. The hunter was reborn seven times as a cow belonging to the same family, and in this way became food for other people.

In Tibet there is a lake called Yamdroktso, where many people from the nearby town used to spend their whole lives fishing. At one time a great Yogi with clairvoyance visited the town and said 'I see the people of this town and the fish in this lake are continually switching their positions.' What he meant was that the people of the town who enjoyed fishing were reborn as the fish, the food of other people, and the fish in the lake were reborn as the people who enjoyed fishing. In this way, changing their physical aspect, they were continually killing and eating each other. This cycle of misery continued from generation to generation.

HOW TO MEDITATE ON THE DANGERS OF
LOWER REBIRTH

First we engage in the following contemplation:

> When the oil of an oil lamp is exhausted, the flame goes out because the flame is produced from the oil; but when our body dies our consciousness is not extinguished, because consciousness is not produced from the body. When we die our mind has to leave this present body, which is just a temporary abode, and find another body, rather like a bird leaving one nest to fly to another. Our mind has no freedom to remain and no choice about where to go. We are blown to the place of our next rebirth by the winds of our actions or karma (our good fortune or misfortune). If the karma that ripens at our death time is negative, we shall definitely take a lower rebirth. Heavy negative karma causes rebirth in hell, middling negative karma causes rebirth as a hungry ghost and lesser negative karma causes rebirth as an animal.

It is very easy to commit heavy negative karma. For example, simply by swatting a mosquito out of anger we create the cause to be reborn in hell. Throughout this and all our countless previous lives we have committed many heavy negative actions. Unless we have already purified these actions by practising sincere confession, their potentialities remain in our mental continuum, and any one of these negative potentialities could ripen when we die. Bearing this in mind, we should ask ourself: 'If I die today, where shall I be tomorrow? It is quite possible that I shall find myself in the animal realm, among the hungry ghosts, or in hell. If someone were to call me a stupid cow today, I would find it difficult to bear, but what shall I do if I actually become a cow, a pig, or a fish – the food of human beings?'

Having repeatedly contemplated these points and understood how beings in the lower realms, such as animals, experience suffering, we generate a strong fear of taking rebirth in the lower realms. This feeling of fear is the object of our meditation. We then hold this without forgetting it; our mind should remain on this feeling of fear single-pointedly for as long as possible. If we lose the object of our meditation we renew the feeling of fear by immediately remembering it or by repeating the contemplation.

During the meditation break we try never to forget our feeling of fear of taking rebirth in the lower realms. In general fear is meaningless, but the fear generated through the above contemplation and meditation has immense meaning, as it arises from wisdom and not from ignorance. This fear is the main cause of seeking refuge in Buddha, Dharma and Sangha, which is the actual protection from such dangers, and helps us to be mindful and conscientious in avoiding non-virtuous actions.

GOING FOR REFUGE

In this context, 'going for refuge' means seeking refuge in Buddha, Dharma and Sangha. The purpose of this practice is to protect ourself permanently from taking lower rebirth. At present, because we are human, we are free from rebirth as an animal, hungry ghost or hell being, but this is only temporary. We are like a prisoner who gets permission to stay at home for a week, but then has to return to prison. We need permanent liberation from the sufferings of this life and countless future lives. This depends upon entering, making progress on and completing the Buddhist path to liberation, which in turn depends upon entering Buddhism.

We enter Buddhism through the practice of going for refuge. For our practice of refuge to be qualified, while visualizing Buddha in front of us we should verbally or mentally make the promise to seek refuge in Buddha, Dharma and Sangha throughout our life. This promise is our refuge vow, and is the gateway through which we enter Buddhism. For as long as we keep this promise we are inside Buddhism, but if we break this promise we are outside. By entering and remaining inside Buddhism we have the opportunity to begin, make progress on and complete the Buddhist path to liberation and enlightenment.

We should never give up our promise to seek refuge in Buddha, Dharma and Sangha throughout our life. Going for refuge to Buddha, Dharma and Sangha means that we apply effort to receiving Buddha's blessings, to putting Dharma into practice and to receiving help from Sangha. These are the three principal commitments of the refuge vow. Through maintaining and sincerely practising these three principal commitments of refuge we can fulfil our final goal.

The main reason why we need to make the determination and promise to seek refuge in Buddha, Dharma and Sangha throughout our life is that we need to attain permanent liberation from suffering. At present we may be free from physical suffering and mental pain, but as mentioned earlier this freedom is only temporary. Later in this life and in our countless future lives we shall have to experience unbearable physical suffering and mental pain continually, in life after life without end.

When our life is in danger or we are threatened by someone, we usually seek refuge in the police. Of course, sometimes the police can protect us from a particular danger, but they cannot give us permanent liberation from death. When we are seriously ill we seek refuge in doctors. Sometimes doctors can cure a particular illness, but no doctor can give us permanent liberation from sickness. What we really need is permanent liberation from all sufferings, and as human beings we can achieve this by seeking refuge in Buddha, Dharma and Sangha.

Buddhas are 'awakened', which means that they have awakened from the sleep of ignorance and are free from the dreams of samsara, the cycle of impure life. They are completely pure beings who are permanently free from all delusions and mistaken appearance. As mentioned earlier, Buddha's function is to bestow mental peace on each and every living being every day by giving blessings. We know that we are happy when our mind is peaceful, and unhappy when it is not. It is therefore clear that our happiness depends upon our having a peaceful mind and not on good external conditions. Even if our external conditions are poor, if we maintain a peaceful mind all the time we shall always be happy. Through continually receiving Buddha's blessings we can maintain a peaceful mind all the time. Buddha is therefore the source of our happiness.

Dharma is the actual protection through which we are permanently released from the sufferings of sickness, ageing, death and rebirth; and Sangha are the supreme spiritual friends who guide us to correct spiritual paths. Through these three precious wishfulfilling jewels, Buddha, Dharma and Sangha – known as the 'Three Jewels' – we can fulfil our own wishes as well as the wishes of all living beings.

Every day from the depths of our heart we should recite requesting prayers to the enlightened Buddhas, while maintaining deep faith in them. This is a simple method for us to receive the Buddhas' blessings continually. We should also join group prayers, known as 'pujas', organized at Buddhist Temples or Prayer Halls, which are powerful methods to receive Buddha's blessings and protection.

HOW TO MEDITATE ON GOING FOR REFUGE

First we engage in the following contemplation:

I want to protect and liberate myself permanently from the sufferings of this life and countless future lives. I can accomplish this only by receiving Buddha's blessings, putting Dharma into practice and receiving help from Sangha – the supreme spiritual friends.

Thinking deeply in this way, we first make the strong determination and then the promise to seek refuge sincerely in Buddha, Dharma and Sangha throughout our life. We should meditate on this determination every day and maintain our promise continually for the rest of our life. As the commitments of our refuge vow we should always apply effort to receive Buddha's blessings, to put Dharma into practice and to receive help from Sangha, our pure spiritual friends including our Spiritual Teacher. This is how we go for refuge to Buddha, Dharma and Sangha. Through this we shall accomplish our aim – permanent liberation from all the sufferings of this life and countless future lives, the real meaning of our human life.

To maintain our promise to go for refuge to Buddha, Dharma and Sangha throughout our life, and so that we and all living beings may receive Buddha's blessings and protection, we recite the following refuge prayer every day with strong faith:

> *I and all sentient beings, until we achieve enlightenment,*
> *Go for refuge to Buddha, Dharma and Sangha.*

WHAT IS KARMA?

The purpose of understanding and believing in karma is to prevent future suffering and to establish the basic foundation for the path to liberation and enlightenment. Generally, karma means 'action'. From non-virtuous actions comes suffering and from virtuous actions comes happiness: if we believe this, we believe in karma. Buddha gave extensive teachings that prove the truth of this statement, and many different examples that show the special connection between the actions of our former lives and our experiences of this life, some of which are explained in *Joyful Path of Good Fortune*.

In our previous lives we performed various kinds of non-virtuous actions that caused others suffering. As a result of these non-virtuous actions, various kinds of miserable conditions and situations arise and we experience endless human suffering and problems. This is the same for all other living beings.

We should judge whether or not we believe that the main cause of suffering is our non-virtuous actions and the main cause of happiness is our virtuous actions. If we do not believe this we shall never apply effort to accumulating virtuous actions, or merit, and we shall never purify our non-virtuous actions, and because of this we shall experience suffering and difficulties continually, in life after life without end.

Every action we perform leaves an imprint on our very subtle mind, and each imprint eventually gives rise to its own effect. Our mind is like a field, and performing actions is like sowing seeds in that field. Virtuous actions sow seeds of future happiness and non-virtuous actions sow seeds of future suffering. These seeds remain dormant in our mind until the conditions for them to ripen occur, and then they produce their effect. In some cases, this can happen many lifetimes after the original action was performed.

The seeds that ripen when we die are very important because they determine what kind of rebirth we shall take in our next life. Which particular seed ripens at death depends upon the state of mind in which we die. If we die with a peaceful mind, this will stimulate a virtuous seed and we shall experience a fortunate rebirth. However, if we die with an unpeaceful mind, such as in a state of anger, this will stimulate a non-virtuous seed and we shall experience an unfortunate rebirth. This is similar to the way in which nightmares are triggered by our being in an agitated state of mind just before falling asleep.

All inappropriate actions, including killing, stealing, sexual misconduct, lying, divisive speech, hurtful speech, idle chatter, covetousness, malice and holding wrong views, are non-virtuous actions. When we abandon non-virtuous actions and apply effort to purifying our previous non-virtuous actions we are practising moral discipline. This will prevent us from experiencing future suffering and from taking a lower rebirth. Examples of virtuous actions are training in all the meditations and other spiritual practices presented in this book. Meditation is a virtuous mental action that is the main cause for experiencing mental peace in the future. Whenever we practise meditation, whether or not our meditation is clear, we are performing a virtuous mental action that is a cause of our future happiness and peace of mind. We are normally concerned mainly about bodily and verbal actions, but in reality mental actions are more important. Our bodily and verbal actions depend upon our mental action, upon our mentally making a decision.

Whenever we perform virtuous actions such as meditation or other spiritual practices we should have the following mental determination:

While riding the horse of virtuous actions
I will guide it into the path of liberation with the reins of
    renunciation;
And through urging this horse onward with the whip of
    effort,
I will quickly reach the Pure Land of liberation and
    enlightenment.

Having contemplated the above explanation, we should think:

Since I myself never wish to suffer and always want to be happy, I must abandon and purify my non-virtuous actions and sincerely perform virtuous actions.

We should meditate on this determination every day, and put our determination into practice.

The Path of a Person of
Middling Scope

In this context, a 'person of middling scope' refers to someone who has a middling capacity for developing spiritual understanding and realizations.

WHAT WE SHOULD KNOW

In *Sutra of the Four Noble Truths* Buddha says: 'You should know sufferings'. In saying this Buddha is advising us that we should know about the unbearable sufferings that we shall experience in our countless future lives, and therefore develop renunciation, the determination to liberate ourself permanently from these sufferings.

In general, everyone who has physical or mental pain, even animals, understands their own suffering; but when Buddha says 'You should know sufferings' he means that we should know the sufferings of our future lives. Through knowing these, we shall develop a strong wish to liberate ourself from them. This practical advice is important for everybody because, if we have the wish to liberate ourself from the sufferings of future lives, we shall definitely use our present human life for the freedom and happiness of our countless future lives. There is no greater meaning than this.

If we do not have this wish, we shall waste our precious human life only for the freedom and happiness of this one short life. This would be foolish because our intention and actions would be no different from the intention and actions of animals who are only concerned with this life alone. The great Yogi Milarepa once said to a hunter called Gonpo Dorje:

Your body is human but your mind is that of an animal.
You, a human being, who possess an animal's mind, please
    listen to my song.

Normally we believe that solving the suffering and problems of our present life is most important, and we dedicate our whole life for this purpose. In reality, the duration of the suffering and problems of this life is very short; if we die tomorrow, they will end tomorrow. However, since the duration of the suffering and problems of future lives is endless, the freedom and happiness of our future lives is vastly more important than the freedom and happiness of this one short life. With the words 'You should know sufferings' Buddha encourages us to use our present human life to prepare for the freedom and happiness of our countless future lives. Those who do this are truly wise.

In future lives, when we are born as an animal, such as a cow or a fish, we shall become the food of other living beings, and we shall have to experience many other kinds of animal suffering. Animals have no freedom, and are used by human beings for food, work and enjoyment. They have no opportunity to improve themselves; even if they hear precious Dharma words it is as meaningless to them as hearing the wind blowing. When we are born as a hungry ghost we shall not have even a tiny drop of water to drink; our only water will be our tears. We shall have to experience the unbearable sufferings of thirst and hunger for many hundreds of years. When we are born as a hell being in the hot hells our body will become inseparable from fire, and others will be able to distinguish between our body and fire only by hearing our suffering cries. We shall have to experience the unbearable torment of our body being burned for millions of years. Like all other phenomena, the hell realms do not exist inherently but exist as mere appearances to mind, like dreams. When we are born as a desire realm god we experience great conflict and dissatisfaction. Even if we experience some superficial enjoyment, still our desires grow stronger, and we have even more mental suffering than human beings. When we are born as a demi-god we are always jealous of the gods' glory and because of this we have great mental suffering. Our jealousy is like a thorn piercing our mind, causing us to experience both mental and physical suffering for long periods of time. When we are born as a human being we shall have to experience various kinds of human suffering such as the sufferings of birth, sickness, ageing and death.

BIRTH

When our consciousness first enters the union of our father's sperm and our mother's ovum, our body is a very hot, watery substance like white yoghurt tinted red. In the first moments after conception we have no gross feelings, but as soon as these develop we begin to experience pain. Our body gradually becomes harder and harder, and as our limbs grow it feels as if our body is being stretched out on a rack. Inside our mother's womb it is hot and dark. Our home for nine months is this small, tightly compressed space full of unclean substances. It is like being squashed inside a small water tank full of filthy liquid with the lid tightly shut so that no air or light can come through.

While we are in our mother's womb we experience much pain and fear all on our own. We are extremely sensitive to everything our mother does. When she walks quickly it feels as if we are falling from a high mountain and we are terrified. If she has sexual intercourse it feels as if we are being crushed and suffocated between two huge weights and we panic. If our mother makes just a small jump it feels as if we are being dashed against the ground from a great height. If she drinks anything hot it feels like boiling water scalding our skin, and if she drinks anything cold it feels like an ice-cold shower in midwinter.

When we are emerging from our mother's womb it feels as if we are being forced through a narrow crevice between two hard rocks, and when we are newly born our body is so delicate that any kind of contact is painful. Even if someone holds us very tenderly, his or her hands feel like thorn bushes piercing our flesh, and the most delicate fabrics feel rough and abrasive. By comparison with the softness and smoothness of our mother's womb, every tactile sensation is harsh and painful. If someone picks us up it feels as if we are being swung over a huge precipice, and we feel frightened and insecure. We have forgotten all that we knew in our previous life; we bring only pain and confusion from our mother's womb. Whatever we hear is as meaningless as the sound of wind, and we cannot comprehend anything we perceive. In the first few weeks we are like someone who is blind, deaf and dumb, and suffering from profound amnesia. When we are hungry we cannot say 'I need food', and when we are in pain we cannot say 'This is hurting me.' The only signs we can make are hot tears and furious gestures. Our mother often has no idea what pains and discomforts we are experiencing. We are completely helpless and have to be taught everything – how to eat, how to sit, how to walk, how to talk.

Although we are most vulnerable in the first few weeks of our life, our pains do not cease as we grow up. We continue to experience various kinds of suffering throughout our life. Just as when we light a fire in a large house, the heat from the fire pervades the whole house and all the heat in the house comes from the fire, so when we are born in samsara, suffering pervades our whole life, and all the miseries we experience arise because we took a contaminated rebirth.

Our human rebirth, contaminated by the poisonous delusion of self-grasping, is the basis of our human suffering; without this basis, there are no human problems. The pains of birth gradually turn into the pains of sickness, ageing and death – they are one continuum.

SICKNESS

Our birth also gives rise to the suffering of sickness. Just as the wind and snow of winter take away the glory of green meadows, trees, forests and flowers, so sickness takes away the youthful splendour of our body, destroying its strength and the power of our senses. If we are usually fit and well, when we become sick we are suddenly unable to engage in all our normal physical activities. Even a champion boxer who is usually able to knock out all his opponents becomes completely helpless when sickness strikes. Sickness makes all our experiences of daily enjoyments disappear and causes us to experience unpleasant feelings day and night.

When we fall ill, we are like a bird that has been soaring in the sky and is suddenly shot down. When a bird is shot, it falls straight to the ground like a lump of lead, and all its glory and power are immediately destroyed. In a similar way, when we become ill we are suddenly incapacitated. If we are seriously ill we may become completely dependent upon others and lose even the ability to control our bodily functions. This transformation is hard to bear, especially for those who pride themselves on their independence and physical well-being.

When we are ill, we feel frustrated as we cannot do our usual work or complete all the tasks we have set ourself. We easily become impatient with our illness and depressed about all the things we cannot do. We cannot enjoy the things that usually give us pleasure, such as sport, dancing, drinking, eating rich foods or the company of our friends. All these limitations make us feel even more miserable; and, to add to our unhappiness, we have to endure all the physical pains the illness brings.

When we are sick, not only do we have to experience all the unwanted pains of the illness itself, but we also have to experience all sorts of other unwished for things. For example, we have to take whatever cure is prescribed, whether it be a foul-tasting medicine, a series of injections, a major operation or abstinence from something we like very much. If we are to have an operation, we have to go to hospital and accept all the conditions there. We may have to eat food we do not like and stay in bed all day long with nothing to do, and we may feel anxiety about the operation. Our doctor may not explain to us exactly what the problem is and whether or not he or she expects us to survive.

If we learn that our sickness is incurable, and we have no spiritual experience, we shall suffer anxiety, fear and regret.

We may become depressed and give up hope, or we may become angry with our illness, feeling that it is an enemy that has maliciously deprived us of all joy.

AGEING

Our birth also gives rise to the pains of ageing. Ageing steals our beauty, our health, our good figure, our fine complexion, our vitality and our comfort. Ageing turns us into objects of contempt. It brings many unwanted pains and takes us swiftly to our death.

As we grow old we lose all the beauty of our youth and our strong, healthy body becomes weak and burdened with illness. Our once firm and well-proportioned figure becomes bent and disfigured, and our muscles and flesh shrink so that our limbs become like thin sticks and our bones poke out. Our hair loses its colour and shine, and our complexion loses its lustre. Our face becomes wrinkled and our features grow distorted. Milarepa said:

> How do old people get up? They get up as if they were heaving a stake out of the ground. How do old people walk about? Once they are on their feet they have to walk gingerly, like bird-catchers. How do old people sit down? They crash down like heavy luggage whose harness has snapped.

We can contemplate the following poem on the sufferings of growing old, written by the scholar Gungtang:

> When we are old, our hair becomes white,
> But not because we have washed it clean;
> It is a sign we shall soon encounter the Lord of Death.

We have wrinkles on our forehead,
But not because we have too much flesh;
It is a warning from the Lord of Death: 'You are about
    to die.'

Our teeth fall out,
But not to make room for new ones;
It is a sign we shall soon lose the ability to eat human
    food.

Our faces are ugly and unpleasant,
But not because we are wearing masks;
It is a sign we have lost the mask of youth.

Our heads shake to and fro,
But not because we are in disagreement;
It is the Lord of Death striking our head with the stick
    he holds in his right hand.

We walk bent and gazing at the ground,
But not because we are searching for lost needles;
It is a sign we are searching for our lost beauty and
    memories.

We get up from the ground using all four limbs,
But not because we are imitating animals;
It is a sign our legs are too weak to support our bodies.

We sit down as if we had suddenly fallen,
But not because we are angry;
It is a sign our body has lost its strength.

Our body sways as we walk,
But not because we think we are important;
It is a sign our legs cannot carry our body.

Our hands shake,
But not because they are itching to steal;
It is a sign the Lord of Death's itchy fingers are stealing
    our possessions.

We eat very little,
But not because we are miserly;
It is a sign we cannot digest our food.

We wheeze frequently,
But not because we are whispering mantras to the sick;
It is a sign our breathing will soon disappear.

When we are young we can travel around the whole
world, but when we are old we can hardly make it to our own
front gate. We become too weak to engage in many worldly
activities, and our spiritual activities are often curtailed. For
example, we have little physical strength to perform virtuous
actions, and little mental energy to memorize, contemplate and
meditate. We cannot attend teachings that are given in places
that are hard to reach or uncomfortable to inhabit. We cannot
help others in ways that require physical strength and good
health. Deprivations such as these often make old people very
sad.

When we grow old, we become like someone who is blind
and deaf. We cannot see clearly, and we need stronger and
stronger glasses until we can no longer read. We cannot hear
clearly, and so it becomes more and more difficult to listen
to music or to the television, or to hear what others are saying. Our memory fades. All activities, worldly and spiritual,
become more difficult. If we practise meditation it becomes
harder for us to gain realizations because our memory and
concentration are too weak. We cannot apply ourself to study.

Thus, if we have not learnt and trained in spiritual practices when we were younger, the only thing to do when we grow old is to develop regret and wait for the Lord of Death to come.

When we are old we cannot derive the same enjoyment from the things we used to enjoy, such as food, drink and sex. We are too weak to play games and we are often too exhausted even for entertainments. As our lifespan runs out we cannot join young people in their activities. When they travel about we have to stay behind. No one wants to take us with them when we are old, and no one wants to visit us. Even our own grandchildren do not want to stay with us for very long. Old people often think to themselves: 'How wonderful it would be if young people would stay with me. We could go out for walks and I could show them things'; but young people do not want to be included in their plans. As their life draws to an end, old people experience the sorrow of abandonment and loneliness. They have many special sorrows.

DEATH

Our birth also gives rise to the sufferings of death. If during our life we have worked hard to acquire possessions, and if we have become very attached to them, we shall experience great suffering at the time of death, thinking 'Now I have to leave all my precious possessions behind.' Even now we find it difficult to lend one of our most treasured possessions to someone else, let alone to give it away. No wonder we become so miserable when we realize that in the hands of death we must abandon everything.

When we die we have to part from even our closest friends. We have to leave our partner, even though we may have been together for years and never spent a day apart. If we are very attached to our friends we shall experience great misery at the time of death, but all we shall be able to do is hold their hands. We shall not be able to halt the process of death, even if they plead with us not to die. Usually when we are very attached to someone we feel jealous if he or she leaves us on our own and spends time with someone else, but when we die we shall have to leave our friends with others forever. We shall have to leave everyone, including our family and all the people who have helped us in this life.

When we die, this body that we have cherished and cared for in so many ways will have to be left behind. It will become mindless like a stone, and will be buried in the ground or cremated. If we do not have the inner protection of spiritual experience, at the time of death we shall experience fear and distress, as well as physical pain.

When our consciousness departs from our body at death, all the potentialities we have accumulated in our mind by performing virtuous and non-virtuous actions will go with it. Other than these we cannot take anything out of this world. All other things deceive us. Death ends all our activities – our conversation, our eating, our meeting with friends, our sleep. Everything draws to a close on the day of our death and we must leave all things behind, even the rings on our fingers. In Tibet beggars carry a stick to defend themselves against dogs. To understand the complete deprivation of death we should remember that at the time of death beggars have to leave even this old stick, the most meagre of human possessions. All over the world we can see that names carved on stone are the only possessions of the dead.

OTHER TYPES OF SUFFERING

We also have to experience the sufferings of separation, having to encounter what we do not like and not fulfilling our wishes – which include the sufferings of poverty, and of being harmed by humans and non-humans and by water, fire, wind and earth. Before the final separation at the time of death we often have to experience temporary separation from the people and things we like, which causes us mental pain. We may have to leave our country where all our friends and relatives live, or we may have to leave the job we like. We may lose our reputation. Many times in this life we have to experience the misery of departing from the people we like, or forsaking and losing the things we find pleasant and attractive; but when we die we have to part forever from all our companions and enjoyments, and from all the outer and inner conditions for our Dharma practice, of this life.

We often have to meet and live with people whom we do not like, or encounter situations that we find unpleasant. Sometimes we may find ourself in a very dangerous situation such as in a fire or a flood, or where there is violence such as in a riot or a battle. Our lives are full of less extreme situations that we find annoying. Sometimes we are prevented from doing the things we want to do. On a sunny day we may set off for the beach but find ourself stuck in a traffic jam. We continually experience interference from our inner demon of delusions, which disturbs our mind and our spiritual practices. There are countless conditions that frustrate our plans and prevent us from doing what we want. It is as if we are naked and living in a thorn bush – whenever we try to move, we are wounded by circumstances. People and things are like thorns piercing our flesh and no situation ever feels entirely comfortable. The more desires and plans we have, the more frustrations we experience. The more we want certain situations, the more we find ourself stuck in situations we do not want. Every desire seems to invite its own obstacle. Undesired situations befall us without our looking for them. In fact, the only things that come effortlessly are the things we do not want. No one wants to die, but death comes effortlessly. No one wants to be sick, but sickness comes effortlessly. Because we have taken rebirth without freedom or control, we have an impure body and inhabit an impure environment, and so undesirable things pour in upon us. In samsara, this kind of experience is entirely natural.

We have countless desires, but no matter how much effort we make we never feel that we have satisfied them. Even when we get what we want, we do not get it in the way we want. We possess the object but we do not derive satisfaction from possessing it. For example, we may dream of becoming wealthy, but if we actually become wealthy our life is not the way we imagined it would be, and we do not feel that we have fulfilled our desire. This is because our desires do not decrease as our wealth increases. The more wealth we have, the more we desire. The wealth we seek is unfindable because we seek an amount that will satiate our desires, and no amount of wealth can do that. To make things worse, in obtaining the object of our desire we create new occasions for discontent. With every object we desire come other objects we do not want. For example, with wealth come taxes, insecurity and complicated financial affairs. These unwished for accessories prevent us from ever feeling fully satisfied. Similarly, we may dream of having a holiday in the South Seas, and we may actually go there on holiday, but the experience is never quite what we expect, and with our holiday come other things such as sunburn and great expense.

If we examine our desires we shall see that they are excessive. We want all the best things in samsara – the best job, the best partner, the best reputation, the best house, the best car, the best holiday. Anything that is not the best leaves us with a feeling of disappointment – still searching for but not finding what we want. No worldly enjoyment, however, can give us the complete and perfect satisfaction we desire. Better things are always being produced. Everywhere, new advertisements announce that the very best thing has just arrived on the market, but a few days later another best thing arrives that is better than the best thing of a few days ago. There is no end of new things to captivate our desires.

Children at school can never satisfy their own or their parents' ambitions. Even if they come top of their class they feel they cannot be content unless they do the same the following year. If they go on to be successful in their jobs, their ambitions will be as strong as ever. There is no point at which they can rest, feeling that they are completely satisfied with what they have done.

We may think that at least people who lead a simple life in the country must be content, but if we look at their situation we shall find that even farmers search for but do not find what they want. Their lives are full of problems and anxieties, and they do not enjoy real peace and satisfaction. Their livelihoods depend upon many uncertain factors beyond their control, such as the weather. Farmers have no more freedom from discontent than businessmen who live and work in the city. Businessmen look smart and efficient as they set off to work each morning carrying their briefcases but, although they look so smooth on the outside, in their hearts they carry many dissatisfactions. They are still searching for but not finding what they want.

If we reflect on this situation we may decide that we can find what we are searching for by abandoning all our possessions. We can see, however, that even poor people are looking for but not finding what they seek, and many poor people have difficulty in finding even the most basic necessities of life; millions of people in the world experience the sufferings of extreme poverty.

We cannot avoid the suffering of dissatisfaction by frequently changing our situation. We may think that if we keep getting a new partner or a new job, or keep travelling about, we shall eventually find what we want; but even if we were to travel to every place on the globe, and have a new lover in every town, we would still be seeking another place and another lover. In samsara there is no real fulfilment of our desires.

Whenever we see anyone in a high or low position, male or female, they differ only in appearance, dress, behaviour and status. In essence they are all equal – they all experience problems in their lives. Whenever we have a problem, it is easy to think that it is caused by our particular circumstances, and that if we were to change our circumstances our problem would disappear. We blame other people, our friends, our food, our government, our times, the weather, society, history and so forth. However, external circumstances such as these are not the main causes of our problems. We need to recognize that all the physical suffering and mental pain we experience are the consequences of our taking a rebirth that is contaminated by the inner poison of delusions. Human beings have to experience various kinds of human suffering because they have taken a contaminated human rebirth; animals have to experience animal suffering because they have taken a contaminated animal rebirth; and hungry ghosts and hell beings have to experience their own sufferings because they have taken contaminated rebirth as hungry ghosts and hell beings. Even gods are not free from suffering because they too have taken a contaminated rebirth. Just as a person trapped inside a raging fire develops intense fear, so we should develop intense fear of the unbearable sufferings of the endless cycle of impure life. This fear is real renunciation and arises from our wisdom.

In conclusion, having contemplated the above explanation we should think:

There is no benefit in denying the sufferings of future lives; when they actually descend upon me it will be too late to protect myself from them. Therefore I definitely need to prepare protection now, while I have this human life that gives me the opportunity to liberate myself permanently from the sufferings of my countless future lives. If I do not apply effort to accomplish this, but allow my human life to become empty of meaning, there is no greater deception and no greater foolishness. I must put effort now into liberating myself permanently from the sufferings of my countless future lives.

We meditate on this determination continually until we develop the spontaneous wish to liberate ourself permanently from the sufferings of countless future lives. This is the actual realization of renunciation. The moment we develop this realization we enter the path to liberation. In this context, liberation refers to the supreme permanent peace of mind known as 'nirvana', which gives us pure and everlasting happiness.

WHAT WE SHOULD ABANDON

In *Sutra of the Four Noble Truths* Buddha says: 'You should abandon origins'. In saying this Buddha is advising us that if we wish to liberate ourself permanently from the sufferings of our countless future lives we should abandon origins. 'Origins' means our delusions, principally our delusion of self-grasping. Self-grasping is called an 'origin' because it is the source of all our suffering and problems, and is also known as the 'inner demon'. Delusions are wrong awarenesses whose function is to destroy mental peace, the source of happiness; they have no function other than to harm us. Delusions such as self-grasping abide at our heart and continually harm us day and night without rest by destroying our peace of mind. In samsara, the cycle of impure life, no one has the opportunity to experience real happiness because their mental peace, the source of happiness, is continually being destroyed by the inner demon of self-grasping.

Our self-grasping ignorance is a mind that mistakenly believes that our self, our body and all the other things that we normally see actually exist. Because of this ignorance we develop attachment to the things we like and anger at the things we do not like. We then perform various kinds of non-virtuous action, and as a result of these actions we experience various kinds of suffering and problems in this life and in life after life.

Self-grasping ignorance is an inner poison that causes far greater harm than any outer poison. Because of being polluted by this inner poison, our mind sees everything in a mistaken way, and as a result we experience hallucination-like sufferings and problems. In reality, our self, our body and all the other things that we normally see do not exist. Self-grasping can be likened to a poisonous tree, all other delusions to its branches, and all our suffering and problems to its fruit; it is the fundamental source of all our other delusions and of all our suffering and problems. Through this we can understand that if we abandon our self-grasping permanently, all our suffering and problems of this life and of countless future lives will cease permanently. The great Yogi Saraha said: 'If your mind is released permanently from self-grasping, there is no doubt that you will be released permanently from suffering.' Understanding this and having contemplated the above explanations, we should think:

I must apply great effort to recognizing, reducing and finally abandoning my ignorance of self-grasping completely.

We should meditate on this determination continually, and put our determination into practice.

WHAT WE SHOULD PRACTISE

In *Sutra of the Four Noble Truths* Buddha says: 'You should practise the path.' In this context, 'path' does not mean an external path that leads from one place to another, but an inner path, a spiritual realization that leads us to the pure happiness of liberation and enlightenment.

The practice of the stages of the path to liberation can be condensed into the three trainings of higher moral discipline, higher concentration and higher wisdom. These trainings are called 'higher' because they are motivated by renunciation. They are therefore the actual path to liberation that we need to practise.

The nature of moral discipline is a virtuous determination to abandon inappropriate actions. When we practise moral discipline we abandon inappropriate actions, maintain pure behaviour and perform every action correctly with a virtuous motivation. Moral discipline is most important for everybody in order to prevent future problems for ourself and for others.

It makes us pure because it makes our actions pure. We need to be clean and pure ourself; just having a clean body is not enough, since our body is not our self. Moral discipline is like a great earth that supports and nurtures the crops of spiritual realizations. Without practising moral discipline, it is very difficult to make progress in spiritual training. Training in higher moral discipline is learning to be deeply familiar with the practice of moral discipline, motivated by renunciation.

The second higher training is training in higher concentration. The nature of concentration is a single-pointed virtuous mind. For as long as we remain with this mind we shall experience mental peace, and thus we shall be happy. When we practise concentration we prevent distractions and concentrate on virtuous objects. It is very important to train in concentration, as with distractions we cannot accomplish anything. Training in higher concentration is learning to be deeply familiar with the ability to stop distractions and concentrate on virtuous objects, with a motivation of renunciation. With regard to any Dharma practice, if our concentration is clear and strong it is very easy to make progress. Normally, distraction is the main obstacle to our Dharma practice. The practice of moral discipline prevents gross distractions, and concentration prevents subtle distractions; together they give rise to quick results in our Dharma practice.

The third higher training is training in higher wisdom. The nature of wisdom is a virtuous intelligent mind that functions to understand meaningful objects such as the existence of past and future lives, karma and emptiness. Understanding these objects brings great meaning to this life and countless future lives. Many people are very intelligent in destroying their enemies, caring for their families, finding what they want and so forth, but this is not wisdom. Even animals have such intelligence. Worldly intelligence is deceptive, whereas wisdom will never deceive us. It is our inner Spiritual Guide who leads us to correct paths, and it is the divine eye through which we can see past and future lives, and the special connection between our actions in past lives and our experiences in this life, known as 'karma'. The subject of karma is very extensive and subtle, and we can understand it only through wisdom. Training in higher wisdom is learning to develop and increase our wisdom realizing emptiness through contemplating and meditating on emptiness, with a motivation of renunciation. This wisdom is extremely profound. Its object, emptiness, is not nothingness but is the real nature of all phenomena. A detailed explanation of emptiness is given in the chapter *Training in Ultimate Bodhichitta*.

The three higher trainings are the actual method to attain permanent liberation from the suffering of this life and countless future lives. This can be understood by the following analogy. When we cut down a tree using a saw, the saw alone cannot cut the tree without the use of our hands, which in turn depend upon our body. Training in higher moral discipline is like our body, training in higher concentration is like our hands, and training in higher wisdom is like the saw. By using these three together, we can cut down the poisonous tree of our self-grasping ignorance, and automatically all other delusions – its branches – and all our suffering and problems – its fruits – will cease completely. Then we shall have attained the permanent cessation of the suffering of this life and future lives – the supreme permanent peace of mind known as 'nirvana', or liberation. We shall have solved all our human problems and accomplished the real meaning of our life.

Contemplating the above explanation we should think:

Since the three higher trainings are the actual method to attain permanent liberation from the suffering of this life and countless future lives, I must put great effort into practising them.

We should meditate on this determination continually, and put our determination into practice.

WHAT WE SHOULD ATTAIN

In *Sutra of the Four Noble Truths* Buddha says: 'You should attain cessations.' In this context, 'cessation' means the permanent cessation of suffering and its root, self-grasping ignorance. In saying this, Buddha is advising us not to be satisfied with a temporary liberation from particular sufferings, but that we should have the intention to accomplish the ultimate goal of human life, the supreme permanent peace of mind (nirvana), and the pure and everlasting happiness of enlightenment.

Every living being without exception has to experience the cycle of the sufferings of sickness, ageing, death and rebirth, in life after life, endlessly. Following Buddha's example, we should develop strong renunciation for this endless cycle. When he was living in the palace with his family, Buddha saw how his people were constantly experiencing these sufferings and he made the strong determination to attain enlightenment, great liberation, and to lead every living being to this state.

Buddha did not encourage us to abandon daily activities that provide necessary conditions for living, or that prevent poverty, environmental problems, particular diseases and so forth. However, no matter how successful we are in these activities, we shall never achieve permanent cessation of such problems. We shall still have to experience them in our countless future lives and, even in this life, although we work very hard to prevent these problems, the sufferings of poverty, environmental pollution and disease are increasing throughout the world. Furthermore, because of the power of modern technology there are now many great dangers developing in the world that have never been experienced before. Therefore, we should not be satisfied with merely temporary freedom from particular sufferings, but apply great effort to attaining permanent freedom while we have this opportunity.

We should remember the preciousness of our human life. Because of their previous deluded views denying the value of spiritual practice, those who have taken rebirth as animals, for example, have no opportunity to engage in spiritual practice, which alone gives rise to a meaningful life. Since it is impossible for them to listen to, understand, contemplate and meditate on spiritual instructions, their present animal rebirth itself is an obstacle. As mentioned earlier, only human beings are free from such obstacles and have all the necessary conditions for engaging in spiritual paths, which alone lead to everlasting peace and happiness. This combination of freedom and the possession of necessary conditions is the special characteristic that makes our human life so precious.

In conclusion, we should think:

I should not be satisfied with a merely temporary cessation of particular sufferings, which even animals can experience. I must attain the permanent cessation of self-grasping ignorance – the root of suffering – through sincerely practising the three higher trainings.

We should meditate on this determination every day, and put our determination into practice. In this way we guide ourself to the liberating path.

The Path of a Person of Great Scope

In this context, a 'person of great scope' refers to someone who has a great capacity for developing spiritual understanding and realizations.

Because this subject is extensive and profound, containing both Sutra and Tantra, a detailed explanation of it will be given in the following chapters.

Je Tsongkhapa

The Supreme Good Heart –
Bodhichitta

We should maintain renunciation – the sincere wish to attain permanent liberation – day and night. It is the door to liberation – the supreme permanent peace of mind – and the basis of more advanced realizations. However, we should not be content with seeking merely our own liberation; we need also to consider the welfare of other living beings. There are countless beings drowning in samsara's ocean experiencing unbearable suffering. Whereas each one of us is just one single person, other living beings are countless in number; therefore the happiness and freedom of others are much more important than our own. For this reason we must enter the Bodhisattva's path, which leads us to the state of full enlightenment.

The gateway through which we enter the Bodhisattva's path is bodhichitta. 'Bodhi' means enlightenment and 'chitta' means mind. Bodhichitta is a mind that spontaneously wishes to attain enlightenment to benefit each and every living being directly. The moment we develop this precious mind of bodhichitta we become a Bodhisattva – a person who spontaneously wishes to attain enlightenment for the benefit of all living beings – and we become a Son or Daughter of the Conqueror Buddhas.

This supreme good heart of bodhichitta cannot be developed without training. Je Tsongkhapa said:

> Through watering the ground of affectionate love with
>   cherishing love,
> And then sowing the seeds of wishing love and
>   compassion,
> The medicinal tree of bodhichitta will grow.

This implies that there are five stages of training in bodhichitta: 1. training in affectionate love; 2. training in cherishing love; 3. training in wishing love; 4. training in universal compassion; and 5. training in actual bodhichitta.

TRAINING IN AFFECTIONATE LOVE

In this training we learn to develop and maintain a warm heart and a feeling of being close to all living beings without exception. This affectionate love makes our mind pure and balanced, and prepares the foundation for generating cherishing love for all living beings. Normally our mind is unbalanced; we feel either too close to someone out of attachment or too distant from others out of anger. It is impossible to develop the supreme good heart of bodhichitta with such an unbalanced mind. This unbalanced mind is the source of all our daily problems. We may think that some people are our enemies because they are harming us, so how can we develop and maintain a warm heart and a feeling of being close to such people? This way of thinking is incorrect. The people who we believe are our enemies are in reality our mothers of former lives. Our mothers of former lives and our mother of this present life are all our mothers and are all equally kind to us.

It is incorrect to reason that our mothers of former lives are no longer our mothers just because a long time has passed since they actually cared for us. If our present mother were to die today, would she cease to be our mother? No, we would still regard her as our mother and pray for her happiness. The same is true of all our previous mothers – they died, yet they remain our mothers. It is only because of the changes in our external appearance that we do not recognize each other.

In our daily life, we see many different living beings, both human and non-human. We regard some as friends, some as enemies, and most as strangers. These distinctions are made by our mistaken minds; they are not verified by valid minds. Rather than following such mistaken minds, we should recognize and believe that all living beings are our mothers. Whoever we meet, we should think 'This person is my mother.' In this way, we shall generate a warm heart and a feeling of being equally close to all living beings. Our belief that all living beings are our mothers is wisdom because it understands a meaningful object, which is that all living beings are our mothers. Through this understanding we shall experience great meaning in this life and in countless future lives. We should never abandon this beneficial belief or view.

We should contemplate as follows:

Since it is impossible to find a beginning to my mental continuum, it follows that I have taken countless rebirths in the past, and, if I have had countless rebirths, I must have had countless mothers. Where are all these mothers now? They are all the living beings alive today.

Having repeatedly contemplated this point we strongly believe that all living beings are our mothers, and we meditate on this belief.

THE KINDNESS OF LIVING BEINGS

Having become convinced that all living beings are our mothers, we contemplate the immense kindness we have received from each of them when they were our mother, as well as the kindness they have shown us at other times.

When we were conceived, had our mother not wanted to keep us in her womb she could have had an abortion. If she had done so, we would not now have this human life. Through her kindness she allowed us to stay in her womb, and so we now enjoy a human life and experience all its advantages. When we were a baby, had we not received her constant care and attention we would certainly have had an accident and could now be disabled or blind. Fortunately, our mother did not neglect us. Day and night, she gave us her loving care, regarding us as more important than herself. She saved our life many times each day. During the night she allowed her sleep to be interrupted, and during the day she forfeited her usual pleasures. She had to leave her job, and when her friends went out to enjoy themselves she had to stay behind. She spent all her money on us, giving us the best food and the best clothes she could afford. She taught us how to eat, how to walk, how to talk. Thinking of our future welfare, she did her best to ensure that we received a good education. Due to her kindness, we are now able to study whatever we choose. It is principally through the kindness of our mother that we now have the opportunity to practise Dharma and eventually to attain enlightenment.

Since there is no one who has not been our mother at some time in our previous lives, and since when we were their child they treated us with the same kindness as our present mother has treated us in this life, all living beings are very kind.

The kindness of living beings is not limited to the times when they have been our mother. All the time, our day-to-day needs are provided through the kindness of others. We brought nothing with us from our former life, yet, as soon as we were born, we were given a home, food, clothes and every-thing we needed – all provided through the kindness of others. Everything we now enjoy has been provided through the kind-ness of other beings, past or present.

We are able to make use of many things with very little effort on our own part. If we consider facilities such as roads, cars, trains, aeroplanes, ships, houses, restaurants, hotels, libraries, hospitals, shops, money and so on, it is clear that many people worked very hard to provide these things. Even though we make little or no contribution towards the provision of these facilities, they are all available for us to use. This shows the great kindness of others.

Both our general education and our spiritual training are provided by others. All our Dharma realizations, from our very first insights up to our eventual attainment of liberation and enlightenment, will be attained in dependence upon the kindness of others. As human beings we generally have the opportunity to attain the supreme happiness of enlightenment. This is because we have the opportunity to enter and follow the path to enlightenment, a spiritual path motivated by com-passion for all living beings. The gateway through which we enter the path to enlightenment is therefore compassion for all living beings – universal compassion – and we develop this compassion only by relying upon all living beings as the objects of our compassion. This shows that it is through the great kindness of all living beings acting as the objects of our compassion that we have the opportunity to enter the path to enlightenment and attain the supreme happiness of enlightenment. It is therefore clear that for us all living beings are supremely kind and precious.

From the depths of our heart we should think:

Each and every living being is supremely kind and precious to me. They provide me with the opportunity to attain the pure and everlasting happiness of enlightenment – the ultimate goal of human life.

Understanding and thinking in this way, we generate a warm heart and a feeling of being equally close to all living beings without exception. We transform our mind into this feeling, and we remain on it single-pointedly for as long as possible. Through continually contemplating and meditating in this way we shall maintain a warm heart and a feeling of being close to each and every living being all the time, in every situation. Having understood the eight benefits of maintaining affectionate love that are listed below in the section *Wishing Love*, we should apply continual effort in this practice.

TRAINING IN CHERISHING LOVE

This training has two stages: 1. equalizing self and others; and 2. exchanging self with others.

EQUALIZING SELF AND OTHERS

This practice is called 'equalizing self and others' because we are learning to believe that the happiness and freedom of ourself and all other living beings are equally important. Learning to cherish others is the best solution to our daily problems, and it is the source of all our future happiness and good fortune.

There are two levels of cherishing others: (1) cherishing others as we cherish a close friend or relative; and (2) cherishing others as we cherish ourself. The second level is more profound. Through cherishing all living beings as we cherish ourself we shall develop the profound universal compassion that functions as the quick path to enlightenment. This is one of the essential points of Kadam Lamrim.

To train in equalizing self and others we engage in the following contemplation, thinking:

I must believe that the happiness and freedom of myself and all other living beings are equally important because:

(1) All living beings have shown me great kindness in both this and previous lives.

(2) Just as I wish to be free from suffering and experience only happiness, so do all other beings. In this respect, I am no different from any other being; we are all equal.

(3) I am only one, whereas others are countless, so how can I be concerned for myself alone while I neglect others? My happiness and suffering are insignificant when compared with the happiness and suffering of countless other living beings.

Having repeatedly contemplated these points, we strongly believe that the happiness and freedom of ourself and all other living beings are equally important. We then remain on this belief single-pointedly for as long as possible. We should continually practise this contemplation and meditation until we spontaneously believe that the happiness and freedom of ourself and all other living beings are equally important, which is the realization of equalizing self and others.

EXCHANGING SELF WITH OTHERS

This training has three stages: 1. contemplating the disadvantages of self-cherishing; 2. contemplating the advantages of cherishing others; and 3. the actual training in exchanging self with others.

CONTEMPLATING THE DISADVANTAGES OF
SELF-CHERISHING

What is self-cherishing? When we think 'I' and 'mine' we perceive an inherently existent I, and we cherish it and believe that its happiness and freedom are the most important. This is self-cherishing. Caring for ourself is not self-cherishing. We need to care for ourself to maintain this human life so that we can continually apply effort to accomplishing its real meaning.

Self-cherishing and self-grasping are different aspects of one mind. Self-grasping grasps at an inherently existent 'I', and self-cherishing believes that such an 'I' is precious and that its happiness and freedom are supremely important. Self-cherishing is our normal view that believes 'I am important' and 'My happiness and freedom are important', and that neglects others' happiness and freedom. It is part of our ignorance because in reality there is no inherently existent I. Our self-cherishing mind nevertheless cherishes this I and believes it to be the most important. It is a foolish and deceptive mind that always interferes with our inner peace, and it is a great obstacle to our accomplishing the real meaning of our human life. We have had this self-cherishing mind in life after life since beginningless time, even while asleep and dreaming.

In *Guide to the Bodhisattva's Way of Life* Shantideva says:

> ... all the suffering there is in this world
> Arises from wishing ourself to be happy.

Sufferings are not given to us as a punishment. They all come from our self-cherishing mind, which wishes ourself to be happy while neglecting the happiness of others. There are two ways to understand this. First, the self-cherishing mind is the creator of all our suffering and problems; and second, self-cherishing is the basis for experiencing all our suffering and problems.

We suffer because in our previous lives we performed actions that caused others to experience suffering, motivated by selfish intention – our self-cherishing. As a result of these actions, we now experience our present suffering and problems. Therefore, the real creator of all our suffering and problems is our self-cherishing mind.

Our present experience of particular suffering and problems has a special connection with particular actions we performed in our previous lives. This is very subtle. We cannot see this hidden connection with our eyes, but as already explained we can understand it through using our wisdom, and in particular through relying upon Buddha's teachings on karma. In general, everyone knows that if they perform bad actions they will experience bad results and if they perform good actions they will experience good results.

The self-cherishing mind is also the basis for experiencing all our suffering and problems. For example, when people are unable to fulfil their wishes, many experience depression, discouragement, unhappiness and mental pain, and some even want to kill themselves. This is because their self-cherishing believes that their own wishes are so important. It is therefore their self-cherishing that is mainly responsible for their problems. Without self-cherishing, there would be no basis for experiencing such suffering.

When we are seriously ill we find it difficult to bear our suffering, but illness harms us only because we cherish ourself. If another person is experiencing a similar illness, we have no problem. Why? Because we do not cherish him or her. However, if we cherished others as we cherish ourself, we would find it difficult to bear their suffering. This is compassion. As Shantideva says:

The suffering I experience
Does not harm others,
But I find it hard to bear
Because I cherish myself.

Likewise, the suffering of others
Does not harm me,
But, if I cherish others,
I shall find their suffering hard to bear.

In life after life, since beginningless time, we have tried to fulfil the wishes of our self-cherishing mind, believing its view to be true. We have put great effort into seeking happiness from external sources, but have nothing to show for it now. Because self-cherishing has deceived us we have wasted countless previous lives. It has driven us to work for our own purpose, but we have gained nothing. This foolish mind has made all our previous lives empty – when we took this human rebirth we brought nothing with us but delusions. In every moment of every day, this self-cherishing mind continues to deceive us.

Having contemplated these points, we think:

Nothing causes me greater harm than the demon of my self-cherishing. It is the source of all my negativity, misfortune, problems and suffering. Therefore I must abandon my self-cherishing.

We should meditate on this determination every day, and put our determination into practice.

CONTEMPLATING THE ADVANTAGES OF CHERISHING OTHERS

When we deeply think that others are important, and that their happiness and freedom are important, we are cherishing others. If we cherish others like this, we shall always have good relationships and live in harmony with others, and our daily life will be peaceful and happy. We can begin this practice with our family, friends and those around us, and then gradually we shall develop and maintain cherishing love for all living beings without exception.

In *Guide to the Bodhisattva's Way of Life*, Shantideva says:

All the happiness there is in this world
Arises from wishing others to be happy

If we think carefully about this, we shall realize that all our present and future happiness depends upon our cherishing others – upon our wanting others to be happy. In our past lives, because we cherished others, we practised virtuous actions such as refraining from killing or harming others and abandoning stealing from and cheating them. We gave them material help and protection, and practised patience. As a result of these virtuous actions, we have now obtained this precious human life with the opportunity to experience human enjoyments.

The immediate effect of cherishing others will be that many of our daily problems, such as those that arise from anger, jealousy and selfish behaviour, will disappear, and our mind will become calm and peaceful. Since we shall act in considerate ways, we shall please others and not become involved in quarrels or disputes. If we cherish others we shall be concerned to help rather than to harm them, so we shall naturally avoid non-virtuous actions. Instead, we shall practise virtuous actions, such as compassion, love, patience, and giving material help and protection, and thus create the cause to attain pure and everlasting happiness in the future.

In particular, if we cherish all other living beings as we cherish ourself we shall find their suffering hard to bear. Our feeling that it is hard to bear the suffering of all other living beings is universal compassion, and this will lead us quickly to the pure and everlasting happiness of enlightenment. Just like all the previous Buddhas, we shall be born an enlightened Buddha from the mother, universal compassion. This is why our cherishing all living beings will enable us to attain enlightenment very quickly.

Contemplating all these benefits, we think:

The precious mind that cherishes all living beings protects both myself and others from suffering, brings pure and everlasting happiness and fulfils the wishes of both myself and others. Therefore I must always cherish all living beings without exception.

We should meditate on this determination every day, and out of meditation put our determination into practice. This means that we should actually cherish each and every living being, including animals.

THE ACTUAL TRAINING IN EXCHANGING
SELF WITH OTHERS

Exchanging self with others means that we change the object of our cherishing from ourself to all other living beings. This is impossible without training. How do we train in exchanging self with others? With an understanding of the great disadvantages of cherishing ourself and the great advantages of cherishing all living beings, as explained above, and remembering that we have made the determination to abandon our self-cherishing and always cherish all living beings without exception, we think from the depths of our heart:

I must give up cherishing myself and instead cherish all other living beings without exception.

We then meditate on this determination. We should continually practise this meditation until we spontaneously believe that the happiness and freedom of each and every other living being are far more important than our own. This belief is the realization of exchanging self with others.

TRAINING IN WISHING LOVE

With the understanding and belief that the happiness and freedom of each and every living being are far more important than our own, we generate wishing love for all living beings, thinking:

How wonderful it would be if all living beings attained the pure and everlasting happiness of enlightenment! May they attain this happiness. I myself will work for this aim.

We remain single-pointedly on this precious mind of wishing love for all living beings for as long as possible. We repeat this meditation again and again until we spontaneously wish that each and every living being may experience the happiness of enlightenment. This spontaneous wish is the actual realization of wishing love.

Wishing love is also called 'immeasurable love' because merely through meditating on wishing love we shall receive immeasurable benefits in this life and in countless future lives. Based on Buddha's teachings, the great scholar Nagarjuna listed eight benefits of affectionate love and wishing love: (1) By meditating on affectionate love and wishing love for just one moment we accumulate greater merit than we would do by giving food three times every day to all those who are hungry in the world.

When we give food to those who are hungry we are not giving real happiness. This is because the happiness that comes from eating food is not real happiness, but just a temporary reduction in the suffering of hunger. However, meditation on affectionate love and wishing love leads us and all living beings to the pure and everlasting happiness of enlightenment.

The remaining seven benefits of meditating on affectionate love and wishing love are that in the future: (2) we shall receive great loving kindness from humans and non-humans; (3) we shall be protected in various ways by humans and non-humans; (4) we shall be mentally happy all the time; (5) we shall be physically healthy all the time; (6) we shall not be harmed by weapons, poison and other harmful conditions; (7) we shall obtain all necessary conditions without effort; and (8) we shall be born in the superior heaven of a Buddha Land.

Having contemplated these benefits we should apply effort in meditating on wishing love many times every day.

TRAINING IN UNIVERSAL COMPASSION

Universal compassion is a mind that sincerely wishes to liberate all living beings from suffering permanently. If, on the basis of cherishing all living beings, we contemplate the fact that they experience the cycle of physical suffering and mental pain in life after life without end, their inability to liberate themselves from suffering, their lack of freedom and how, by engaging in negative actions, they create the causes of future suffering, we shall develop deep compassion for them. We need to empathize with them and feel their pain as keenly as we feel our own.

No one wants to suffer, yet out of ignorance living beings create suffering by performing non-virtuous actions. We should therefore feel equal compassion for all living beings without exception; there is no single living being who is not a suitable object of our compassion.

All living beings suffer because they take contaminated rebirths. Human beings have no choice but to experience immense human sufferings because they have taken human rebirth, which is contaminated by the inner poison of delusions. Similarly, animals have to experience animal suffering, and hungry ghosts and hell beings have to experience all the sufferings of their respective realms. If living beings were to experience all this suffering for just one single life, it would not be so bad, but the cycle of suffering continues life after life, endlessly.

To develop renunciation, we previously contemplated how in our countless future lives we shall have to experience the unbearable sufferings of animals, hungry ghosts, hells beings, humans, demi-gods and gods. Now, at this point, to develop compassion for all living beings who are our mothers, we contemplate how in their countless future lives they will have to experience the unbearable sufferings of animals, hungry ghosts, hells beings, humans, demi-gods and gods.

Having contemplated this we should think:

> *I cannot bear the suffering of these countless mother beings. Drowning in the vast and deep ocean of samsara, the cycle of contaminated rebirth, they have to experience unbearable physical suffering and mental pain in this life and in countless future lives. I must permanently liberate all these living beings from their suffering.*

We should meditate continually on this determination, which is universal compassion, and apply great effort to fulfilling its aim.

TRAINING IN ACTUAL BODHICHITTA

The moment we develop bodhichitta we become a Bodhisattva, a person who spontaneously wishes to attain enlightenment for the benefit of all living beings. Initially we shall be a Bodhisattva on the path of accumulation. Then, by following the path to enlightenment with the vehicle of bodhichitta, we can progress from being a Bodhisattva on the path of accumulation to being a Bodhisattva on the path of preparation, a Bodhisattva on the path of seeing, and then a Bodhisattva on the path of meditation. From there we shall reach the Path of No More Learning, which is the actual state of enlightenment. As already mentioned, enlightenment is the inner light of wisdom that is permanently free from all mistaken appearance, and whose function is to bestow mental peace upon each and every living being every day. When we attain a Buddha's enlightenment we shall be able to benefit each and every living being directly through bestowing blessings and through our countless emanations.

In Sutra teachings, Buddha says:

In this impure life of samsara
No one experiences real happiness;
The actions they perform
Will always be the causes of suffering.

The happiness that we normally experience through having good conditions, such as a good reputation, a good position, a good job, good relationships, seeing attractive forms, hearing good news or beautiful music, eating, drinking and sex is not real happiness, but changing suffering – a reduction in our previous suffering. Out of ignorance, however, we believe that only these things bring happiness, and because of this we never wish to attain real happiness, the pure and everlasting happiness of liberation and enlightenment, even for our own benefit. We are always searching for happiness in this impure life of samsara, like the thief who searched for gold in Milarepa's empty cave and found nothing. The great Yogi Milarepa heard a thief rummaging around his cave one night and called out to him, 'How do you expect to find anything valuable here at night, when I cannot find anything valuable here during the day?'

When, through training, we develop the precious mind of enlightenment, bodhichitta, we spontaneously think:

How wonderful it would be if I and all living beings attained real happiness, the pure and everlasting happiness of enlightenment! May we attain this happiness. I myself will work for this aim.

We need to have this precious mind of bodhichitta in our heart. It is our inner Spiritual Guide, who leads us directly to the state of supreme happiness of enlightenment; and it is the real wishfulfilling jewel through which we can fulfil our own and others' wishes. There is no greater beneficial intention than this precious mind.

Having contemplated the above explanation, we think from the depths of our heart:

> *I am one single person but other living beings are countless, and they are all my kind mothers. These countless mother beings have to experience unbearable physical suffering and mental pain in this life and in their countless future lives. Compared with the suffering of these countless living beings, my own suffering is insignificant. I must liberate all living beings from suffering permanently, and for this purpose I must attain a Buddha's enlightenment.*

We meditate on this determination, which is bodhichitta, single-pointedly. We should practise this contemplation and meditation continually until we develop the spontaneous wish to attain enlightenment to benefit each and every living being directly, and then we should apply great effort to fulfilling our bodhichitta wish.

Training in the Path of Bodhichitta

There are three stages of training in the path of bodhichitta: 1. training in the six perfections; 2. training in taking in conjunction with the practice of the six perfections; and 3. training in giving in conjunction with the practice of the six perfections.

TRAINING IN THE SIX PERFECTIONS

The six perfections are the actual path to enlightenment, and they are also the path of bodhichitta and the Bodhisattva's path. Through following this path with the vehicle of bodhichitta we shall definitely reach the state of enlightenment. Our bodhichitta wish is to attain enlightenment to benefit each and every living being directly. To fulfil this wish, in front of our Spiritual Guide or an image of Buddha regarded as the living Buddha, we should promise to engage in the Bodhisattva's path or training while reciting the following ritual prayer three times. This promise is the Bodhisattva's vow.

Just as all the previous Sugatas, the Buddhas,
Generated the mind of enlightenment, bodhichitta,
And accomplished all the stages
Of the Bodhisattva's training,

So will I too, for the sake of all beings,
Generate the mind of enlightenment
And accomplish all the stages
Of the Bodhisattva's training.

When we take the Bodhisattva's vow we are taking the commitment to engage in the path to enlightenment, the Bodhisattva's training, which is the practice of the six perfections. Normally, when we start a job, we commit ourself to fulfilling our employer's wishes; otherwise we shall quickly lose our job. In the same way, having generated bodhichitta – the determination to attain enlightenment to benefit each and every living being directly – we need to commit ourself to engaging in the practice of the six perfections. If we do not make this commitment by taking the Bodhisattva's vow, we shall lose our opportunity to attain enlightenment. Through contemplating this we should encourage ourself to take the Bodhisattva's vow and sincerely practise the six perfections.

The six perfections are the practices of giving, moral discipline, patience, effort, concentration and wisdom, motivated by bodhichitta. We should recognize that the six perfections are our daily practice.

In the practice of giving we should practise: (1) giving material help to those in poverty, including giving food to animals; (2) giving practical help to those sick or physically weak; (3) giving protection by always trying to save others' lives, including those of insects; (4) giving love, learning to cherish all living beings by always believing that their happiness and freedom are important; and (5) giving Dharma, helping others to solve their problems of anger, attachment and ignorance by giving Dharma teachings or meaningful advice.

In the practice of moral discipline we should abandon any inappropriate actions including those that cause others suffering. We should especially abandon breaking our commitments of the Bodhisattva's vow. This is the basic foundation upon which we can make progress on the Bodhisattva's path. By doing this our actions of body, speech and mind will be pure, so that we become a pure being.

In the practice of patience we should never allow ourself to become angry or discouraged, by temporarily accepting any difficulties or harm from others. When we practise patience we are wearing the supreme inner armour that directly protects us from physical sufferings, mental pain and other problems. Anger destroys our merit, or good fortune, so that we shall continually experience many obstacles, and because of lacking good fortune it will be difficult to fulfil our wishes, especially our spiritual aims. There is no greater evil than anger. With the practice of patience we can accomplish any spiritual aim; there is no greater virtue than patience.

In the practice of effort we should rely upon irreversible effort to accumulate the great collections of merit and wisdom, which are the main causes of attaining Buddha's Form Body (Rupakaya), and Truth Body (Dharmakaya); and especially we should emphasize contemplation and meditation on emptiness, the way things really are. By doing this we can easily make progress on the path to enlightenment. With effort we can accomplish our aim, whereas with laziness we cannot achieve anything.

In the practice of concentration, at this stage we should emphasize accomplishing the concentration of tranquil abiding observing emptiness. An explanation is given below in the section *A Simple Training in Ultimate Bodhichitta*. When, through the power of this concentration, we experience a special wisdom called 'superior seeing' that realizes the emptiness of all phenomena very clearly, we shall have progressed from being a Bodhisattva on the path of accumulation to being a Bodhisattva on the path of preparation.

In the practice of wisdom, at this stage we need to emphasize increasing the power of our wisdom of superior seeing by continually meditating on the emptiness of all phenomena with bodhichitta motivation. Through this, when our superior seeing transforms into the path of seeing, which is the direct realization of the emptiness of all phenomena, we shall have progressed from being a Bodhisattva on the path of preparation to being a Bodhisattva on the path of seeing. The moment we attain the path of seeing we are a Superior Bodhisattva and no longer experience samsara's sufferings. Even if someone cuts our body piece by piece with a knife we have no pain because we have the direct realization of the way things really are.

Having completed the path of seeing, to make further progress we need to engage continually in the meditation on the emptiness of all phenomena with bodhichitta motivation. This meditation is called the 'path of meditation'. When we reach this stage we shall have progressed from being a Bodhisattva on the path of seeing to being a Bodhisattva on the path of meditation.

Having completed the path of meditation, when our wisdom of the path of meditation transforms into an omniscient wisdom that is permanently free from all mistaken appearances, this omniscient wisdom is called the 'Path of No More Learning', which is actual enlightenment. When we reach this stage we shall have progressed from being a Bodhisattva on the path of meditation to being an enlightened being, a Buddha. We shall have completed the ultimate goal of living beings.

The Bodhisattva's initial training in accumulating merit or wisdom is the Bodhisattva's path of accumulation; the Bodhisattva's training in accumulating merit or wisdom that is a preparation for attaining the path of seeing is the Bodhisattva's path of preparation; the Bodhisattva's training that is the initial direct realization of emptiness is the Bodhisattva's path of seeing; after completing the path of seeing the Bodhisattva's training that meditates continually on emptiness is the Bodhisattva's path of meditation; and Buddha's omniscient wisdom that is attained through completing all the trainings of Sutra and Tantra is the Path of No More Learning, the state of enlightenment.

TRAINING IN TAKING IN CONJUNCTION WITH THE PRACTICE OF THE SIX PERFECTIONS

There are four main benefits of the meditations on taking and giving: they are powerful methods (1) to purify the potentialities of non-virtuous actions that cause us to experience incurable diseases such as cancer; (2) to accumulate a great collection of merit; (3) to ripen our potentiality to be able to benefit all living beings; and (4) to purify our mind.

There was once a Lamrim practitioner called Kharak Gomchen who was seriously afflicted by leprosy. The treatments given by his doctors did not work, and each year his condition grew worse. Finally, his doctors told him that there was nothing they could do to cure his disease. Believing that he would soon die, Gomchen left his home and went to a cemetery to prepare for death. While staying in the cemetery, he concentrated day and night on practising the meditations on taking and giving

with strong compassion for all living beings. Through this practice he was completely cured and returned home healthy and
with a happy mind. There are many other similar examples.

At the moment we are unable to benefit all living beings
but we have the potential for this ability, which is part of our
Buddha nature. Through practising the meditations on taking
and giving with strong compassion for all living beings, the
potential to be able to benefit all living beings will ripen, and
when this happens we shall become an enlightened being, a
Buddha. When we purify our mind through the practices of
taking and giving, every spiritual realization will grow easily
in our mind. Through contemplating the four main benefits of
meditating on taking and giving, we should encourage ourself
to practise these meditations sincerely.

'Taking' in this context means taking others' sufferings upon
ourself through meditation. When we meditate on taking our
motivation should be compassion, thinking:

*I must permanently liberate all living beings from their
suffering and fears in this life and countless future lives.*

In this way, by giving protection we are practising the
perfection of giving; by abandoning self-cherishing we are
practising the perfection of moral discipline; by willingly
accepting any adverse conditions obstructing our practice of
taking we are practising the perfection of patience; by applying
effort to practising this meditation continually, free from laziness, we are practising the perfection of effort; by concentrating
single-pointedly on the meditation on taking, free from distraction, we are practising the perfection of concentration; and by
realizing that we ourself, all living beings, and their suffering
all exist as mere names and do not inherently exist we are
practising the perfection of wisdom. This is how we should

train in the meditation on taking in conjunction with practising the six perfections. This is a very profound method of practising the six perfections. We should apply this same method to all other meditations, such as the meditation on death, so that we can quickly make progress along the path to enlightenment.

There are two stages to the meditation on taking: 1. meditation on taking focusing on all living beings; and 2. meditation on taking focusing on particular living beings.

MEDITATION ON TAKING FOCUSING ON ALL LIVING BEINGS

In this first stage we focus on the assembly of all living beings without exception, and then think from the depths of our heart:

In their countless future lives these living beings will continually experience without choice the sufferings of humans, animals, hungry ghosts, hell beings, demi-gods and gods. How wonderful it would be if all these living beings were permanently freed from the suffering and fears in this life and countless future lives! May they achieve this. I myself will work for them to achieve this. I must do this.

Thinking in this way, we imagine that the sufferings of all living beings gather together in the aspect of black smoke. This dissolves into our ignorance of self-grasping and self-cherishing at our heart. We then strongly believe that all living beings are permanently freed from suffering, and that our ignorance of self-grasping and self-cherishing is completely destroyed. We meditate on this belief single-pointedly for as long as possible.

With compassion for all living beings we should continually practise this meditation until we experience signs that indicate our mind has been purified. These signs can include the curing of any sickness we may have, the reducing of our delusions, our having a more peaceful and happy mind, the increasing of our faith, correct intention and correct view, and especially the strengthening of our experience of universal compassion.

MEDITATION ON TAKING FOCUSING ON
PARTICULAR LIVING BEINGS

In this meditation we can focus, for example, on the assembly of living beings who experience the suffering of sickness. We then think:

These living beings experience the suffering of sickness in this life and in their countless future lives without end. How wonderful it would be if these living beings were permanently freed from sickness! May they achieve this. I myself will work for them to achieve this. I must do this.

Thinking in this way, we imagine that the suffering of sickness of all living beings gathers together in the aspect of black smoke. This dissolves into our ignorance of self-grasping and self-cherishing at our heart. We then strongly believe that all these living beings are permanently freed from sickness, and that our ignorance of self-grasping and self-cherishing is completely destroyed. We meditate on this belief single-pointedly for as long as possible.

In the same way, we can practise the meditation on taking while focusing on a particular individual or group of living beings who are experiencing other sufferings such as poverty, fighting and famine.

In particular, we should apply effort to developing deep familiarity with the meditation on taking focusing on all living beings. This meditation makes our mind pure, which in turn makes our actions pure so that we become a pure being. If we die with strong compassion for all living beings we shall definitely be born in the Pure Land of a Buddha. This is because our compassion that manifests when we are dying will directly cause our potential for taking rebirth in the Pure Land of a Buddha to ripen. This is the good result of a good heart. The result of maintaining the good heart of sincerely wishing to liberate permanently all living beings from suffering is that we ourself shall experience permanent liberation from suffering by taking rebirth in the Pure Land of a Buddha.

For example, when Geshe Chekhawa was dying he developed the sincere wish to be reborn in hell in order to help hell beings directly, but he received clear visions that he would be reborn in Sukhavati, the Pure Land of Buddha Amitabha. He told his assistant 'Unfortunately my wish will not be fulfilled.' The assistant asked him 'What is your wish?', and Geshe Chekhawa replied: 'My wish is to take rebirth in hell so that I can help hell beings directly, but I have seen clear signs that I shall be born in the Pure Land of Buddha Amitabha.' Although Geshe Chekhawa wanted to take rebirth in hell, his compassion for all living beings prevented him from taking a lower rebirth; he had no choice but to go to a Buddha's Pure Land where he experienced permanent liberation from suffering. However, although Geshe Chekhawa took rebirth in a Pure Land, he was able to help hell beings through his emanations.

We may think our belief that living beings have attained permanent liberation from suffering through our meditation is incorrect, because living beings have not actually attained this. Although it is true that living beings have not actually attained permanent liberation, our belief is still correct because it arises from our compassion and wisdom. Meditating on this belief will cause our potentiality of being able to liberate all living beings permanently from suffering to ripen quickly, so that we shall attain enlightenment quickly. Therefore we should never abandon such a beneficial belief, which is the nature of wisdom. Meditation on taking is the quick path to enlightenment, and has a similar function to Tantric practice. It is said that Tantric realizations can be achieved simply through relying upon correct belief and imagination. This practice is very simple; all we need to do is to become deeply familiar with meditation on correct belief and imagination as presented in Tantra, by applying continual effort.

TRAINING IN GIVING IN CONJUNCTION WITH THE PRACTICE OF THE SIX PERFECTIONS

'Giving' in this context means giving our own happiness to others through meditation. In general, in the cycle of impure life, samsara, there is no real happiness at all. As mentioned previously, the happiness that we normally experience through eating, drinking, sex and so forth is not real happiness, but merely a reduction of a previous problem or dissatisfaction. For example, if the happiness we experience from sex is real happiness, then it would follow that sex itself would be a real cause of happiness. If this were true, then the more we had sex, the more our happiness would increase, but actually the opposite would happen; instead of happiness increasing, our suffering would increase. In *Four Hundred Verses* the Buddhist Master Aryadeva says:

The experience of suffering will never be changed by the same cause,
But we can see the experience of happiness will be changed by the same cause.

This means that, for example, the suffering caused by fire will never be changed into happiness by that fire, but we can see that the happiness caused, for example, by eating will change into suffering just through eating.

How do we meditate on giving? In *Guide to the Bodhisattva's Way of Life* Shantideva says:

... to accomplish the welfare of all living beings
I will transform my body into an enlightened
    wishfulfilling jewel.

We should regard our continuously residing body, our very subtle body, as the real wishfulfilling jewel; this is our Buddha nature through which the wishes of ourself and all other living beings will be fulfilled. We then think:

All living beings wish to be happy all the time, but they do not know how to do this. They never experience real happiness, because out of ignorance they destroy their own happiness by developing delusions such as anger and performing non-virtuous actions. How wonderful it would be if all these living beings experienced the pure and everlasting happiness of enlightenment! May they experience this happiness. I will now give my own future happiness of enlightenment to each and every living being.

Thinking in this way we imagine that from our continuously residing body at our heart we emanate infinite rays of light, which are in nature our future happiness of enlightenment. These reach all living beings of the six realms, and we strongly believe that each and every living being experiences the pure and everlasting happiness of enlightenment. We meditate on this belief single-pointedly for as long as possible. We should continually practise this meditation until we spontaneously believe that all living beings have actually received our future happiness of enlightenment now. Through this practice we are like a Bodhisattva who practises shepherd-like bodhichitta. Just as a shepherd wishes to provide protection and necessary conditions for his flock before he himself relaxes, a Bodhisattva who practises shepherd-like bodhichitta wishes to prepare protection and ultimate happiness for all beings before accomplishing it for himself.

This meditation has four main benefits: (1) it increases our wishing love for all living beings; (2) it ripens our potential ability to benefit all living beings; (3) it accumulates a great collection of merit, or good fortune; and (4) it causes our ordinary appearances and conceptions to cease.

Our future happiness of enlightenment is the result of our generating compassion for all living beings. The meditation on giving brings this future result into the path, and is therefore a quick path to enlightenment that has a similar function to Tantric practice. We should apply great effort to practise this meditation so that we can quickly make progress on the path to enlightenment.

When we are meditating on giving, our motivation should be wishing love. By giving love in this way we are practising the perfection of giving; by abandoning self-cherishing we are practising the perfection of moral discipline; by willingly accepting any adverse conditions obstructing our practice of giving we are practising the perfection of patience; by applying effort to practising this meditation continually, free from laziness, we are practising the perfection of effort; by concentrating single-pointedly on the meditation on giving, free from distraction, we are practising the perfection of concentration; and by realizing that we ourself, all living beings, and their happiness all exist as mere names and do not inherently exist we are practising the perfection of wisdom. This is how we should train in the meditation on giving in conjunction with practising the six perfections.

Training in giving is a special meditation on wishing love that sincerely wishes all living beings to attain real happiness – the pure and everlasting happiness of liberation and enlightenment. As mentioned above, meditation on wishing love is also called 'immeasurable love' because just by meditating on wishing love we receive immeasurable benefits in this life and in countless future lives.

Buddha of Compassion

Training in Ultimate Bodhichitta

When we meditate on emptiness to develop or increase ultimate bodhichitta, we are training in ultimate bodhichitta. Actual ultimate bodhichitta is a wisdom that directly realizes emptiness motivated by bodhichitta. It is called 'ultimate bodhichitta' because its object is ultimate truth, emptiness, and it is one of the main paths to enlightenment. The bodhichitta that has been explained so far is conventional bodhichitta, and this is the nature of compassion, whereas ultimate bodhichitta is the nature of wisdom. These two bodhichittas are like the two wings of a bird with which we can fly to the enlightened world.

If we do not know the meaning of emptiness there is no basis for training in ultimate bodhichitta, because emptiness is the object of ultimate bodhichitta. Je Tsongkhapa said:

> The knowledge of emptiness is superior to any other knowledge,
> The Teacher who teaches emptiness unmistakenly is superior to any other teacher,
> And the realization of emptiness is the very essence of Buddhadharma.

WHAT IS EMPTINESS?

Emptiness is the way things really are. It is the way things exist as opposed to the way they appear. We naturally believe that the things we see around us, such as tables, chairs and houses are truly existent, because we believe that they exist in exactly the way that they appear. However, the way things appear to our senses is deceptive and completely contradictory to the way in which they actually exist. Things appear to exist from their own side, without depending upon our mind. This book that appears to our mind, for example, seems to have its own independent, objective existence. It seems to be 'outside' whereas our mind seems to be 'inside'. We feel that the book can exist without our mind; we do not feel that our mind is in any way involved in bringing the book into existence. This way of existing independent of our mind is variously called 'true existence', 'inherent existence', 'existence from its own side' and 'existence from the side of the object'.

Although things appear directly to our senses to be truly, or inherently, existent, in reality all phenomena lack, or are empty of, true existence. This book, our body, our friends, we ourself, and the entire universe are in reality just appearances to mind, like things seen in a dream. If we dream of an elephant, the elephant appears vividly in all its detail – we can see it, hear it, smell it and touch it – but when we wake up we realize that it was just an appearance to mind. We do not wonder 'Where is the elephant now?', because we understand that it was simply a projection of our mind and had no existence outside our mind. When the dream awareness that apprehended the elephant ceased, the elephant did not go anywhere – it simply disappeared, for it was just an appearance to the mind and did not exist separately from the mind. Buddha said that the same is true for all phenomena; they are mere appearances to mind, totally dependent upon the minds that perceive them.

The world we experience when we are awake and the world we experience when we are dreaming are both mere appearances to mind that arise from our mistaken conceptions. If we want to say that the dream world is false, we also have to say that the waking world is false; and if we want to say that the waking world is true, we also have to say that the dream world is true. The only difference between them is that the dream world is an appearance to our subtle dreaming mind whereas the waking world is an appearance to our gross waking mind. The dream world exists only for as long as the dream awareness to which it appears exists, and the waking world exists only for as long as the waking awareness to which it appears exists. Buddha said: 'You should know that all phenomena are like dreams.' When we die, our gross waking minds dissolve into our very subtle mind and the world we experienced when we were alive simply disappears. The world as others perceive it will continue, but our personal world will disappear as completely and irrevocably as the world of last night's dream.

Buddha also said that all phenomena are like illusions. There are many different types of illusion, such as mirages, rainbows or drug-induced hallucinations. In ancient times, there used to be magicians who would cast a spell over their audience, causing them to see objects, such as a piece of wood, as something else, such as a tiger. Those deceived by the spell would see what appeared to be a real tiger and develop fear, but those who arrived after the spell had been cast would simply see a piece of wood. What all illusions have in common is that the way they appear does not coincide with the way they exist. Buddha likened all phenomena to illusions because, through the force of the imprints of self-grasping ignorance accumulated since beginningless time, whatever appears to our mind naturally appears to be truly existent and we instinctively assent to this appearance, but in reality everything is totally empty of true existence. Like a mirage that appears to be water but is not in fact water, things appear in a deceptive way. Not understanding their real nature we are fooled by appearances, and grasp at books and tables, bodies and worlds as truly existent. The result of grasping at phenomena in this way is that we develop self-cherishing, attachment, hatred, jealousy and other delusions, our mind becomes agitated and unbalanced, and our peace of mind is destroyed. We are like travellers in a desert who exhaust themselves running after mirages, or like someone walking down a road at night mistaking the shadows of the trees for criminals or wild animals waiting to attack.

THE EMPTINESS OF OUR BODY

To understand how phenomena are empty of true, or inherent, existence we should consider our own body. Once we have understood how our body lacks true existence we can easily apply the same reasoning to other objects.

In *Guide to the Bodhisattva's Way of Life* Bodhisattva Shantideva says:

> Therefore, there is no body,
> But, because of ignorance, we see a body within the
>   hands and so forth,
> Just like a mind mistakenly apprehending a person
> When observing the shape of a pile of stones at dusk.

On one level we know our body very well – we know whether it is healthy or unhealthy, beautiful or ugly, and so forth.

However, we never examine it more deeply, asking ourself: 'What precisely is my body? Where is my body? What is its real nature?' If we did examine our body in this way we would not be able to find it – instead of finding our body the result of this examination would be that our body disappears. The meaning of the first part of Shantideva's verse, 'Therefore, there is no body', is that if we search for our 'real' body, there is no body; our body exists only if we do not search for a real body behind its mere appearance.

There are two ways of searching for an object. An example of the first way, which we can call a 'conventional search', is searching for our car in a car park. The conclusion of this type of search is that we find the car, in the sense that we see the thing that everyone agrees is our car. However, having located our car in the car park, suppose we are still not satisfied with the mere appearance of the car and we want to determine exactly what the car is. We might then engage in what we can call an 'ultimate search' for the car, in which we look within the object itself to find something that is the object. To do this we ask ourself: 'Are any of the individual parts of the car, the car? Are the wheels the car? Is the engine the car? Is the chassis the car?' and so forth. When conducting an ultimate search for our car we are not satisfied with just pointing to the bonnet, wheels and so forth, and then saying 'car'; we want to know what the car really is. Instead of just using the word 'car' as ordinary people do, we want to know what the word really refers to. We want to mentally separate the car from all that is not car, so that we can say 'This is what the car really is.' We want to find a car, but in truth there is no car; we can find nothing. In *Condensed Perfection of Wisdom Sutra* Buddha says: 'If you search for your body with wisdom you cannot find it.' This also applies to our car, our house and all other phenomena.

In *Guide to the Bodhisattva's Way of Life* Shantideva says:

When examined in this way,
Who is living and who is it who will die?
What is the future and what is the past?
Who are our friends and who are our relatives?

I beseech you who are just like me,
Please know that all things are empty, like space.

The essential meaning of these words is that when we search
for things with wisdom, there is no person who is living
or dying, there is no past or future, and there is no present,
including our friends and relatives. We should know that all
phenomena are empty, like space, which means we should
know that all phenomena are not other than emptiness.

To understand Shantideva's claim that in reality there is no
body, we need to conduct an ultimate search for our body. If
we are ordinary beings, all objects, including our body, appear
to exist inherently. As mentioned above, objects seem to be
independent of our mind and independent of other phenomena. The universe appears to consist of discrete objects that
have an existence from their own side. These objects appear
to exist in themselves as stars, planets, mountains, people
and so forth, 'waiting' to be experienced by conscious beings.
Normally it does not occur to us that we are involved in any
way in the existence of these phenomena. For example, we feel
that our body exists from its own side and does not depend
upon our mind, or anyone else's, to bring it into existence.
However, if our body did exist in the way that we instinctively
grasp it – as an external object rather than just a projection of
mind – we should be able to point to our body without pointing to any phenomenon that is not our body. We should be able

to find it amongst its parts or outside its parts. Since there is no third possibility, if our body cannot be found either amongst its parts or outside its parts we must conclude that our body that we normally see does not exist.

It is not difficult to understand that the individual parts of our body are not our body – it is absurd to say that our back, our legs, or our head are our body. If one of the parts, say our back, is our body, then the other parts are equally our body, and it would follow that we have many bodies. Furthermore, our back, legs and so forth cannot be our body because they are parts of our body. The body is the part-possessor, and the back, legs and so forth are the possessed parts; and possessor and possessed cannot be one and the same.

Some people believe that although none of the individual parts of the body is the body, the collection of all the parts assembled together is the body. According to them, it is possible to find our body when we search for it analytic-ally because the collection of all the parts of our body is our body. However, this assertion can be refuted with many valid reasons. The force of these reasons may not be immediately obvious to us, but if we contemplate them carefully with a calm and positive mind we shall come to appreciate their validity.

Since none of the individual parts of our body is our body, how can the collection of all the parts be our body? For example, a collection of dogs cannot be a human being, because none of the individual dogs is human. As each indi-vidual member is 'non-human', how can this collection of non-humans magically transform into a human? Similarly, since the collection of the parts of our body is a collection of things that are not our body, it cannot be our body. Just as the collection of dogs remains simply dogs, so the collection of all the parts of our body remains simply parts of our body – it does not magically transform into the part-possessor, our body.

We may find this point difficult to understand, but if we think about it for a long time with a calm and positive mind, and discuss it with more experienced practitioners, it will gradually become clearer. We can also consult authentic books on the subject, such as *Heart of Wisdom* and *Ocean of Nectar*.

There is another way in which we can know that the collection of the parts of our body is not our body. If we can point to the collection of the parts of our body and say that this is, in itself, our body, then the collection of the parts of our body must exist independently of all phenomena that are not our body. Thus it would follow that the collection of the parts of our body exists independently of the parts themselves. This is clearly absurd – if it were true, we could remove all the parts of our body and the collection of the parts would remain. We can therefore conclude that the collection of the parts of our body is not our body.

Since the body cannot be found within its parts, either as an individual part or as the collection, the only possibility that remains is that it exists separately from its parts. If this is the case, it should be possible mentally or physically to remove all the parts of our body and still be left with the body. However, if we remove our arms, our legs, our head, our trunk and all the other parts of our body, no body is left. This proves that there is no body separate from its parts. It is because of ignorance that whenever we point to our body we are pointing only to a part of our body, which is not our body.

We have now searched in every possible place and have been unable to find our body either amongst its parts or anywhere else. We can find nothing that corresponds to the vividly appearing body that we normally grasp at. We are forced to agree with Shantideva that, when we search for our body, there is no body to be found. This clearly proves that our body that we normally see does not exist. It is almost as if our body does not exist at all. Indeed, the only sense in which we can say that our body does exist is if we are satisfied with the mere name 'body' and do not expect to find a real body behind the name. If we try to find, or point to, a real body to which the name 'body' refers, we shall not find anything at all. Instead of finding a truly existent body, we shall perceive the mere absence of our body that we normally see. This mere absence of our body that we normally see is the way our body actually exists. We shall realize that the body we normally perceive, grasp at and cherish does not exist at all. This non-existence of the body we normally grasp at is the emptiness of our body, the true nature of our body.

The term 'true nature' is very meaningful. Not being satisfied with the mere appearance and name 'body' we examined our body to discover its true nature. The result of this examination was a definite non-finding of our body. Where we expected to find a truly existent body, we discovered the utter non-existence of that truly existent body. This non-existence, or emptiness, is the true nature of our body. Apart from the mere absence of a truly existent body, there is no other true nature of our body – every other attribute of the body is just part of its deceptive nature. Since this is the case, why do we spend so much time focusing on the deceptive nature of our body? At present we ignore the true nature of our body and other phenomena, and concentrate only on their deceptive nature; yet the result of concentrating all the time on deceptive objects is that our mind becomes disturbed and we remain in the miserable life of samsara. If we wish to experience pure happiness, we must acquaint our mind with the truth. Instead of wasting our energy focusing only on meaningless, deceptive objects, we should focus on the true nature of things.

Although it is impossible to find our body when we search for it analytically, when we do not engage in analysis our body appears very clearly. Why is this? Shantideva says that because of ignorance we see our body within the hands and other parts of our body. In reality, our body does not exist within its parts. Just as at dusk we might see a pile of stones as a man even though there is no man within the stones, so in the same way our ignorant mind sees a body within the collection of arms, legs and so forth, even though no body exists there. The body we see within the collection of arms and legs is simply a hallucination of our ignorant mind. Not recognizing it as such, however, we grasp at it very strongly, cherish it and exhaust ourself in trying to protect it from any discomfort.

The way to familiarize our mind with the true nature of the body is to use the above reasoning to search for our body and then, when we have searched in every possible place and not found it, to concentrate on the space-like emptiness that is the mere absence of the body that we normally see. This space-like emptiness is the true nature of our body. Although it resembles empty space, it is a meaningful emptiness. Its meaning is the utter non-existence of the body that we normally see, the body that we grasp at so strongly and have cherished all our life.

Through becoming familiar with the experience of the space-like ultimate nature of the body, our grasping at our body will be reduced. As a result we shall experience far less suffering, anxiety and frustration in relation to our body. Our physical tension will diminish and our health will improve, and even when we do become sick our physical discomfort will not disturb our mind. Those who have a direct experience of emptiness do not feel any pain even if they are beaten or shot. Knowing that the real nature of their body is like space, for them being beaten is like space being beaten and being shot is like space being shot. Moreover, good and bad external conditions no longer have the power to disturb their mind, because they realize them to be like a magician's illusion, with no existence separate from the mind. Instead of being pulled about by changing conditions like a puppet on a string, their minds remain free and tranquil in the knowledge of the equal and unchanging ultimate nature of all things. In this way, a person who directly realizes emptiness, the true nature of phenomena, experiences peace and happiness day and night, life after life.

We need to distinguish between the conventionally existent body that does exist and the inherently existent body that does not exist; but we must take care not to be misled by the words into thinking that the conventionally existent body is anything more than a mere appearance to mind. It is perhaps less confusing simply to say that for a mind that directly sees the truth, or emptiness, there is no body. A body exists only for an ordinary mind to which a body appears.

Shantideva advises us that unless we wish to understand emptiness we should not examine conventional truths such as our body, possessions, places and friends, but instead be satisfied with their mere names, as are worldly people. Once a worldly person knows an object's name and purpose he is satisfied that he knows the object and does not investigate further. We must do the same, unless we want to meditate on emptiness. However, we should remember that if we did examine objects more closely we would not find them, for they would simply disappear, just as a mirage disappears if we try to look for it.

The same reasoning that we have used to prove the lack of true existence of our body can be applied to all other phenomena. This book, for example, seems to exist from its own side, somewhere within its parts; but when we examine the book more precisely we discover that none of the individual pages nor the collection of the pages is the book, yet without them there is no book. Instead of finding a truly existent book we are left beholding an emptiness that is the non-existence of the book we previously held to exist. Because of our ignorance the book appears to exist separately from our mind, as if our mind were inside and the book outside, but through analyzing the book we discover that this appearance is completely false. There is no book outside the mind. There is no book 'out there', within the pages. The only way the book exists is as a mere appearance to mind, a mere projection of the mind.

All phenomena exist by way of convention; nothing is inherently existent. This applies to mind, to Buddha, and even to emptiness itself. Everything is merely imputed by mind. All phenomena have parts – physical phenomena have physical parts, and non-physical phenomena have various parts, or attributes, that can be distinguished by thought. Using the same type of reasoning as above, we can realize that any phenomenon is not one of its parts, not the collection of its parts, and not separate from its parts. In this way we can realize the emptiness of all phenomena, the mere absence of all phenomena that we normally see or perceive.

It is particularly helpful to meditate on the emptiness of objects that arouse in us strong delusions like attachment or anger. By analyzing correctly we shall realize that the object we desire, or the object we dislike, does not exist from its own side. Its beauty or ugliness, and even its very existence, are imputed by mind. By thinking in this way we shall discover that there is no basis for attachment or anger.

THE EMPTINESS OF OUR MIND

In *Training the Mind in Seven Points,* after outlining how to engage in analytical meditation on the emptiness of inherent existence of outer phenomena such as our body, Geshe Chekhawa continues by saying that we should then analyze our own mind to understand how it lacks inherent existence.

Our mind is not an independent entity, but an ever-changing continuum that depends upon many factors, such as its previous moments, its objects and the inner energy winds upon which our minds are mounted. Like everything else, our mind is imputed upon a collection of many factors and therefore lacks inherent existence. A primary mind, or consciousness, for example, has five parts or 'mental factors': feeling, discrimination, intention, contact and attention. Neither the individual mental factors nor the collection of these mental factors is the primary mind itself, because they are mental factors and therefore parts of the primary mind. However, there is no primary mind that is separate from these mental factors. A primary mind is merely imputed upon the mental factors that are its basis of imputation, and therefore it does not exist from its own side.

Having identified the nature of our primary mind, which is an empty like space that perceives or understands objects, we then search for it within its parts – feeling, discrimination, intention, contact and attention – until finally we realize its unfindability. This unfindability is its ultimate nature, or emptiness. We then think:

All phenomena that appear to my mind are the nature of my mind. My mind is the nature of emptiness.

In this way we feel that everything dissolves into emptiness. We perceive only the emptiness of all phenomena and we

meditate on this emptiness. This way of meditating on emptiness is more profound than the meditation on the emptiness of
our body. Gradually our experience of emptiness will become
clearer and clearer until finally we gain an undefiled wisdom
that directly realizes the emptiness of all phenomena.

THE EMPTINESS OF OUR I

The object we grasp at most strongly is our self or I. Due to
the imprints of self-grasping ignorance accumulated over time
without beginning, our I appears to us as inherently existent,
and our self-grasping mind automatically grasps at it in this
way. Although we grasp at an inherently existent I all the time,
even during sleep, it is not easy to identify how it appears to
our mind. To identify it clearly, we must begin by allowing it
to manifest strongly by contemplating situations in which we
have an exaggerated sense of I, such as when we are embar-
rassed, ashamed, afraid or indignant. We recall or imagine
such a situation and then, without any comment or analysis,
try to gain a clear mental image of how the I naturally appears
at such times. We have to be patient at this stage because it may
take many sessions before we gain a clear image. Eventually
we shall see that the I appears to be completely solid and real,
existing from its own side without depending upon the body
or the mind. This vividly appearing I is the inherently existent
I that we cherish so strongly. It is the I that we defend when we
are criticized and that we are so proud of when we are praised.

Once we have an image of how the I appears in these extreme
circumstances, we should try to identify how it appears normally, in less extreme situations. For example, we can observe
the I that is presently reading this book and try to discover how
it appears to our mind. Eventually we shall see that although

in this case there is not such an inflated sense of I, nevertheless the I still appears to be inherently existent, existing from its own side without depending upon the body or the mind. Once we have an image of the inherently existent I, we focus on it for a while with single-pointed concentration. Then in meditation we proceed to the next stage, which is to contemplate valid reasons to prove that the inherently existent I we are grasping at does not in fact exist. The inherently existent I and our self that we normally see are the same; we should know that neither exists, both are objects negated by emptiness.

If the I exists in the way that it appears, it must exist in one of four ways: as the body, as the mind, as the collection of the body and mind, or as something separate from the body and mind; there is no other possibility. We contemplate this carefully until we become convinced that this is the case and then we proceed to examine each of the four possibilities:

(1) If our I is our body, there is no sense in saying 'my body', because the possessor and the possessed are identical.

If our I is our body, there is no future rebirth because the I ceases when the body dies.

If our I and our body are identical, then since we are capable of developing faith, dreaming, solving mathematical puzzles and so on, it follows that flesh, blood and bones can do the same.

Since none of this is true, it follows that our I is not our body.

(2) If our I is our mind, there is no sense in saying 'my mind', because the possessor and the possessed are identical; but usually when we focus on our mind

we say 'my mind'. This clearly indicates that our I is not our mind.

If our I is our mind, then since we have many types of mind, such as the six consciousnesses, conceptual minds and non-conceptual minds, it follows that we have just as many I's. Since this is absurd, our I cannot be our mind.

(3) Since our body is not our I and our mind is not our I, the collection of our body and mind cannot be our I. The collection of our body and mind is a collection of things that are not our I, so how can the collection itself be our I? For example, in a herd of cows none of the animals is a sheep, therefore the herd itself is not sheep. In the same way, in the collection of our body and mind, neither our body nor our mind is our I, therefore the collection itself is not our I.

(4) If our I is not our body, not our mind, and not the collection of our body and mind, the only possibility that remains is that it is something separate from our body and mind. If this is the case, we must be able to apprehend our I without either our body or our mind appearing, but if we imagine that our body and our mind were completely to disappear there would be nothing remaining that could be called our I. Therefore it follows that our I is not separate from our body and mind.

We should imagine that our body gradually dissolves into thin air, and then our mind dissolves, our thoughts scatter with the wind, our feelings, wishes and awareness melt into nothingness. Is there anything left that is our I? There is nothing. Clearly our I is not something separate from our body and mind.

We have now examined all four possibilities and have failed to find our I or self. Since we have already decided that there is no fifth possibility, we must conclude that our I that we normally grasp at and cherish does not exist at all. Where there previously appeared an inherently existent I, there now appears an absence of that I. This absence of an inherently existent I is emptiness, ultimate truth.

We contemplate in this way until there appears to us a generic, or mental, image of the absence of our self that we normally see. This image is our object of placement meditation. We try to become completely familiar with it by continually meditating on it single-pointedly for as long as possible.

Because we have grasped at our inherently existent I since beginningless time, and have cherished it more dearly than anything else, the experience of failing to find our self in meditation can be quite shocking at first. Some people develop fear, thinking 'I have become completely non-existent.' Others feel great joy, as if the source of all their problems were vanishing. Both reactions are good signs and indicate correct meditation. After a while these initial reactions will subside and our mind will settle into a more balanced state. Then we shall be able to meditate on the emptiness of our self in a calm, controlled manner.

We should allow our mind to become absorbed in space-like emptiness for as long as possible. It is important to remember that our object is emptiness, the mere absence of our self that we normally see, not mere nothingness. Occasionally we should check our meditation with alertness. If our mind has wandered to another object, or if we have lost the meaning of emptiness and are focusing on mere nothingness, we should return to the contemplations to bring the emptiness of our self clearly to mind once again.

We may wonder: 'If my self that I normally see does not exist, then who is meditating? Who will get up from meditation, speak to others and reply when my name is called?' Although our self that we normally see does not exist, this does not mean that our self does not exist at all. We exist as a mere imputation. So long as we are satisfied with the mere imputation of our 'self', there is no problem. We can think 'I exist', 'I am going to town', and so on. The problem arises only when we look for our self other than the mere conceptual imputation 'I', our 'self'. Our mind grasps at an I that ultimately exists, independently of conceptual imputation, as if there were a 'real' I existing behind the label. If such an I existed, we would be able to find it, but we have seen that our I cannot be found upon investigation. The conclusion of our search was a definite non-finding of our self. This unfindability of our self is the emptiness of our self, the ultimate nature of our self. Our self that exists as mere imputation is the conventional nature of our self.

When we first realize emptiness we do so conceptually, by means of a generic image. By continuing to meditate on emptiness over and over again, the generic image gradually becomes more and more transparent until it disappears entirely and we see emptiness directly. This direct realization of emptiness will be our first completely non-mistaken awareness, or undefiled mind. Until we realize emptiness directly, all our minds are mistaken awarenesses because, due to the imprints of self-grasping or true-grasping ignorance, their objects appear as inherently existent.

Most people veer towards the extreme of existence, thinking that if something exists it must exist inherently, thus exaggerating the way in which things exist without being satisfied with them as mere name. Others may veer towards the extreme of non-existence, thinking that if phenomena do not exist inherently they do not exist at all, thus exaggerating their lack of inherent existence. We need to realize that although phenomena lack any trace of existence from their own side, they do exist conventionally as mere appearances to a valid mind.

The conceptual minds grasping at our I and other phenomena as being truly existent are wrong awarenesses and should therefore be abandoned, but I am not saying that all conceptual thoughts are wrong awarenesses and should therefore be abandoned. There are many correct conceptual minds that are useful in our day-to-day lives, such as the conceptual mind remembering what we did yesterday or the conceptual mind understanding what we will do tomorrow. There are also many conceptual minds that need to be cultivated on the spiritual path. For example, conventional bodhichitta in the mental continuum of a Bodhisattva is a conceptual mind because it apprehends its object, great enlightenment, by means of a generic image. Moreover, before we can realize emptiness directly with a non-conceptual mind, we need to realize it by means of an inferential cognizer, which is a conceptual mind. Through contemplating the reasons that refute inherent existence, there appears to our mind a generic image of the absence, or emptiness, of inherent existence. This is the only way that emptiness of inherent existence can initially appear to our mind. We then meditate on this image with stronger and stronger concentration until finally we perceive emptiness directly.

There are some people who say that the way to meditate on emptiness is simply to empty our mind of all conceptual thoughts, arguing that just as white clouds obscure the sun as much as black clouds, so positive conceptual thoughts obscure our mind as much as negative conceptual thoughts. This view is completely mistaken, for if we make no effort to gain a conceptual understanding of emptiness, but try instead to suppress all conceptual thoughts, actual emptiness will never appear to our mind. We may achieve a vivid experience of a space-like vacuity, but this is just the absence of conceptual thought – it is not emptiness, the true nature of phenomena. Meditation on this vacuity may temporarily calm our mind, but it will never destroy our delusions nor liberate us from samsara and its sufferings.

THE EMPTINESS OF THE EIGHT EXTREMES

If all the necessary atmospheric causes and conditions come together, clouds will appear. If these are absent, clouds cannot form. The clouds are completely dependent upon causes and conditions for their development; without these they have no power to develop. The same is true for mountains, planets, bodies, minds and all other produced phenomena. Because they depend upon factors outside themselves for their existence, they are empty of inherent, or independent, existence and are mere imputations of the mind.

Contemplating the teachings on karma, actions and their effects, can help us to understand this. Where do all our good and bad experiences come from? According to Buddhism they are the result of the positive and negative karma we created in the past. As a result of positive karma, attractive and agreeable people appear in our life, pleasant material conditions arise and we live in a beautiful environment; but as a result of negative karma, unpleasant people and things appear. This world is the effect of the collective karma created by the beings who inhabit it. Because karma originates in the mind – specifically in our mental intentions – we can see that all worlds arise from the mind. This is similar to the way in which appearances arise in a dream. Everything we perceive when we are dreaming is the result of the ripening of karmic potentials in our mind and has no existence outside of our mind. When our mind is calm and pure, positive karmic imprints ripen and pleasant dream appearances arise; but when our mind is agitated and impure, negative karmic imprints ripen and unpleasant, nightmarish appearances arise. In a similar way, all the appearances of our waking world are simply the ripening of positive, negative, or neutral karmic imprints in our mind.

Once we understand how things arise from their inner and outer causes and conditions and have no independent existence, then just seeing or thinking about the production of phenomena will remind us of their emptiness. Instead of reinforcing our sense of the solidity and objectivity of things, we shall begin to see things as manifestations of their emptiness, with no more concrete existence than a rainbow arising out of an empty sky.

Just as the production of things depends upon causes and conditions, so too does the disintegration of things. Therefore, neither production nor disintegration can be truly existent. For example, if our new car were destroyed we would feel unhappy because we grasp at both the car and the disintegration of the car as truly existent; but if we understood that our car is merely an appearance to our mind, like a car in a dream, its destruction would not disturb us. This is true for all objects of our attachment: if we realize that both objects and their cessations lack true existence, there is no basis for becoming upset if we are separated from them.

All functioning things – our environments, enjoyments, body, mind and our self – change from moment to moment. They are impermanent in the sense that they do not last for a second moment. The book you are reading in this moment is not the same book that you were reading a moment ago, and it could only come into existence because the book of a moment ago ceased to exist. When we understand subtle impermanence – that our body, our mind, our self and so forth do not abide for a second moment – it is not difficult to understand that they are empty of inherent existence.

Even though we may agree that impermanent phenomena are empty of inherent existence, we might think that because permanent phenomena are unchanging and do not arise from causes and conditions, they must exist inherently. However, even permanent phenomena such as emptiness and unproduced space – the mere absence of physical obstruction – are dependent-related phenomena because they depend upon their parts, their bases and the minds that impute them; and therefore they are not inherently existent. Although emptiness is ultimate reality, it is not independent or inherently existent for it too depends upon its parts, its bases and the minds that impute it. Just as a gold coin does not exist separately from its gold, so the emptiness of our body does not exist separately from our body, because it is simply our body's lack of inherent existence.

Whenever we go anywhere we develop the thought 'I am going', and grasp at an inherently existent act of going. In a similar way, when someone comes to visit us we think 'They are coming', and we grasp at an inherently existent act of coming. Both these conceptions are self-grasping and wrong awarenesses. When someone goes away we feel that a truly existent person has truly left, and when they come back we feel that a truly existent person has truly returned. However, the coming and going of people is like the appearance and disappearance of a rainbow in the sky. When the causes and conditions for a rainbow to appear are assembled a rainbow appears, and when the causes and conditions for the continued appearance of the rainbow disperse the rainbow disappears; but the rainbow does not come from anywhere, nor does it go anywhere.

When we observe one object, such as our I, we strongly feel that it is a single, indivisible entity, and that its singularity is inherently existent. In reality, however, our I has many parts, such as the parts that look, listen, walk and think, or the parts that are, for example, a teacher, a mother, a daughter and a wife. Our I is imputed upon the collection of all these parts. As with each individual phenomenon it is a singularity, but its singularity is merely imputed, like an army that is merely imputed upon a collection of soldiers or a forest that is imputed upon a collection of trees.

When we see more than one object, we regard the multiplicity of these objects to be inherently existent. However, just as singularity is merely imputed, likewise plurality is just an imputation by mind and does not exist from the side of the object. For example, instead of looking at a collection of soldiers or trees from the point of view of the individual soldiers or trees, we could look at them as an army or a forest, that is, as a singular collection or whole, in which case we would be looking at a singularity rather than a plurality.

In summary, singularity does not exist from its own side because it is just imputed upon a plurality – its parts. In the same way, plurality does not exist from its own side because it is just imputed upon a singularity – the collection of its parts. Therefore singularity and plurality are mere imputations by conceptual mind and they lack true existence. If we realize this clearly, there is no basis for developing attachment and anger towards objects, either singular or plural. We tend to project the faults or qualities of the few onto the many, and then develop hatred or attachment on the basis of, for example, race, religion or country. Contemplating the emptiness of singularity and plurality can be helpful in reducing such hatred and attachment.

Although production, disintegration and so forth do exist, they do not exist inherently. It is our conceptual minds of self-grasping ignorance that grasp them as inherently existent. These conceptions grasp at the eight extremes: inherently existent production, inherently existent disintegration, inherently existent impermanence, inherently existent permanence, inherently existent going, inherently existent coming, inherently existent singularity and inherently existent plurality. Although these extremes do not exist, due to our ignorance we are always grasping them. The conceptions of these extremes lie at the root of all other delusions, and because delusions give rise to our performing contaminated actions that keep us trapped in the prison of samsara, these conceptions are the root of samsara, the cycle of impure life.

Inherently existent production is the same as the production that we normally see, and we should know that in reality neither of these exists. This is the same for the remaining seven extremes. For example, inherently existent disintegration and destruction and the disintegration and destruction that we normally see are the same, and we should know that neither of these exists. Our minds that grasp at these eight extremes are different aspects of our self-grasping ignorance. Because it is our self-grasping ignorance that causes us to experience endless suffering and problems, when this ignorance ceases permanently through meditation on the emptiness of all phenomena, all our suffering of this life and countless future lives will cease permanently and we shall accomplish the real meaning of human life.

The subject of the eight extremes is profound and requires detailed explanation and lengthy study. Buddha explains them in detail in the *Perfection of Wisdom Sutras*; and in *Fundamental Wisdom*, a commentary to the *Perfection of Wisdom Sutras*, Nagarjuna also uses many profound and powerful reasons to prove that the eight extremes do not exist by showing how all phenomena are empty of inherent existence. Through analyzing conventional truths he establishes their ultimate nature, and shows why it is necessary to understand both the conventional and ultimate natures of an object in order to understand that object fully.

CONVENTIONAL AND ULTIMATE TRUTHS

Whatever exists is either a conventional truth or an ultimate truth, and, since ultimate truth refers just to emptiness, everything except emptiness is a conventional truth. For example, things such as houses, cars and tables are all conventional truths.

All conventional truths are false objects because the way they appear and the way they exist do not correspond. If someone appears to be friendly and kind but his real intention is to gain our confidence in order to rob us, we would say that he is false or deceptive because there is a discrepancy between the way he appears and his real nature. Similarly, objects such as forms and sounds are false or deceptive because they appear to exist inherently but in reality are completely devoid of inherent existence. Because the way they appear does not coincide with the way they exist, conventional truths are known as 'deceptive phenomena'. A cup, for instance, appears to exist independently of its parts, its causes and the mind that apprehends it, but in reality it totally depends upon these things. Because the way the cup appears to our mind and the way it exists do not correspond, the cup is a false object.

Although conventional truths are false objects, nevertheless they actually exist because a mind directly perceiving a conventional truth is a valid mind, a completely reliable mind. For instance, an eye consciousness directly perceiving a cup on the table is a valid mind because it will not deceive us – if we reach out to pick up the cup we shall find it where our eye consciousness sees it. In this respect, an eye consciousness perceiving a cup on the table is different from an eye consciousness mistaking a cup reflected in a mirror for a real cup, or an eye consciousness seeing a mirage as water. Even though a cup is a false object, for practical purposes the eye consciousness that directly perceives it is a valid, reliable mind. However, although it is a valid mind it is nevertheless a mistaken awareness insofar as the cup appears to that mind to be truly existent. It is valid and non-deceptive with respect to the conventional characteristics of the cup – its position, size, colour and so forth – but mistaken with respect to its appearance.

To summarize, conventional objects are false because, although they appear to exist from their own side, in reality they are mere appearances to mind, like things seen in a dream. Within the context of a dream, however, dream objects have a relative validity, and this distinguishes them from things that do not exist at all. Suppose in a dream we steal a diamond and someone then asks us whether it was we who stole it. Even though the dream is merely a creation of our mind, if we answer 'yes' we are telling the truth whereas if we answer 'no' we are telling a lie. In the same way, even though in reality the whole universe is just an appearance to mind, within the context of the experience of ordinary beings we can distinguish between relative truths and relative falsities.

Conventional truths can be divided into gross conventional truths and subtle conventional truths. We can understand how all phenomena have these two levels of conventional truth by considering the example of a car. The car itself, the car depending on its causes, and the car depending on its parts are all gross conventional truths of the car. They are called 'gross' because they are relatively easy to understand. The car depending on its basis of imputation is quite subtle and is not easy to understand, but it is still a gross conventional truth. The basis of imputation of the car is the parts of the car. To apprehend car, the parts of the car must appear to our mind; without the parts appearing, there is no way to develop the thought 'car'. For this reason, the parts are the basis of imputation of the car. We say 'I see a car', but strictly speaking all we ever see is parts of the car. However, when we develop the thought 'car' by seeing its parts, we see the car. There is no car other than its parts, there is no body other than its parts, and so on. The car existing merely as an imputation by thought is the subtle conventional truth of the car. We have understood this when we realize that the car is nothing more than a mere imputation by a valid mind. We cannot understand subtle conventional truths unless we have understood emptiness. When we thoroughly realize subtle conventional truth we have realized both conventional truth and ultimate truth.

Strictly speaking, truth, ultimate truth and emptiness are synonymous because conventional truths are not real truths but false objects. They are true only for the minds of those who have not realized emptiness. Only emptiness is true because only emptiness exists in the way that it appears. When the mind of any sentient being directly perceives conventional truths, such as forms, they appear to exist from their own side. When the mind of a Superior being directly perceives emptiness, however, nothing appears other than emptiness; this mind is totally mixed with the mere absence of inherently existent phenomena. The way in which emptiness appears to the mind of a non-conceptual direct perceiver corresponds exactly to the way in which emptiness exists.

It should be noted that although emptiness is ultimate truth it is not inherently existent. Emptiness is not a separate reality existing behind conventional appearances, but the real nature of those appearances. We cannot talk about emptiness in isolation, for emptiness is always the mere lack of inherent existence of something. For example, the emptiness of our body is the lack of inherent existence of our body, and without our body as its basis this emptiness cannot exist. Because emptiness necessarily depends upon a basis, it lacks inherent existence.

In *Guide to the Bodhisattva's Way of Life* Shantideva defines ultimate truth as a phenomenon that is true for the uncontaminated mind of a Superior being. An uncontaminated mind is a mind that realizes emptiness directly. This mind is the only unmistaken awareness and is possessed exclusively by Superior beings. Because uncontaminated minds are completely unmistaken, anything directly perceived by them to be true is necessarily an ultimate truth. In contrast, anything that is directly perceived to be true by the mind of an ordinary being is necessarily not an ultimate truth, because all minds of ordinary beings are mistaken, and mistaken minds can never directly perceive the truth.

Because of the imprints of conceptual thoughts that grasp at the eight extremes, everything that appears to the minds of ordinary beings appears to be inherently existent. Only the wisdom of meditative equipoise that directly realizes emptiness is undefiled by the imprints, or stains, of these conceptual thoughts. This is the only wisdom that has no mistaken appearance.

When a Superior Bodhisattva meditates on emptiness his or her mind mixes with emptiness completely, with no appearance of inherent existence. He develops a completely pure, uncontaminated wisdom that is ultimate bodhichitta. When he arises from meditative equipoise, however, due to the imprints of true-grasping, conventional phenomena again appear to his mind as inherently existent, and his uncontaminated wisdom temporarily becomes non-manifest. Only a Buddha can manifest uncontaminated wisdom at the same time as directly perceiving conventional truths. An uncommon quality of a Buddha is that a single moment of a Buddha's mind realizes both conventional truth and ultimate truth directly and simultaneously. There are many levels of ultimate bodhichitta. For instance, the ultimate bodhichitta attained through Tantric practice is more profound than that developed through Sutra practice alone, and the supreme ultimate bodhichitta is that of a Buddha.

If through valid reasoning we realize the emptiness of the first extreme, the extreme of production, we shall easily be able to realize the emptiness of the remaining seven extremes. Once we have realized the emptiness of the eight extremes we have realized the emptiness of all phenomena. Having gained this realization, we continue to contemplate and meditate on the emptiness of produced phenomena and so forth, and as our meditations deepen we shall feel all phenomena dissolving into emptiness. We shall then be able to maintain a single-pointed concentration on the emptiness of all phenomena.

To meditate on the emptiness of produced phenomena we can think:

My self who was born, through causes and conditions, as a human being is unfindable when I search for it with wisdom within my body and my mind, or separate from my body and mind. This proves that my self that I normally see does not exist at all.

Having contemplated in this way we feel our self that we normally see disappears and we perceive a space-like emptiness that is the mere absence of our self that we normally see. We feel that our mind enters into this space-like emptiness and remains there single-pointedly. This meditation is called 'space-like meditative equipoise on emptiness'.

Just as eagles soar through the vast expanse of the sky without meeting any obstructions, needing only minimal effort to maintain their flight, so advanced meditators concentrating on emptiness can meditate on emptiness for a long time with little effort. Their minds soar through space-like emptiness, undistracted by any other phenomenon. When we meditate on emptiness we should try to emulate these meditators. Once we have found our object of meditation, the mere absence of our self that we normally see, we should refrain from further analysis and simply rest our mind in the experience of this emptiness. From time to time we should check to make sure that we have lost neither the clear appearance of emptiness nor the recognition of its meaning, but we should not check too forcefully as this will disturb our concentration. Our meditation should not be like the flight of a small bird, which never stops flapping its wings and is always changing direction, but like the flight of an eagle, which soars gently with only occasional adjustments to its wings. Through meditating in this way we shall feel our mind dissolving into and becoming one with emptiness.

If we are successful in doing this, then during our meditation we are free from manifest self-grasping. If, on the other hand, we spend all our time checking and analyzing, never allowing our mind to relax into the space of emptiness, we shall never gain this experience and our meditation will not serve to reduce our self-grasping.

In general we need to improve our understanding of emptiness through extensive study, approaching it from many angles and using many different lines of reasoning. It is also important to become thoroughly familiar with one complete meditation on emptiness through continuous contemplation, understanding exactly how to use the reasoning to lead to an experience of emptiness. We can then concentrate on emptiness single-pointedly and try to mix our mind with it, like water mixing with water.

THE UNION OF THE TWO TRUTHS

The union of the two truths means that conventional truths, such as our body, and ultimate truths, such as the emptiness of our body, are the same nature. When something such as our body appears to us, both the body and the inherently existent body appear simultaneously. This is dualistic appearance, which is subtle mistaken appearance. Only Buddhas are free from such mistaken appearances. The main purpose of understanding and meditating on the union of the two truths is to prevent dualistic appearances – appearances of inherent existence to the mind that is meditating on emptiness – and thereby enable our mind to dissolve into emptiness. Once we can do this, our meditation on emptiness will be very powerful in eliminating our delusions. If we correctly identify and negate the inherently existent body, the body that we normally see, and meditate on the mere absence of such a body with strong concentration, we shall feel our normal body dissolving into emptiness. We shall understand that the real nature of our body is emptiness and that our body is merely a manifestation of emptiness.

Emptiness is like the sky and our body is like the blue of the sky. Just as the blue is a manifestation of the sky itself and cannot be separated from it, so our blue-like body is simply a manifestation of the sky of its emptiness and cannot be separated from it. If we realize this, when we focus on the emptiness of our body we feel that our body itself dissolves into its ultimate nature. In this way, we can easily overcome the conventional appearance of the body in our meditations, and our mind naturally mixes with emptiness.

In the *Heart Sutra*, Bodhisattva Avalokiteshvara says: 'Form is not other than emptiness.' This means that conventional phenomena, such as our body, do not exist separately from their emptiness. When we meditate on the emptiness of our body with this understanding, we know that the emptiness appearing to our mind is the very nature of our body, and that apart from this emptiness there is no body. Meditating in this way will greatly weaken our self-grasping mind. If we really believed that our body and its emptiness were the same nature, our self-grasping would definitely become weaker.

Although we can divide emptinesses from the point of view of their bases, and speak of the emptiness of the body, the emptiness of the I and so forth, in truth all emptinesses are the same nature. If we look at ten bottles, we can distinguish ten different spaces inside the bottles, but in reality these spaces are the same nature; and if we break the bottles, the spaces become indistinguishable. In the same way, although we can speak of the emptiness of the body, the mind, the I and so forth, in reality they are the same nature and indistinguishable. The only way in which they can be distinguished is by their conventional bases.

There are two principal benefits of understanding that all emptinesses are the same nature: in the meditation session our mind will mix with emptiness more easily, and in the meditation break we shall be able to see all appearances as equal manifestations of their emptiness.

For as long as we feel that there is a gap between our mind and emptiness – that our mind is 'here' and emptiness is 'there' – our mind will not mix with emptiness. Knowing that all emptinesses are the same nature helps to close this gap. In ordinary life we experience many different objects – good, bad, attractive, unattractive – and our feelings towards them differ. Because we feel that the differences exist from the side of the objects, our mind is unbalanced and we develop attachment to attractive objects, aversion to unattractive objects and indifference to neutral objects. It is very difficult to mix such an uneven mind with emptiness. To mix our mind with emptiness we need to know that, although phenomena appear in many different aspects, in essence they are all empty. The differences we see are just appearances to mistaken minds; from the point of view of ultimate truth all phenomena are equal in emptiness. For a qualified meditator single-pointedly absorbed in emptiness, there is no difference between production and disintegration, impermanence and permanence, going and coming, singularity and plurality – everything is equal in emptiness and all problems of attachment, anger and self-grasping ignorance are solved. In this experience, everything becomes very peaceful and comfortable, balanced and harmonious, joyful and wonderful. There is no heat, no cold, no lower, no higher, no here, no there, no self, no other, no samsara – everything is equal in the peace of emptiness. This realization is called the 'yoga of equalizing samsara and nirvana', and is explained in detail in both the Sutras and Tantras.

Since all emptinesses are the same nature, the ultimate nature of a mind that is meditating on emptiness is the same nature as the ultimate nature of its object. When we first meditate on emptiness our mind and emptiness appear to be two separate phenomena, but when we understand that all emptinesses are the same nature we shall know that this feeling of separation is simply the experience of a mistaken mind. In reality our mind and emptiness are ultimately of one taste. If we apply this knowledge in our meditations, it will help to prevent the appearance of the conventional nature of our mind and allow our mind to dissolve into emptiness.

Having mixed our mind with emptiness, when we arise from meditation we shall experience all phenomena equally as manifestations of their emptiness. Instead of feeling that the attractive, unattractive and neutral objects we see are inherently different, we shall know that in essence they are the same nature. Just as both the gentlest and most violent waves in an ocean are equally water, likewise both attractive forms and repulsive forms are equally manifestations of emptiness. Realizing this, our mind will become balanced and peaceful. We shall recognize all conventional appearances as the magical play of the mind, and we shall not grasp strongly at their apparent differences.

When Milarepa once taught emptiness to a woman, he compared emptiness to the sky and conventional truths to clouds and told her to meditate on the sky. She followed his instructions with great success, but she had one problem – when she meditated on the sky of emptiness everything disappeared, and she could not understand how phenomena could exist conventionally. She said to Milarepa: 'I find it easy to meditate on the sky but difficult to establish the clouds. Please teach me how to meditate on the clouds.' Milarepa replied: 'If your meditation on the sky is going well, the clouds will not be a problem. Clouds simply appear in the sky – they arise from the sky and dissolve back into the sky. As your experience of the sky improves, you will naturally come to understand the clouds.'

In Tibetan, the word for both sky and space is 'namkha', although space is different from sky. There are two types of space, produced space and unproduced space. Produced space is the visible space we can see inside a room or in the sky. This space may become dark at night and light during the day, and as it undergoes change in this way it is an impermanent phenomenon. The characteristic property of produced space is that it does not obstruct objects – if there is space in a room we can place objects there without obstruction. Similarly, birds are able to fly through the space of the sky because it lacks obstruction, whereas they cannot fly through a mountain! Therefore it is clear that produced space lacks, or is empty of, obstructive contact. This mere lack, or emptiness, of obstructive contact is unproduced space.

Because unproduced space is the mere absence of obstructive contact it does not undergo momentary change and is therefore a permanent phenomenon. Whereas produced space is visible and quite easy to understand, unproduced space is a mere absence of obstructive contact and is rather more subtle. However, once we understand unproduced space we shall find it easier to understand emptiness.

The only difference between emptiness and unproduced space is their object of negation. The object of negation of unproduced space is obstructive contact whereas the object of negation of emptiness is inherent existence. Because unproduced space is the best analogy for understanding emptiness, it is used in the Sutras and in many scriptures. Unproduced space is a non-affirming negative phenomenon – a phenomenon that is realized by a mind that merely eliminates its negated object without realizing another positive phenomenon. Produced space is an affirmative, or positive, phenomenon – a phenomenon that is realized without the mind explicitly eliminating a negated object. More details on these two types of phenomenon can be found in *Heart of Wisdom* and *Ocean of Nectar*.

THE PRACTICE OF EMPTINESS IN OUR DAILY ACTIVITIES

In our daily activities, we should believe that all appearances are illusory. Although things appear to us as inherently existent we should remember that these appearances are deceptive and that in reality the things that we normally see do not exist. As mentioned earlier, in *King of Concentration Sutra* Buddha says:

A magician creates various things
Such as horses, elephants and so forth.
His creations do not actually exist;
You should know all things in the same way.

The last two lines of this verse mean that just as we know that the horses and elephants created by the magician do not exist, in the same way we should know that all the things that we normally see do not actually exist. This chapter *Training in Ultimate Bodhichitta* has extensively explained how all the things that we normally see do not exist.

When a magician creates an illusory horse, a horse appears very clearly to his mind but he knows that it is just an illusion. Indeed, the very appearance of the horse reminds him that there is no horse in front of him. In the same way, when we are very familiar with emptiness, the very fact that things appear to be inherently existent will remind us that they are not inherently existent. We should therefore recognize that whatever appears to us in our daily life is like an illusion and lacks inherent existence. In this way our wisdom will increase day by day, and our self-grasping ignorance and other delusions will naturally diminish.

Between meditation sessions we should be like an actor. When an actor plays the part of a king, he dresses, speaks and acts like a king, but he knows all the time that he is not a real king. In the same way we should live and function in the conventional world yet always remember that we ourself, our environment and the people around us that we normally see do not exist at all.

If we think like this we shall be able to live in the conventional world without grasping at it. We shall treat it lightly and have the flexibility of mind to respond to every situation in a constructive way. Knowing that whatever appears to our mind is mere appearance, when attractive objects appear we shall not grasp at them and develop attachment, and when unattractive objects appear we shall not grasp at them and develop aversion or anger.

In *Training the Mind in Seven Points*, Geshe Chekhawa says: 'Think that all phenomena are like dreams.' Some of the things we see in our dreams are beautiful and some are ugly, but they are all mere appearances to our dreaming mind. They do not exist from their own side, and are empty of inherent existence. It is the same with the objects we perceive when we are awake –

they too are mere appearances to mind and lack inherent existence.

All phenomena lack inherent existence. When we look at a rainbow it appears to occupy a particular location in space, and it seems that if we searched we would be able to find where the rainbow touches the ground. However, we know that no matter how hard we search we shall never be able to find the end of the rainbow, for as soon as we arrive at the place where we saw the rainbow touch the ground, the rainbow will have disappeared. If we do not search for it, the rainbow appears clearly; but when we look for it, it is not there. All phenomena are like this. If we do not analyze them they appear clearly, but when we search for them analytically, trying to isolate them from everything else, they are not there.

If something did exist inherently, and we investigated it by separating it from all other phenomena, we would be able to find it. However, all phenomena are like rainbows – if we search for them we shall never find them. At first we might find this idea very uncomfortable and difficult to accept, but this is quite natural. With greater familiarity we shall find this reasoning more acceptable, and eventually we shall realize that it is true.

It is important to understand that emptiness does not mean nothingness. Although things do not exist from their own side, independent of the mind, they do exist in the sense that they are understood by a valid mind. The world we experience when we are awake is similar to the world we experience when we are dreaming. We cannot say that dream things do not exist, but if we believe that they exist as more than mere appearances to the mind, existing 'out there', then we are mistaken, as we shall discover when we wake up.

As mentioned before, there is no greater method for experiencing peace of mind and happiness than to understand and meditate on emptiness. Since it is our self-grasping that keeps us bound to the prison of samsara and is the source of all our suffering, meditation on emptiness is the universal solution to all our problems. It is the medicine that cures all mental and physical diseases, and the nectar that bestows the everlasting happiness of nirvana and enlightenment.

A SIMPLE TRAINING IN ULTIMATE BODHICHITTA

We begin by thinking:

I must attain enlightenment to benefit directly each and every living being every day. For this purpose I shall attain a direct realization of the way things really are.

With this bodhichitta motivation, we contemplate:

Normally I see my body within its parts – the hands, back and so forth – but neither the individual parts nor the collection of the parts are my body because they are the parts of my body and not the body itself. However, there is no 'my body' other than its parts. Through searching with wisdom for my body in this way, I realize that my body is unfindable. This is a valid reason to prove that my body that I normally see does not exist at all.

Through contemplating this point we try to perceive the mere absence of the body that we normally see. This mere absence of the body that we normally see is the emptiness of our body, and we meditate on this emptiness single-pointedly for as long as possible.

We should continually practise this contemplation and meditation, and then move to the next stage, meditation on the emptiness of our self. We should contemplate and think:

Normally I see my self within my body and mind, but neither my body, nor my mind, nor the collection of my body and mind are my self, because these are my possessions and my self is the possessor; and possessor and possessions cannot be the same. However, there is no 'my self' other than my body and mind. Through searching with wisdom for my self in this way, I realize that my self is unfindable. This is a valid reason to prove that my self that I normally see does not exist at all.

Through contemplating this point we try to perceive the mere absence of our self that we normally see. This mere absence of our self that we normally see is the emptiness of our self, and we meditate on this emptiness single-pointedly for as long as possible.

We should continually practise this contemplation and meditation, and then move to the next stage, meditation on the emptiness of all phenomena. We should contemplate and think:

As with my body and my self, all other phenomena are unfindable when I search for them with wisdom. This is a valid reason to prove that all phenomena that I normally see or perceive do not exist at all.

Through contemplating this point we try to perceive the mere absence of all phenomena that we normally see or perceive. This mere absence of all phenomena that we normally see or perceive is the emptiness of all phenomena. We meditate continually on this emptiness of all phenomena with bodhichitta motivation until we are able to maintain our concentration clearly for one minute every time we meditate on it. Our concentration that has this ability is called 'concentration of placing the mind'.

In the second stage, with the concentration of placing the mind, we meditate continually on the emptiness of all phenomena until we are able to maintain our concentration clearly for five minutes every time we meditate on it. Our concentration that has this ability is called 'concentration of continual placement'. In the third stage, with the concentration of continual placement we meditate continually on the emptiness of all phenomena until we are able to immediately remember our object of meditation – the mere absence of all phenomena that we normally see or perceive – whenever we lose it during meditation. Our concentration that has this ability is called 'concentration of replacement'. In the fourth stage, with the concentration of replacement we meditate continually on the emptiness of all phenomena until we are able to maintain our concentration clearly during the entire meditation session without forgetting the object of meditation. Our concentration that has this ability is called 'concentration of close placement'. At this stage we have very stable and clear concentration focused on the emptiness of all phenomena.

Then, with the concentration of close placement, we meditate continually on the emptiness of all phenomena until finally we attain the concentration of tranquil abiding focused on emptiness, which causes us to experience special physical and mental suppleness and bliss. With this concentration of tranquil abiding we shall develop a special wisdom that realizes the emptiness of all phenomena very clearly. This wisdom is called 'superior seeing'. Through continually meditating on the concentration of tranquil abiding associated with superior seeing, our wisdom of superior seeing will transform into the wisdom that directly realizes the emptiness of all phenomena.

This direct realization of emptiness is the actual ultimate bodhichitta. The moment we attain the wisdom of ultimate bodhichitta we become a Superior Bodhisattva. As mentioned before, conventional bodhichitta is the nature of compassion and ultimate bodhichitta is the nature of wisdom. These two bodhichittas are like the two wings of a bird with which we can fly and very quickly reach the enlightened world.

In *Advice from Atisha's Heart* Atisha says:

Friends, until you attain enlightenment, the Spiritual Teacher is indispensible, therefore rely upon the holy Spiritual Guide.

We need to rely upon our Spiritual Guide until we attain enlightenment. The reason for this is very simple. The ultimate goal of human life is to attain enlightenment, and this depends upon continually receiving the special blessings of Buddha through our Spiritual Guide. Buddha attained enlightenment with the sole intention of leading all living beings along the stages of the path to enlightenment through his emanations. Who is his emanation who is leading us along the stages of the path to enlightenment? It is clearly our present Spiritual Teacher who is sincerely and correctly leading us along the paths of renunciation, bodhichitta and the correct view of emptiness by giving these teachings and showing a practical example of someone who is sincerely practising them. With this understanding we should strongly believe that our Spiritual Guide is an emanation of Buddha, and develop and maintain deep faith in him or her.

Atisha also says:

Until you realize ultimate truth, listening is indispensible, therefore listen to the instructions of the Spiritual Guide.

Even if we were mistakenly to see two moons in the sky, this mistaken appearance would remind us that in fact there are not two moons, but only one. In a similar way, if seeing inherently existent things reminds us there are no inherently existent things, this indicates that our understanding of emptiness, ultimate truth, is correct. Until our understanding of emptiness is perfect, and to prevent ourself from falling into one of the two extremes – the extreme of existence and the extreme of non-existence – we should listen to, read and contemplate the instructions of our Spiritual Guide. A more detailed explanation of relying upon our Spiritual Guide can be found in *Joyful Path of Good Fortune*.

All the contemplations and meditations presented in Part One of this book, from *The Preciousness of our Human Life* to *A Simple Training in Ultimate Bodhichitta* should be practised in conjunction with the preliminary practices for meditation presented in Appendix II: *Prayers for Meditation*. These preliminary practices will enable us to purify our mind, accumulate merit and receive the blessings of the enlightened beings, thus ensuring that our meditation practice is successful.

Arya Tara

Examination of our Lamrim Practice

Through practising the stages of the paths of persons of initial scope, middling scope and great scope we may have developed some experience of renunciation, bodhichitta and the correct view of emptiness, which are known as the 'three principal paths'. We should now examine ourself to see whether or not our experiences of renunciation, bodhichitta and the correct view of emptiness are qualified. Through judging our mind, if we realize that our attachment to the things of this life still remains, this is the sign that our renunciation is unqualified; if our self-cherishing that believes our own happiness and freedom are important, while neglecting others' happiness and freedom, still remains, this is the sign that our bodhichitta is unqualified; and if our self-grasping that grasps at ourself, our body and all other things that we normally see still remains, this is the sign that our understanding of emptiness is unqualified.

We therefore need to apply great effort to become deeply familiar with the trainings in renunciation, bodhichitta and the correct view of emptiness. We need to practise these trainings continually until our attachment, self-cherishing and

self-grasping reduce and we are able to control these delusions. When we have accomplished this, we have 'passed our
examination' and we have the 'position' of being a great Yogi
or Yogini.

PART TWO:

Tantra

Wisdom Dharma Protector

The Preciousness of Tantra

In his Sutra teachings Buddha gives us great encouragement to accomplish the ultimate goal of human life. This goal will be accomplished quickly through the practice of Tantra. Tantra, also known as 'Secret Mantra' or 'Vajrayana', is a special method to purify our world, our self, our enjoyments and our activities; and if we put this method into practice we shall very quickly attain enlightenment. As explained in Part One, our world does not exist from its own side; like a dream world, it is a mere appearance to our mind. In dreams we can see and touch our dream world, but when we wake up we realize that it was simply a projection of our mind and had no existence outside our mind. In the same way, the world we see when we are awake is simply a projection of our mind and has no existence outside our mind. Milarepa said:

> You should know that all appearances are the nature of mind, and mind is the nature of emptiness.

Because our world, our self, our enjoyments and our activities are the nature of our mind, when our mind is impure they are impure, and when our mind becomes pure through purification practice they become pure. There are many different levels of purifying our mind. The subtle mistaken appearance of our mind cannot be purified through the practice of Sutra alone; we need to engage in the practice of Highest Yoga Tantra. When we completely purify our mind through Tantric practice, our world, our self, our enjoyments and our activities also become completely pure – this is the state of enlightenment. Attaining enlightenment is therefore very simple; all we need to do is apply effort to purifying our mind.

We know that when our mind is impure because we are feeling angry with our friend, we see him as bad; but when our mind is pure because we are feeling affectionate love for the same friend, we see him as good. Therefore, it is because of changing our own mind from pure to impure or from impure to pure that for us our friend changes from good to bad or from bad to good. This indicates that everything that is good, bad or neutral for us is a projection of our mind and has no existence outside our mind. Through practising Tantra we shall completely purify our mind and thus experience the complete purity of our world, our self, our enjoyments and our activities – the 'four complete purities'.

Although Tantra is very popular, not many people understand its real meaning. Some people deny Buddha's Tantric teachings, whereas others misuse them for worldly attainments; and many people are confused about the union of Sutra and Tantra practice, mistakenly believing that Sutra and Tantra are contradictory. In *Condensed Heruka Root Tantra* Buddha says:

> You should never abandon Highest Yoga Tantra,
> But realize that it has inconceivable meaning
> And is the very essence of Buddhadharma.

When we understand the real meaning of Tantra there will be no basis for misusing it, and we shall see that there are no contradictions at all between Sutra and Tantra. Practising Sutra teachings is the basic foundation for practising Tantric teachings, and the practice of Tantra is the quick method to fulfil the ultimate goal of Sutra teachings. For example, in his Sutra teachings Buddha encourages us to abandon attachment, and in Tantra he encourages us to transform our attachment into the spiritual path. Some people may think this a contradiction, but it is not, because Buddha's Tantric instructions on how to transform attachment into the spiritual path are the quick method for abandoning attachment! In this way, they are the method to fulfil the aims of Sutra teachings.

We should take care not to misunderstand the meaning of transforming attachment into the spiritual path. Attachment itself cannot be transformed directly into the spiritual path; it is a delusion, an inner poison, and an object to be abandoned in both Sutra and Tantra. Transforming attachment into the path means that we transform the causes of attachment – our experiences of worldly pleasure – into the spiritual path. There are many methods for doing this that are explained in Tantric teachings.

The universal compassion accomplished through the practice of Sutra teachings, and the wisdom of Mahamudra Tantra accomplished through the practice of Tantric teachings, are like the two wings of a bird. Just as both wings are equally important for a bird to fly, so both Sutra and Tantra are equally important for practitioners seeking enlightenment.

Tantra is defined as an inner realization that functions to prevent ordinary appearances and conceptions and to accomplish the four complete purities. Although Buddha's Tantric scriptures are sometimes called 'Tantra' because they reveal

Tantric practices, actual Tantra is necessarily an inner realization that protects living beings from ordinary appearances and conceptions, which are the root of samsara's sufferings. Ordinary appearance is our perception of all the things that we normally see, such as our self and body. This appearance is subtle mistaken appearance. It is mistaken because our self, our body and all other things that we normally see do not exist, even though we always mistakenly see them; and it is subtle because for us it is difficult to understand that this appearance is mistaken. Our subtle mistaken appearance is the root of self-grasping, which is the root of all other delusions and suffering. We can abandon this subtle mistaken appearance completely only through the practice of Highest Yoga Tantra. When we do this we shall have accomplished the four complete purities mentioned above.

In general, our experience of worldly pleasure or enjoyments gives rise to attachment, which is the source of all suffering. However, through practising Tantra we can transform our experience of worldly pleasure into a profound spiritual path that leads us very quickly to the supreme happiness of enlightenment. The instructions of Tantra are therefore superior to all other instructions.

For living beings, the experience of worldly pleasures is the main cause of increasing their attachment, and therefore the main cause of increasing their problems. To stop attachment arising from the experience of worldly pleasures, Buddha taught Tantra as a method to transform worldly pleasures into the path to enlightenment. In accordance with the different levels of transforming worldly pleasures into the path, Buddha taught four levels or classes of Tantra: Action Tantra, Performance Tantra, Yoga Tantra and Highest Yoga Tantra. The first three are called the 'lower Tantras'. In Highest Yoga

Tantra, Buddha taught the most profound instructions for transforming sexual bliss into the quick path to enlightenment. Since the effectiveness of this practice depends upon gathering and dissolving the inner winds into the central channel through the power of meditation, these instructions were not explained by Buddha in the lower Tantras. In the lower Tantras, Buddha taught instructions on how to transform worldly pleasures – other than sexual bliss – into the path to enlightenment through imagination, which is a simpler practice of Tantra.

The gateway through which we enter Tantra is receiving a Tantric empowerment. An empowerment bestows upon us special blessings that heal our mental continuum and awaken our Buddha nature. When we receive a Tantric empowerment we are sowing the special seeds of the four bodies of a Buddha upon our mental continuum. These four bodies are the Nature Truth Body, the Wisdom Truth Body, the Enjoyment Body and the Emanation Body. Ordinary beings do not possess more than one body, whereas Buddhas possess four bodies simultaneously. A Buddha's Emanation Body is his or her gross body, which can be seen by ordinary beings; the Enjoyment Body is his subtle body, which can be seen only by practitioners who have gained higher realizations; and the Nature and Wisdom Truth Bodies are his very subtle bodies that only Buddhas themselves can see.

In Tantra, the principal objects to be abandoned are ordinary conceptions and ordinary appearances. The terms 'ordinary conceptions' and 'ordinary appearances' are best explained by the following example. Suppose there is a Heruka practitioner called John. Normally he appears to himself as John that he normally sees, and his environment, enjoyments, body and mind appear as those of John that he normally sees. These appearances are ordinary appearances. The mind that assents to these ordinary appearances by holding them to be true is ordinary conception. The appearances we have of an inherently existent 'I', 'mine' and other phenomena are also ordinary appearances; self-grasping and all other delusions are ordinary conceptions. Ordinary conceptions are obstructions to liberation, and ordinary appearances are obstructions to enlightenment. In general, all sentient beings, except Bodhisattvas who have attained the vajra-like concentration of the path of meditation, have ordinary appearances.

Now if John were to meditate on the generation stage of Heruka, strongly regarding himself as Heruka and believing his surroundings, experiences, body and mind to be those of Heruka, at that time he would have the divine pride that prevents ordinary conceptions. If he were also to attain clear appearance of himself as Heruka, with the environment, enjoyments, body and mind of Heruka, at that time he would have the clear appearance that prevents him from developing ordinary appearances.

At the beginning, ordinary conceptions are more harmful than ordinary appearances. How this is so is illustrated by the following analogy. Suppose a magician conjures up an illusion of a tiger in front of an audience. The tiger appears to both the audience and the magician, but whereas the audience believe that the tiger actually exists, and consequently become afraid, the magician does not assent to the appearance of the tiger and so remains calm. The problem for the audience is not so much that a tiger appears to them, as their conception that the tiger actually exists. It is this conception rather than the mere appearance of the tiger that causes them to experience fear. If like the magician they had no conception that the tiger existed, then even though they still had an appearance of a tiger they would not be afraid. In the same way, even though things appear to us as ordinary, if we do not conceptually grasp them as ordinary this will not be so harmful. Similarly, it is less damaging to our spiritual development that our Spiritual Guide appears to us as ordinary and yet we hold him or her to be in essence a Buddha, than it is for our Spiritual Guide to appear to us as ordinary and for us to believe that he or she is ordinary. The conviction that our Spiritual Guide is a Buddha, even though he or she may appear to us as an ordinary person, helps our spiritual practice to progress rapidly.

To reduce ordinary appearances and conceptions Buddha taught the Tantra of generation stage; and to abandon these two obstructions completely Buddha taught the Tantra of completion stage, especially Mahamudra Tantra. By completing our training in these Tantras we shall become a Tantric enlightened being, such as Heruka, with the four complete purities.

Twelve-armed Heruka

The Tantra of Generation Stage

The following chapters present the instructions on the practices of Heruka and Vajrayogini, which are the very essence of Highest Yoga Tantra. The practice of Highest Yoga Tantra can be divided into two stages: generation stage and completion stage. In generation stage, through the power of correct imagination arising from wisdom, Tantric practitioners generate themselves as Tantric enlightened Deities such as Heruka, and their environment, body, enjoyments and activities as those of Heruka. This imagined new world of Heruka is their object of meditation and they meditate on this new generation with single-pointed concentration. Through continually training in this meditation, Heruka practitioners will gain deep realizations of themselves as Heruka, and their environment, body, enjoyments and activities as those of Heruka. This inner realization is generation stage Tantra.

Generation stage Tantra is defined as an inner realization of a creative yoga that is attained through training in divine pride and clear appearance of being an enlightened Deity. It is called a 'creative yoga' because the object of meditation is created by imagination and wisdom. The main function of generation stage Tantra is to purify ordinary death, intermediate state and rebirth, and to accomplish a Buddha's Truth Body, Enjoyment Body and Emanation Body. It is the quick method to ripen our Buddha nature.

Heruka is an enlightened Deity of Highest Yoga Tantra who is the manifestation of the compassion of all Buddhas. In generation stage Heruka practice, practitioners emphasize training in divine pride and clear appearance of being Heruka. Before training in divine pride, practitioners need to learn to perceive their body and mind as Heruka's body and mind. Having accomplished this, they then use their imagined Heruka's body and mind as the basis of imputation for their 'I' or 'self' and develop the thought 'I am Buddha Heruka.' They then meditate on this divine pride with single-pointed concentration. Through training in this meditation they will gain a deep realization of divine pride, which spontaneously believes that they are Heruka. At this time they have changed the basis of imputation for their I.

From beginningless time, in life after life, the basis of imputation for our self or I has been only a contaminated body and mind. Because our self or I is imputed upon a contaminated body and mind, whenever we develop the thought 'I' we simultaneously develop self-grasping ignorance, a mind grasping at an inherently existent 'I' and 'mine', which is the root of all our suffering. However, for qualified Heruka practitioners, their deep realization of divine pride prevents self-grasping ignorance from arising so there is no basis for their experiencing suffering; they will enjoy their pure environment, enjoyments, body and mind of Heruka.

We may ask how, if these practitioners are not yet actually Buddha Heruka, they can believe that they are; and how it is possible for them to gain the realization of divine pride if their view that believes themselves to be Heruka is a mistaken view? Although these practitioners are not actually Buddha Heruka, nevertheless they can believe that they are because they have changed their basis of imputation from their contaminated aggregates to the uncontaminated aggregates of Heruka. Their view that believes they are Buddha Heruka is not a mistaken view because it is non-deceptive and arises from the wisdom realizing that the inherently existent 'I' and 'mine' do not exist. Their realization of divine pride that spontaneously believes themselves to be Heruka therefore has the power to prevent self-grasping ignorance, the root of samsara, from arising.

As explained earlier, things do not exist from their own side. There are no inherently existent 'I', 'mine' and other phenomena; all phenomena exist as mere imputations. Things are imputed upon their basis of imputation by thought. What does 'basis of imputation' mean? For example, the parts of a car are the basis of imputation for the car. The parts of a car are not the car, but there is no car other than its parts. Car is imputed upon its parts by thought. How? Through perceiving any of the parts of the car we naturally develop the thought 'This is the car'. Similarly, our body and mind are not our self but are the basis of imputation for our self. Our self is imputed upon our body or mind by thought. Through perceiving our body or mind we naturally develop the thought 'I' or 'mine'. Without a basis of imputation things cannot exist; everything depends upon its basis of imputation.

Why is it necessary to change the basis of imputation for our self? As mentioned above, since beginningless time, in life after life until now, the basis of imputation for our self has only been the contaminated aggregates of body and mind. Because the basis of imputation for our self is contaminated by the poison of self-grasping ignorance, we experience the endless cycle of

suffering. To free ourself from suffering permanently we therefore need to change our basis of imputation from contaminated
aggregates to uncontaminated aggregates.

How can we change our basis of imputation? In general, we
have changed our basis of imputation countless times. In our
previous lives we took countless rebirths, and each time the
basis of imputation for our self was different. When we took a
human rebirth our basis of imputation was a human body and
mind, and when we took an animal rebirth our basis of imputation was an animal's body and mind. Even in this life, when
we were a baby our basis of imputation was a baby's body and
mind, when we were a teenager our basis of imputation was
a teenager's body and mind, and when we grow old our basis
of imputation will be an old person's body and mind. All these
countless bases of imputation are contaminated aggregates.
We have never changed our basis of imputation from contaminated to uncontaminated aggregates. Only through relying
upon Buddha's Tantric teachings can we accomplish this.

We change our basis of imputation from contaminated to
uncontaminated aggregates by training in clear appearance
and divine pride of being Heruka. As Buddha explained in
his Tantric teachings, first we learn to purify our body and
mind by meditating on the emptiness of the body, mind and
all other phenomena. Perceiving only emptiness, we then
generate ourself as an enlightened Deity such as Heruka. We
then learn to perceive clearly our body and mind as Heruka's
body and mind, our world as Heruka's Pure Land, and all
those around us as enlightened Heroes and Heroines. This is
called 'training in clear appearance'. Perceiving our body and
mind as the uncontaminated aggregates of Heruka's body and
mind, we develop the thought 'I am Buddha Heruka'. We then
meditate on this divine pride continually with single-pointed

concentration, until we gain a deep realization of divine pride that spontaneously believes we are Buddha Heruka. At this time we have changed our basis of imputation from contaminated to uncontaminated aggregates.

If we are normally called John, for example, we should never believe that John is Buddha Heruka, but feel that John disappeared into emptiness before we generated as Buddha Heruka. We then believe that our I, which is imputed upon Heruka's body and mind, is Buddha Heruka. This belief is not a mistaken view, because it arises from wisdom, whereas mistaken views necessarily arise from ignorance. The realization of divine pride arises from wisdom and is a powerful method for accumulating great merit and wisdom.

Even if we have the realization that spontaneously believes that we are Buddha Heruka we should never indicate or declare this to others, as such behaviour is inappropriate in normal society. People will still see us as John and not Heruka, and we also know that John is not Heruka. The realizations of divine pride and clear appearance are inner experiences that have the power to control our delusions, and from which pure actions will naturally develop. There is therefore no basis for us to show inappropriate behaviour; we must continue to engage in our daily activities and communicate with others as normal.

As mentioned before, Tantric realizations can be achieved simply through relying upon correct belief and imagination. This practice is very simple: all we need to do is to become deeply familiar with meditation on correct belief and imagination as presented in Tantra, by applying continual effort. Understanding this we should be confident in our ability to accomplish generation stage realizations of Highest Yoga Tantra. Also, because our world and our self that we normally see do not exist, we have the precious opportunity to generate our new world and our self that are completely pure; this is generation stage. If our world and our self that we normally see existed it would be impossible to generate our world and our self as completely pure. When the strong perception of our world and our self that we normally see ceases through training in generation stage, we shall naturally experience our world and our self as completely pure. It is most important that our motivation for training in generation stage is the compassionate mind of bodhichitta.

The Tantra of Completion Stage

Generation stage is like drawing the basic outline of a picture and completion stage is like completing the picture. Whereas the principal objects of generation stage meditation – the mandala and Deities – are generated by correct imagination, the principal objects of completion stage meditation – the channels, drops and winds – already exist within our body and there is no need to generate them through the power of imagination. For this reason completion stage is not a creative yoga.

Completion stage Tantra is defined as an inner realization of learning developed in dependence upon the inner winds entering, abiding and dissolving within the central channel through the force of meditations. The objects of these meditations are the central channel, the indestructible drop, and the indestructible wind and mind.

THE CENTRAL CHANNEL

The central channel is located exactly midway between the left and right halves of the body, but is closer to the back than the front. Immediately in front of the spine is the life channel, which is quite thick, and in front of this is the central channel. It begins at the point between the eyebrows, from where it ascends in an arch to the crown of the head, and then descends in a straight line to the tip of the sex organ.

The central channel is pale blue on the outside and has four attributes: (1) it is very straight, like the trunk of a plantain tree; (2) inside it is an oily red colour, like pure blood; (3) it is very clear and transparent, like a candle flame; and (4) it is very soft and flexible, like a lotus petal.

At either side of the central channel, with no intervening space, are the right and left channels. The right channel is red in colour and the left is white. The right channel begins at the tip of the right nostril and the left channel at the tip of the left nostril. From there, they both ascend in an arch to the crown of the head, at either side of the central channel. From the crown of the head down to the navel, these three main channels are straight and adjacent to one another. As the left channel continues down below the level of the navel, it curves a little to the right, separating slightly from the central channel and rejoining it at the tip of the sex organ. There it functions to hold and release sperm, blood and urine. As the right channel continues down below the level of the navel, it curves a little to the left and terminates at the tip of the anus, where it functions to hold and release faeces and so forth.

The right and left channels coil around the central channel at various places, thereby forming the so-called 'channel knots'. The four places at which these knots occur are, in ascending order: the navel channel wheel, or navel chakra, the heart channel wheel, the throat channel wheel and the crown channel wheel. At each of these places, except at the heart, there is a twofold knot formed by a single coil of the right channel and a single coil of the left. As the right and left channels ascend to these places, they coil around the central channel by crossing in front and then looping around it. They then continue upward to the level of the next knot. At the heart level, the same thing happens, except that here there is a sixfold knot formed by three overlapping loops of each of the flanking channels. The channels are the paths through which the inner winds and drops flow. To begin with, it is sufficient simply to become familiar with the description and visualization of the three channels. A more detailed explanation of channels can be found in Appendix III.

THE INDESTRUCTIBLE DROP

There are two types of drop in the body: white drops and red drops. The former are the pure essence of white seminal fluid or sperm, and the latter are the pure essence of blood. Both have gross and subtle forms. It is easy to recognize gross drops, but it is more difficult to recognize subtle drops.

The principal seat of the white drop (also known as 'white bodhichitta') is the crown channel wheel, and it is from here that the white seminal fluid originates. The principal seat of the red drop (also known as 'red bodhichitta') is the navel channel wheel, and it is from here that the blood originates. The red drop at the navel is also the foundation of the warmth of the body and the basis for attaining inner fire, or tummo, realizations. When the drops melt and flow through the channels, they give rise to an experience of bliss.

As just explained, at the heart channel wheel there is a sixfold knot formed by the right and left channels coiling around the central channel and constricting it. This is the most difficult knot to loosen, but when it is loosened through meditation we shall develop great power – the realization of clear light. Because the central channel at the heart is constricted by this sixfold knot, it is blocked like a tube of bamboo. Inside the central channel, at the very centre of this sixfold knot, is a small vacuole, and inside this is a drop called the 'indestructible drop'. It is the size of a small pea, with the upper half white in colour and the lower half red. The substance of the white half is the very clear essence of sperm, and the substance of the red half is the very clear essence of blood. This drop, which is very pure and subtle, is the very essence of all drops. All the ordinary red and white drops throughout the body originally come from this drop.

The indestructible drop is like a small pea that has been cut in half, slightly hollowed out, and then rejoined. It is called the 'indestructible drop' because its two halves never separate until death. When we die, all the inner winds dissolve into the indestructible drop, and this causes the drop to open. As the two halves separate, our consciousness immediately leaves our body and goes to the next life.

THE INDESTRUCTIBLE WIND AND MIND

The nature of the indestructible wind is a very subtle 'inner wind'. Inner winds are energy winds that flow through the channels of the body, and they are much more subtle than outer winds. They are associated with, and act as mounts for, various minds. Without these winds our mind cannot move from one object to another. It is said that inner winds are like someone who is blind but who has legs, because they cannot perceive anything but can move from one place to another. Minds are like someone who has eyes but no legs, because minds can see but cannot move without their mount, the inner winds. Because minds are always mounted upon their associated inner winds, they can both see and move.

Inner winds that flow through the left and right channels are impure and harmful because they act as mounts for the minds of self-grasping, self-cherishing and other delusions. We need to make great effort to bring and dissolve these inner winds into the central channel so that we can prevent these delusions from arising.

For ordinary beings, inner winds enter, abide and dissolve within the central channel only during the death process and deep sleep. At these times the indestructible wind and mind manifest, but ordinary beings cannot recognize them because their memory or mindfulness is unable to function then. Completion stage Tantric practitioners can cause their inner winds to enter, abide and dissolve within the central channel at any time through the power of their meditation on the channels, drops and winds. They can therefore accomplish the realizations of the five stages of completion stage Tantra: (1) the initial realization of spontaneous great bliss (isolated body and speech of completion stage); (2) ultimate example clear light; (3) illusory body; (4) meaning clear light; and (5) the union of meaning clear light and the pure illusory body. From the fifth stage, practitioners will attain actual enlightenment within a few months.

There are five root and five branch winds. The root winds are: (1) the life-supporting wind; (2) the downward-voiding wind; (3) the upward-moving wind; (4) the equally-abiding wind; and (5) the pervading wind. The five branch winds are: (1) the moving wind; (2) the intensely-moving wind; (3) the perfectly-moving wind; (4) the strongly-moving wind; and (5) the definitely-moving wind. A detailed explanation of inner winds can be found in Appendix IV.

The indestructible wind is the very subtle wind that is associated with, and acts as the mount for, the very subtle mind. It is called the 'continuously residing body' because we have had this body continuously in life after life. Although our mind of self-cherishing believes that our present body is our own body and cherishes it, in reality our present body is a part of others' bodies because it is part of our parents' bodies. Our self imputed upon our present body and mind will cease at the end of the death process, whereas our self imputed upon our continuously residing body and mind will never cease, but goes from one life to the next. It is this person or I that will finally become an enlightened being. Through this we can understand that, according to Highest Yoga Tantra, in the mental continuum of each and every living being there is a deathless person or I who possesses a deathless body. However, without relying upon the profound instructions of Highest Yoga Tantra we cannot recognize our own deathless body and deathless I, our actual self. A Yogi once said:

First, due to fear of death, I ran towards Dharma.
Then I trained in the state of deathlessness.
Finally I realized there is no death and I relaxed!

Inside the indestructible drop resides the indestructible wind and mind, the union of our very subtle wind and very subtle mind. The very subtle wind is our own body, or continuously residing body. The very subtle mind, or indestructible mind, is our own mind, or continuously residing mind, and is mounted upon the very subtle wind. Because the union of our very subtle wind and very subtle mind never ceases, it is called the 'indestructible wind and mind'. Our indestructible wind and mind have never separated since beginningless time, and they will never separate in the future. The potential to communicate possessed by the combination of our very subtle body and mind is our very subtle speech, which is our own speech, or continuously residing speech. This will become a Buddha's speech in the future. In short, inside the indestructible drop is our own body, speech and mind, which in the future will become the enlightened body, speech and mind of a Buddha. These three, our very subtle body, speech and mind, are our real Buddha nature.

Having gained some experience of generation stage Tantra, which is like drawing the basic outline of a picture, we need to engage in the meditations on completion stage Tantra in order to complete the picture. These are the meditations on the central channel, indestructible drop, and indestructible wind and mind, known as the 'yogas of the channel, drop and wind'.

HOW TO MEDITATE ON THE CENTRAL CHANNEL

First, we should learn to perceive what our central channel looks like, contemplating as follows:

My central channel is located exactly midway between the left and right halves of my body, but is closer to the back than the front. Immediately in front of the spine, there is the life channel, which is quite thick, and in front of this is the central channel. It begins at the point between my eyebrows, from where it ascends in an arch to the crown of my head, and then descends in a straight line to the tip of my sex organ. It is pale blue in colour on the outside, and it is an oily red colour on the inside. It is clear and transparent, and very soft and flexible.

At the very beginning we can, if we wish, visualize the central channel as being fairly wide, and then gradually visualize it as being thinner and thinner until finally we are able to visualize it as being the width of a drinking straw. We contemplate like this repeatedly until we perceive a generic image of our central channel. Then, while believing that our mind is inside the central channel at our heart, we focus single-pointedly on the central channel at the level of our heart and meditate on this. We should train continually in this way until we gain deep experience of this meditation.

HOW TO MEDITATE ON THE INDESTRUCTIBLE DROP

To perceive our indestructible drop, we contemplate as follows:

Inside my central channel at the level of my heart there is a small vacuole. Inside this is my indestructible drop. It is the size of a small pea, with the upper half white in colour and the lower half red. It is like a pea that has been cut in half, slightly hollowed out, and then rejoined. It is the very essence of all drops and is very pure and subtle. Even though it is the substance of blood and sperm, it has a very clear nature, like a tiny ball of crystal that radiates five-coloured rays of light.

We contemplate like this repeatedly until we perceive a clear generic image of our indestructible drop at our heart inside our central channel. With the feeling that our mind is inside our indestructible drop at our heart, we meditate on this drop single-pointedly without distraction.

This meditation is a powerful method for causing our inner winds to enter, abide and dissolve within the central channel. Master Ghantapa said:

We should meditate single-pointedly
On the indestructible drop that always abides at our heart.
Those who are familiar with this meditation
Will definitely develop exalted wisdom.

Here 'exalted wisdom' means the wisdom of the clear light of
bliss experienced when the knots at the heart channel wheel
are loosened. Of all the knots in the central channel, these
are the most difficult to loosen; but if from the beginning of
our completion stage practice we concentrate on our heart
channel wheel, this will help us to loosen these knots. This
meditation, therefore, is a powerful method for gaining qualified completion stage realizations.

HOW TO MEDITATE ON THE INDESTRUCTIBLE
WIND AND MIND

To gain deeper experience of the wisdom of the clear light
of bliss, we engage in meditation on the indestructible wind
and mind. First we find the object of this meditation, that is,
the clear perception of our indestructible wind and mind, by
contemplating as follows:

*Inside my indestructible drop is the union of my indestructible
wind and mind in the aspect of a tiny nada, which symbolizes
Heruka's mind of clear light. It is reddish-white in colour and
radiates five-coloured rays of light. My indestructible drop,
located inside my central channel at my heart, is like a cave,
and the union of my indestructible wind and mind is like
someone living inside this cave.*

An illustration of the nada appears in Appendix VIII. We contemplate repeatedly in this way until we perceive the nada,

which is the nature of the union of our indestructible wind and mind. With the strong recognition that the nada is the union of our very subtle wind and mind, and feeling that our mind has entered into this nada, we meditate single-pointedly on the nada without forgetting it.

Through gaining deep experience of the meditations on the central channel, the indestructible drop and the union of the indestructible wind and mind, our inner winds will enter, abide and dissolve within the central channel, and we shall experience special signs. We can tell whether or not the winds have entered the central channel by checking our breathing. Normally there are imbalances in our breath – more air is exhaled through one nostril than through the other, and the air begins to leave one nostril before the other. However, when the winds have entered the central channel as a result of the meditations explained above, the pressure and the timing of the breath will be the same for both nostrils during inhalation and exhalation. Therefore, the first sign to be noticed is that we will be breathing evenly through both nostrils. Another noticeable imbalance in the normal breath is that the inhalation is stronger than the exhalation, or vice versa. The second sign that the winds have entered the central channel is that the pressure of the inhalation will be exactly equal to that of the exhalation.

There are also two signs indicating that the winds are abiding in the central channel: (1) our breathing becomes weaker and weaker, eventually ceasing completely, and (2) all abdominal movement normally associated with the breath stops. In the normal course of events, if our breathing were to stop we would be filled with panic and think that we were close to death, but if we are able to stop breathing through the force of meditation, far from panicking our mind will become even more confident, comfortable and flexible.

When the winds are abiding within the central channel, we no longer have to rely upon gross air to survive. Normally our breathing stops only at the time of death. During sleep our breathing becomes much more subtle, but it never stops completely. During completion stage meditation, however, our breath can come to a complete halt without our becoming unconscious. After the winds have been abiding in the central channel for five or ten minutes, it is possible that they will escape again into the right and left channels. If this happens, we shall resume breathing. Air flowing through the nostrils is an indication that the winds are not abiding within the central channel.

What are the signs that the winds have dissolved within the central channel? There are seven winds that must dissolve, and each has a specific sign indicating that its dissolution has been completed. The seven winds are: (1) the earth element wind; (2) the water element wind; (3) the fire element wind; (4) the wind element wind; (5) the wind mounted by the mind of white appearance; (6) the wind mounted by the mind of red increase; and (7) the wind mounted by the mind of black near-attainment. The first four of these winds are gross and the last three are subtle. These seven winds dissolve gradually in sequence, and with each dissolution there is a particular appearance.

The earth element wind supports and increases everything that is associated with the earth element in our body, such as our bones, cartilage and fingernails. When this wind dissolves within the central channel, we perceive an appearance known as the 'mirage-like appearance'. This is like the appearance of shimmering water that is sometimes seen on the floor of a desert. There are three levels on which this mirage-like appearance is perceived, depending upon the degree to which the earth element wind has dissolved within the central channel. If the dissolution is only slight the appearance will be vague, the least clear, and very difficult to recognize; if the dissolution is almost complete the appearance will be clearer and more vivid; and if the wind dissolves completely the appearance will be unmistakably clear and vivid, and impossible not to perceive. When the earth element wind has dissolved and the mirage-like appearance has been perceived, the next wind will dissolve and a different appearance will manifest. The more completely the first wind dissolves, the more vivid will be our perception of this next appearance.

The second wind to dissolve is the water element wind, which supports and increases the liquid elements of the body such as the blood. The appearance associated with this dissolution is called the 'smoke-like appearance'. Some texts say that this appearance is like smoke billowing from a chimney, but this is not the actual appearance. There is an appearance like billowing smoke, but this occurs just prior to the actual dissolution of the water element wind. It is not until this initial appearance has subsided that the actual smoke-like appearance is perceived. This is like thin wisps of wafting blue smoke drifting in the air in a slowly swirling haze. As before, there are three levels on which this appearance is perceived, depending upon the degree to which the water element wind has dissolved.

Next comes the dissolution of the fire element wind. This wind supports and increases the fire element in the body and is responsible for bodily heat and so forth. The sign that this wind has dissolved is the 'sparkling-fireflies-like appearance'. This appearance is sometimes described in terms of an open crackling fire seen at night, with the mass of ascending sparks swirling above the fire resembling the sparkling-fireflies-like appearance. Once again, there are three levels on which this appearance is perceived, depending upon the degree of dissolution.

Following this, the wind element wind dissolves. This is the wind mounted by gross conceptual thought. It powers gross dualistic appearances and the gross conceptual thoughts that result from holding these appearances to be true. The sign that the fourth of the gross winds has started to dissolve is the 'candle-flame-like appearance'. This is like the steady, erect flame of a candle in a draughtless room. Once again there are three levels on which this appearance is perceived.

When the earth element wind has dissolved within the central channel and the power of the earth element is thereby diminished, it may seem as though the water element has increased because, as the power of the former element diminishes, the latter is perceived more clearly. For this reason, the dissolution of the earth element wind into the central channel is often described as 'the earth element dissolving into the water element'. For similar reasons, the subsequent dissolutions are referred to as 'the water element dissolving into the fire element', 'the fire element dissolving into the wind element', and 'the wind element dissolving into consciousness'.

After the candle-flame-like appearance, all gross conceptual minds have ceased functioning because the winds upon which they are mounted have dissolved and disappeared. When the meditator has completed the dissolution of the fourth wind, the first subtle mind – the mind of white appearance – arises. With this mind, the meditator perceives an appearance of whiteness, like the bright light of the moon pervading an empty sky on a clear autumn night. As before, there are three levels of clarity to this appearance depending upon the ability of the meditator.

At this point the mind is completely free from gross conceptions, such as the eighty indicative conceptions listed in *Clear Light of Bliss*, and the only perception is that of white, empty space. Ordinary beings also perceive this appearance, for example, at the time of death, but they are unable to recognize it or to prolong it because at this stage the ordinary gross level of mindfulness has ceased to function. However, even though there is no gross mindfulness at this stage, those who have trained properly according to the practices of completion stage Tantra are able to use the subtle mindfulness they have developed during meditation to recognize and prolong the white appearance, something that ordinary beings are unable to do.

When the subtle wind mounted by the mind of white appearance dissolves, the mind of red increase arises. This mind and its mounted wind are more subtle than the mind and wind of white appearance. The sign that occurs when this mind arises is an appearance like red sunlight pervading an empty sky. Once again, there are three levels of clarity to this appearance.

When the subtle wind mounted by the mind of red increase dissolves, the mind of black near-attainment arises. This mind and its mounted wind are even more subtle than the mind and wind of red increase. The mind of black near-attainment has two levels: the upper part and the lower part. The upper part of the mind of black near-attainment still possesses subtle mindfulness, but the lower part has no mindfulness at all. It is experienced as an overwhelming unconsciousness, like that of a very deep faint. At this point, we would appear to others to be dead.

The sign that occurs when the mind of black near-attainment arises is an appearance like a very black, empty sky. This appearance comes with the upper part of the mind of black near-attainment, immediately after the cessation of the mind of red increase. As the experience of black near-attainment progresses and we approach complete unconsciousness, our subtle mindfulness ceases. The more strongly the wind dissolves into the central channel, the more deeply unconscious we become during the mind of black near-attainment; and the more deeply unconscious we become at this time, the more vividly we shall perceive the subsequent appearance of clear light. This is similar to the experience of someone who stays in a dark room for a long time; the longer he stays there, the brighter the outside world will appear when he eventually emerges. Thus, the degree of brightness experienced depends upon the depth and duration of the previous darkness.

When the subtle wind mounted by the mind of black near-attainment dissolves, the mind of clear light arises. This mind and its mounted wind are the most subtle of all. The sign that occurs when this mind arises is an appearance like an autumn sky at dawn – perfectly clear and empty.

When the mind of clear light arises, a very subtle mindfulness is restored, according to the meditator's level of development. The very subtle wind and the very subtle mind that is mounted upon it, reside in the indestructible drop in the centre of the heart channel wheel. Normally the very subtle mind does not function, but at the time of the clear light it manifests and becomes active. If we have trained in the techniques of completion stage Tantra, and have become proficient in them, we shall be able to perceive and maintain the appearance of clear light. Eventually, by learning to use the very subtle mindfulness developed at this stage, we shall be able to focus our very subtle mind on emptiness, and in this way use the mind of clear light as the means for attaining a Buddha's Truth Body.

Our mind cannot become more subtle than the mind of clear light. During the first four appearances (mirage-like, smoke-like, sparkling-fireflies-like and candle-flame-like) the gross winds dissolve; and during the next three (white appearance, red increase and black near-attainment) the subtle winds dissolve. Then, with the appearance of the clear light, the very subtle mind and its mounted wind manifest and become active. These cannot dissolve because they are indestructible. After death, they simply pass to the next life.

Of the three subtle winds mounted by the three subtle minds, the least subtle is that mounted by the mind of white appearance. This mind is called 'white appearance' because all that is perceived is an appearance of white, empty space. It is also called 'empty' because the mind of white appearance perceives this white space as empty. At this stage the appearance of white and the appearance of empty are of equal strength.

When the wind mounted by the mind of white appearance dissolves, the second of the three subtle minds – the mind of red increase – arises. The mounted wind of this mind is more subtle than that mounted by the mind of white appearance. This mind is called 'red increase' because the appearance of red space is increasing. It is also called 'very empty' because the appearance of empty is stronger than that of the previous mind. At this stage the appearance of empty is stronger than the appearance of red.

When the wind of the mind of red increase dissolves, the third subtle mind – the mind of black near-attainment – arises. This mind is called 'near-attainment' because the experience of clear light is now close at hand. It is also called 'great empty' because the appearance of empty is even greater than that of the previous mind.

When the third subtle wind, that mounted by the mind of black near-attainment, dissolves, the mind of clear light arises.

This mind is called 'clear light' because its nature is very lucid and clear, and because it perceives an appearance like the light of an autumn dawn. It is also called 'all-empty' because it is empty of all gross and subtle winds and perceives only an empty appearance. The object of the mind of clear light is very similar in appearance to the object perceived by a Superior being in meditative equipoise on emptiness. Collectively, the four minds – the mind of white appearance, the mind of red increase, the mind of black near-attainment and the mind of clear light – are referred to as the 'four empties'.

If a completion stage meditator is highly accomplished, he or she will have a very vivid experience of clear light and will be able to maintain that experience for a long time. Just how vivid our experience of clear light is depends upon how vivid the previous seven appearances were, and this in turn depends upon how strongly the winds dissolve within the central channel. If the winds dissolve very strongly, the meditator will have a vivid experience of all the appearances and will be able to prolong the experience of each one. The longer we are able to remain with the experience of each appearance, the longer we shall be able to remain with the clear light itself.

If a person dies a violent death, he or she progresses through these appearances very rapidly, but if the death is slow or natural the appearances from mirage-like to clear light will be experienced more gradually and for longer. If we have developed the realization of ultimate example clear light, we shall be able to have exactly the same experience of these appearances while in deep concentration that we would have if we were actually dying. Moreover, if we have trained well in the meditations explained above, we shall be able to meditate on emptiness throughout all four empties, except during the time spent in the swoon, or faint, of the mind of black near-attainment.

To be able to perceive the four empties clearly, exactly as in the death process, we must be able to dissolve all the winds into the indestructible drop in the centre of the heart channel wheel. If they dissolve into another channel wheel of the central channel, such as the navel channel wheel, we shall experience similar appearances, but they will be artificial – not the true appearances that occur when the winds dissolve into the indestructible drop, as they do at the time of death.

Although an accomplished meditator can abide within the clear light for a long time, he or she must eventually move on. When we arise from the clear light, the first thing we experience is the mind of black near-attainment of reverse order. Then we experience in sequence the mind of red increase, the mind of white appearance, the eighty gross conceptual minds, the minds of the candle-flame-like appearance and so forth, as the minds evolve in an order that is the reverse of that in which they previously dissolved.

Thus the mind of clear light is the foundation of all other minds. When the gross and subtle minds and their mounted winds dissolve into the indestructible drop at the heart, we remain with only the clear light, and then it is from this clear light that all the other minds evolve, each one grosser than the previous one.

These sequences of serial and reverse order are experienced by ordinary beings during sleep and the initial stages of waking up, during death and the initial stages of their next rebirth, and by qualified completion stage practitioners during meditation. Because enlightened beings have attained permanent cessation of the seven winds listed above, they experience only the very subtle mind of clear light – even their compassion and bodhichitta are part of their mind of clear light.

The Completion Stage of Mahamudra

The term 'Mahamudra' is Sanskrit. 'Maha' means 'great' and refers to great bliss, and 'mudra' here means 'non-deceptive' and refers to emptiness. Mahamudra is the union of great bliss and emptiness. Mahamudra Tantra is defined as a mind of fully qualified clear light that experiences great bliss and realizes emptiness directly. Because emptiness is explained in detail in Buddha's Sutra teachings and is a part of Mahamudra, some texts say that it is Sutra Mahamudra; but actual Mahamudra is necessarily a realization of Highest Yoga Tantra.

The instructions on Mahamudra Tantra given by the Wisdom Buddha Je Tsongkhapa Losang Dragpa are superior to those given by other scholars. As the scholar Gungtang says in *Prayer for the Flourishing of the Doctrine of Je Tsongkhapa*:

> The emptiness that is explained in Buddha's Sutra
>   teachings,
> And the great bliss that is explained in Buddha's
>   Tantric teachings –
> The union of these two is the very essence of Buddha's
>   eighty-four thousand teachings.

Ghantapa

May the doctrine of Conqueror Losang Dragpa flourish for evermore.

The nature of Mahamudra is a fully qualified clear light. As mentioned previously there are many different levels of the experience of clear light depending upon the degree of dissolution of the inner winds into the central channel. The realization of great bliss developed in dependence upon the inner winds entering, abiding and dissolving within the central channel, prior to attaining the fully qualified clear light, is the first of the five stages of completion stage. It is called 'isolated body and speech of completion stage', which means that at this stage the practitioner is free, or isolated, from gross ordinary appearances and conceptions of body and speech.

A fully qualified clear light mind experiencing great bliss that realizes emptiness with a generic image is called 'ultimate example clear light'. This realization is called 'ultimate' because it is a fully qualified clear light. It is called 'example' because by using this realization as an example, practitioners understand that they can accomplish a fully qualified clear light mind experiencing great bliss that realizes emptiness directly, which is called 'meaning clear light'. The realization of ultimate example clear light is the second of the five stages of completion stage. It is also called 'isolated mind' because at this stage practitioners are free, or isolated, from gross ordinary appearances and conceptions of mind.

When practitioners arise from the concentration of ultimate example clear light, their indestructible wind – their continuously residing body – transforms into the illusory body. This is a divine body, which in nature is wisdom light having the aspect of the divine body of an enlightened Deity such as Heruka. The colour of the illusory body is white. The realization of this illusory body is the third of the five stages of completion stage, and is called 'illusory body of the third stage'.

Practitioners who have attained the illusory body of the third stage meditate on emptiness again and again with their clear light mind of bliss until they directly realize the emptiness of all phenomena. When they accomplish this they attain 'meaning clear light', a fully qualified clear light mind experiencing great bliss that realizes the emptiness of all phenomena directly. This realization of meaning clear light is the fourth of the five stages of completion stage, and is called 'meaning clear light of the fourth stage'. 'Meaning clear light' and 'Mahamudra Tantra' are synonymous.

When practitioners arise from the concentration of meaning clear light they attain the pure illusory body and completely abandon ordinary conceptions and all other delusions. When these practitioners manifest meaning clear light again, they will attain the union of meaning clear light and pure illusory body. The realization of this union is the fifth of the five stages of completion stage, and is called 'union of the fifth stage'. From this fifth stage practitioners will attain actual enlightenment – the Path of No More Learning, or Buddhahood.

As mentioned above, Mahamudra is the union of great bliss and emptiness. This means that Mahamudra Tantra is a single mind that is both bliss and wisdom: it experiences great bliss and realizes emptiness directly. Mahamudra Tantra is a collection of merit that is the main cause of a Buddha's Form Body, and a collection of wisdom that is the main cause of a Buddha's Truth Body, or Dharmakaya. When training in the meditations of Mahamudra Tantra we are transforming our continuously residing body and mind into a Buddha's Form

Body and Truth Body. Mahamudra Tantra, therefore, gives inconceivable meaning to our life.

GREAT BLISS

The bliss explained by Buddha in completion stage Tantra is unequalled among all other types of bliss and is therefore called 'great bliss'.

In general, there are many different types of bliss. For example, ordinary beings sometimes experience some artificial bliss when they engage in sexual activity, and qualified meditators experience a special bliss of suppleness during deep meditation due to their pure concentration, especially when they attain tranquil abiding and accomplish the concentration of the absorption of cessation. Moreover when Dharma practitioners, through training in higher moral discipline, higher concentration and higher wisdom, attain permanent inner peace by abandoning self-grasping, they experience a profound bliss of inner peace day and night in life after life. These types of bliss are mentioned in Buddha's Sutra teachings. The bliss of completion stage, however, is quite different from all of these, and is vastly superior. The bliss of completion stage – great bliss – is a bliss that possesses two special characteristics: (1) its nature is a bliss arisen from the melting of the drops inside the central channel; and (2) its function is to prevent subtle mistaken appearance. No other form of bliss possesses these two characteristics.

A bliss possessing these two characteristics can be experienced only by those who are engaged in Highest Yoga Tantra practice, and by Buddhas. Even many high Bodhisattvas abiding in Pure Lands have no opportunity to experience it because, although they have very high realizations, their bodies lack the necessary physical conditions for generating bliss possessing the two characteristics. What are these conditions? They are the three elements of flesh, skin and blood that come from the mother; and the three elements of bone, marrow and sperm that come from the father. These six elements are essential for accomplishing this bliss, which is the quick path to Buddhahood. It was because humans possessed these conditions that Buddha explained Tantric teachings to us in the first place. Therefore, from this point of view, we are more fortunate than many high Bodhisattvas abiding in Pure Lands who are experiencing great enjoyments. It is said that these Bodhisattvas pray to be born in the human world so that they can meet a qualified Vajra Master and practise the quick path to enlightenment. In *Song of the Spring Queen*, Je Tsongkhapa says that without experiencing this bliss there is no possibility of attaining liberation in this life. It goes without saying, therefore, that without this bliss there is no possibility of attaining full enlightenment in this life.

If we develop and maintain this bliss through the practice of completion stage meditation, we can transform our attachment into a special method for completing the quick path to enlightenment. Before we attain this bliss, our attachment causes us to be reborn in samsara, but once we have this bliss our attachment causes us to be released from samsara. Moreover, once we attain this bliss we shall be able to stop our samsaric rebirths very quickly. The cause of samsara is our mind of self-grasping. According to the teachings of Highest Yoga Tantra, self-grasping depends upon its mounted wind, which flows through the right and left channels. For human beings, without this wind self-grasping cannot develop. By gaining the bliss of completion stage, we can gradually reduce the inner winds of the right and left channels until finally they cease completely.

When they cease, our self-grasping ceases, and we experience liberation from samsara.

From this we can see that in Sutra alone there is no liberation, not to mention full enlightenment. The Highest Yoga Tantra teachings are Buddha's ultimate intention, and the Sutra teachings are like the basic foundation. Although there are many explanations of how to attain liberation or nirvana in the Sutra teachings, if we check precisely it is very difficult to understand from Sutra teachings how nirvana can be attained. 'Nirvana' means 'the state beyond sorrow' – the permanent cessation of self-grasping and its mounted wind – and its nature is emptiness. If we have never heard Highest Yoga Tantra teachings and someone asks us precisely how we attain such a nirvana, we cannot give a perfect answer. As Je Tsongkhapa said, the final answer can be found only in teachings on Highest Yoga Tantra.

The bliss that arises from the melting of drops inside channels other than the central channel has no special qualities. When ordinary beings engage in sexual intercourse, for example, this causes their downward-voiding wind to move upwards, and this in turn causes their ordinary inner heat, or tummo, to increase in their right and left channels, principally in the left. As a result the red drops of the woman and the white drops of the man melt and flow through the left channel. This flowing of the drops causes them to experience some bliss, but it is very short-lived and the drops are soon released. Having had this brief experience of bliss, they are not left with any good results, except maybe a baby!

By contrast, when a qualified Tantric practitioner practises the completion stage meditations that are explained above, he or she will cause his inner winds to gather, abide and dissolve within the central channel. This will cause the downward-voiding wind located just below the navel to move upwards. Normally this wind functions to release the drops, but because it is now rising within the central channel, the inner heat located at the navel will increase inside the central channel, thereby causing the drops to melt and flow also inside the central channel.

For the practitioner of a male Deity, the white drop begins to flow down from the crown and, when it reaches the throat, the practitioner experiences a very special bliss possessing the two characteristics, or qualities. As the drop flows down to the heart, the bliss becomes stronger and more qualified; as it flows down to the navel, the bliss becomes even stronger and more qualified; and finally, as it flows down to the tip of the sex organ, the practitioner experiences spontaneous great bliss – the great bliss of completion stage. Because the downward-voiding wind is reversed, the drop is not released at this point but flows up again through the central channel, causing the practitioner to experience even greater bliss. For such a practitioner, the drops are never released and so they flow up and down the central channel for a very long time, giving rise to unceasing bliss. The practitioner can cause such bliss to manifest at any time simply by penetrating the central channel with concentration.

The stronger this bliss becomes, the more subtle our mind becomes. Gradually our mind becomes very peaceful, all conceptual distractions disappear, and we experience very special suppleness. This mind is infinitely superior to the experience of tranquil abiding explained in Sutra teachings. Moreover, as our mind becomes more subtle our subtle mistaken appearance is reduced, and eventually our mind becomes the very subtle mind of the clear light of bliss. This is a very high realization. When the clear light of bliss concentrates on emptiness it mixes with emptiness very easily because subtle mistaken appearance is greatly reduced. Finally it realizes emptiness directly, and whereas previously it felt as if our bliss and emptiness were two things, now they have become one nature. This mind is the union of great bliss and emptiness, or meaning clear light.

The initial realization of the union of great bliss and emptiness is the path of seeing of Highest Yoga Tantra. However, even though it is only the path of seeing, it has the power to eliminate both the intellectually-formed delusions and innate delusions together. When the practitioner rises from this concentration of the union of bliss and emptiness, he or she has abandoned all the delusions and has attained liberation. At the same time, he or she has attained the pure illusory body. From that moment, the practitioner's body is a vajra body, which means a deathless body, and he or she will never again experience ageing, sickness or contaminated rebirth.

As mentioned above, previously when the practitioner was ordinary, he or she was using a body taken from others – from his or her parents. We normally say 'My body, my body' as if our present gross body is our real body, but this is not our actual body because originally it was part of our parents' bodies. When a Tantric practitioner attains a vajra body, however, he has manifested his own body, the continuously residing body. When he perceives this vajra body he develops the thoughts 'I' and 'mine'. Such a practitioner has now become a deathless person.

We have had our very subtle body, very subtle speech and very subtle mind since beginningless time. These are the continuously residing body, the continuously residing speech and the continuously residing mind, and they are our actual Buddha nature. The Buddha nature explained in Sutra is not actual Buddha nature because it is a gross object that will cease; actual Buddha nature is explained only in Highest Yoga Tantra. Normally, for ordinary beings, the only times their very subtle body, speech and mind become manifest are during deep sleep and death. However, even though they are not normally manifest, our very subtle body is the seed of a Buddha's body, our very subtle speech is the seed of a Buddha's speech, and our very subtle mind is the seed of a Buddha's mind.

As already mentioned, the very subtle body is the very subtle wind upon which the very subtle mind is mounted. This very subtle body and very subtle mind are always together. Since they are the same nature, and are never separated, they are called the 'indestructible wind' and the 'indestructible mind'. The union of the indestructible wind and mind is normally located inside the indestructible drop, inside the central channel at the heart.

Our very subtle mind manifests only when all our inner winds dissolve within our central channel. When this happens we gradually experience the eight signs described previously, as we pass through the different levels of dissolution. Finally, with the last level of dissolution, the very subtle mind of clear light becomes manifest. At the same time, the very subtle body also becomes manifest.

During death, the inner winds dissolve naturally and fully within the central channel and the very subtle mind and very subtle body naturally become manifest, but we cannot recognize them. However, by practising the completion stage meditations explained above, we can cause our very subtle mind and body to become manifest during meditation. Until we attain the realization of illusory body, our very subtle body will not maintain a definite shape or colour. When we attain the union of bliss and emptiness, our very subtle mind transforms into meaning clear light and, when we rise from that meditation, our very subtle body transforms into the vajra body, or pure illusory body, which does have definite shape, colour and so forth.

For example, if we are a Heruka practitioner, whenever we do self-generation as Heruka with a blue-coloured body, four faces, twelve arms and so on, we are building the basic foundation for the illusory body. In the future, when our very subtle body transforms into the illusory body it will look like real Heruka. Previously it was merely an imagined body, but at this time it will become real. This is a very good reason for now practising generation stage very sincerely.

When we attain the pure illusory body, we shall no longer think of our gross body as our body. The basis for imputing our I will have completely changed, and we shall now impute I in dependence upon our subtle body. When we have reached this attainment, we shall have become deathless because our body and mind will never separate. Death is the permanent separation of body and mind, but the body and mind of those who have attained the illusory body never separate because they are indestructible. Finally, our pure illusory body will transform into Buddha's Form Body and our union of bliss and emptiness will transform into Buddha's Truth Body, and we shall experience the union of Buddha's Form Body and Truth Body, the Union of No More Learning.

In the section on the benefits of bodhichitta in *Guide to the Bodhisattva's Way of Life* Shantideva says:

Just like the supreme elixir that transmutes into gold,
Bodhichitta can transform this impure body we have taken
Into the priceless jewel of a Buddha's form;
Therefore, firmly maintain bodhichitta.

Here, 'elixir' refers to a special substance that can transform iron into gold, like that used by great Masters such as Nagarjuna. This verse says that bodhichitta is a special method that, like a supreme elixir, has the power to transform our impure body into a Buddha's Form Body. How can it do this? According to Sutra, a practitioner cannot attain enlightenment in one life but must practise for many lives until finally he or she is born into Akanishta Pure Land with a pure body. It is only with this pure body that he or she can attain Buddhahood. There is no method in either Sutra or Tantra for transforming our present impure body into a Buddha's body. This impure body must eventually die; it must be left behind. Even the holy Buddha Shakyamuni himself left behind the gross body that came from his parents when he passed away. Thus, if we ask how bodhichitta can transform this impure body into a Buddha's body, there is no correct answer within Sutra teachings. This is because, according to Sutra teachings, the gross body is the real body; the Sutras never mention the continuously residing body, the vajra body, or the deathless body.

By following the Tantric view, however, we can answer this question as follows. The body referred to by Shantideva is not the gross body, but our own body, our continuously residing body, which is the very subtle wind upon which our very subtle mind is mounted. At present this is an impure body because it is obscured by delusions and other obstructions, like a blue sky covered by clouds. These defilements are not the nature of our subtle body, but are temporary defilements. The method for transforming this impure body into a Buddha's Form Body is not conventional bodhichitta, but the ultimate bodhichitta of Highest Yoga Tantra, the union of great bliss and emptiness. This ultimate bodhichitta can directly transform our impure continuously residing body first into the pure illusory body and finally into the Form Body of a Buddha. Since Shantideva himself was a sincere Tantric practitioner, we can be certain that this was his intended meaning.

As mentioned previously, to generate the bliss that possesses two special qualities we need to gather and dissolve our inner winds within our central channel. There are two ways to do this: by penetrating our own body or by penetrating another's body.

We begin by penetrating our own body. Here, the term 'our own body' refers to our channels, drops and winds, and 'penetrate' to concentrating on our central channel, drops and winds, as already explained. Meditation on the central channel is called the 'yoga of the central channel', meditation on the drops is called the 'yoga of the drop', and meditation on the winds is called the 'yoga of wind'.

Penetrating another's body means relying upon an action mudra, or consort, and engaging in sexual intercourse. However, just penetrating another's body will not bring our inner winds into our central channel if we do not already have deep experience of and familiarity with the yoga of the central channel, the yoga of the drop and the yoga of wind. This means that we must have gained the experience of dissolving some of our inner winds within the central channel at the heart channel wheel and, through this practice, be able to perceive clearly the eight signs of dissolution from the mirage-like appearance to the clear light. Only when we have such experience is it the right time to rely upon an action mudra. This order of practice is very important.

There are only ten doors through which the winds can enter the central channel. They are located along the central channel as follows: (1) the upper tip of the central channel: the point between the eyebrows; (2) the lower tip: the tip of the sex organ; (3) the centre of the crown channel wheel: located in the apex of the cranium; (4) the centre of the throat channel wheel: located near the back of the throat; (5) the centre of the heart channel wheel: located between the two breasts; (6) the centre of the navel channel wheel; (7) the centre of the secret place channel wheel: four finger-widths below the navel; (8) the centre of the jewel channel wheel: located in the centre of the sex organ, near its tip; (9) the wheel of wind: the centre of the forehead channel wheel; and (10) the wheel of fire: the centre of the channel wheel located midway between the throat and the heart channel wheels. Just as we can enter a house through any of the doors leading in from the outside, so the winds can enter the central channel through any of these ten doors.

The central channel is in reality one single channel, but it is divided into different sections: the central channel of the crown channel wheel, the central channel of the throat channel wheel, the central channel of the heart channel wheel, the central channel of the navel channel wheel, and so forth. Because there are these different locations, when a practitioner wants to bring his or her winds into the central channel, he or she must choose one of these points at which to concentrate.

In *Clear Light of Bliss*, I explain how to bring the inner winds into the central channel through the sixth of the ten doors, the centre of the navel channel wheel. We do this by visualizing our inner heat, known as tummo, inside our central channel at the navel in the aspect of a short-AH and meditating on this. This common practice, known as 'tummo meditation', accords with the tradition of the Six Yogas of Naropa. It was originally explained in *Hevajra Root Tantra* by Buddha Vajradhara, and since then has been used by many practitioners such as Milarepa and his disciples, and later by practitioners in

Je Tsongkhapa's tradition. However, the instructions of the Ganden Oral Lineage present an uncommon Mahamudra Tantra practice. This is a very special practice of Mahamudra that Je Tsongkhapa received directly from Manjushri, who had received it directly from Buddha. The lineage of this instruction, the Ganden Oral Lineage, which is a close lineage, was then passed to Togden Jampel Gyatso, Baso Chokyi Gyaltsen, Mahasiddha Dharmavajra, and so on. A full list of the lineage Gurus of this special instruction is given in *Clear Light of Bliss*. These Spiritual Guides are the close lineage Gurus.

In this Mahamudra Tantra practice, we choose the centre of the heart channel wheel from among the ten doors to bring the winds into the central channel. This practice is indicated in the following verse from the sadhana *Offering to the Spiritual Guide*, which is the uncommon preliminary practice of Mahamudra Tantra according to Je Tsongkhapa's tradition:

I seek your blessings, O Protector, that you may place
  your feet
On the centre of the eight-petalled lotus at my heart,
So that I may manifest within this life
The paths of illusory body, clear light, and union.

These words actually reveal that penetrating the central channel of the heart channel wheel, the ` and the indestructible wind – the three yogas explained above – are meditations on isolated body. These lead to the meditations on isolated speech and isolated mind, which in turn lead to the meditations on illusory body, meaning clear light and union.

Because penetrating and concentrating on the indestructible drop at the heart is a powerful method for attaining the realizations of completion stage, Buddha Vajradhara praises this method in *Ambhidana Tantra*, where he says:

Those who meditate on the drop
That always abides at the heart,
Single-pointedly and without change,
Will definitely attain realizations.

The Practice of Heruka Body Mandala

As mentioned above, Heruka – also known as Chakrasambara – is an enlightened Deity of Highest Yoga Tantra who is the manifestation of the compassion of all Buddhas.

To lead living beings to the supreme happiness of enlightenment, all the Buddhas' compassion appears in the form of Heruka who has a blue-coloured body, four faces and twelve arms, and embraces the consort Vajravarahi. Every part of Heruka's body is the nature of wisdom light. Although each aspect of Heruka's body has great meaning, as explained in the commentary to Heruka body mandala practice called *Essence of Vajrayana*, at first we should be satisfied with the mere name Heruka. There is no need to search closely for Heruka's body, because like a rainbow the closer we search for it the more it will disappear. The name Heruka has three parts, 'He' 'ru' and 'ka'. 'He' refers to the emptiness of all phenomena, 'ru' refers to great bliss and 'ka' refers to the union of great bliss and emptiness. This indicates that through relying upon

Heruka with faith we shall attain the realization of the union of great bliss and emptiness, which is the actual quick path to enlightenment.

Heruka imputed upon Buddha's Enjoyment Body is 'Enjoyment Body Heruka', and Heruka imputed upon Buddha's Emanation Body is 'Emanation Body Heruka'; together they are called 'interpretative Heruka'. Emanation Body Heruka can be seen even by ordinary beings who have a special pure mind. When, through training, we are able to believe spontaneously that our Spiritual Guide is an emanation of Heruka, we shall see Emanation Body Heruka. Heruka imputed upon Buddha's Truth Body, or Dharmakaya, is called 'definitive Heruka', and always lacks form, shape and colour. Because its basis of imputation, Buddha's Truth Body, is extremely subtle, definitive Heruka can be seen only by Buddhas and not by other beings. It is also called 'wisdom being Buddha Heruka'. Definitive Heruka pervades the entire universe; there is no single place where definitive Heruka is absent.

Buddha expounded extensive, middling and condensed Heruka root Tantras. The *Condensed Root Tantra* and many of its commentaries written by Indian Buddhist Tantric scholars, including the great Yogis Ghantapa and Naropa, were translated from Sanskrit into Tibetan. Later, many Tibetan Tantric scholars, including the great translator Marpa, the founder of the Kagyu tradition, and Je Tsongkhapa, the founder of the Gelug tradition, wrote commentaries to the practice of Heruka Tantra. In this present age, the great Lama Je Phabongkhapa wrote special commentaries to the practices of Heruka body mandala and Vajrayogini. He also wrote many profound ritual prayers, or sadhanas, and gave extensive teachings on these. It is through the great kindness of Je Phabongkhapa and his heart disciple, Kyabje Trijang Rinpoche, that even in these times of extreme spiritual degeneration the profound practices of Heruka body mandala and Vajrayogini are flourishing both in the East and the West.

Je Phabongkhapa had direct visions of Heruka. At one time Heruka told him: 'For seven generations, the practitioners of your instructions of Heruka and Vajrayogini will have the special good fortune to accomplish easily the realizations of these practices.' Whenever I contemplate this I think 'How fortunate we are'. It is said that as the general level of spirituality decreases, it becomes increasingly difficult for practitioners to receive the blessings of other Deities, such as Guhyasamaja and Yamantaka; but the opposite is the case with Heruka and Vajrayogini – the more times degenerate the more easily practitioners can receive their blessings. This is because the people of this world have a special karmic connection with Heruka and Vajrayogini, and the emanations of Heruka and Vajrayogini and their places – the Pure Lands of Keajra – pervade everywhere throughout this world.

The first lineage holder of these instructions on Heruka body mandala is the great Yogi Ghantapa. He received the empowerment and instructions of Heruka body mandala direct from Heruka. Ghantapa lived deep in a forest in Odivisha, (present-day Orissa), in India, where he engaged in intensive meditation on Heruka and Vajrayogini. Since he was living in such an isolated place his diet was poor and his body became emaciated. One day the king of Odivisha was out hunting in the forest when he came across Ghantapa. Seeing how thin and weak he was, the king asked Ghantapa why he lived in the forest on such a poor diet, and encouraged him to return with him to the city where he would give him food and shelter. Ghantapa replied that just as a great elephant could not be led from the forest by a fine thread, so he could not be tempted to leave the forest by the riches of a king. Angered by Ghantapa's refusal, the king returned to his palace threatening revenge.

Such was the king's anger that he summoned a number of women from the city and told them about the arrogant monk in the forest. He offered great wealth to any one of them who could seduce him and force him to break his vows of celibacy. One woman, a wine-seller, boasted that she could do this and she set out for the forest to look for Ghantapa. When eventually she found him she asked if she could become his servant. Ghantapa had no need of a servant, but he realized that they had a strong relationship from previous lives and so he allowed her to stay. Ghantapa gave her spiritual instructions and empowerments and they engaged sincerely in meditation. After twelve years they both attained the Union of No More Learning, full enlightenment.

One day Ghantapa and the former wine-seller decided to encourage the people of the city to develop a greater interest in Dharma. Accordingly, the woman returned to the king and reported that she had seduced the monk. At first the king doubted the truth of her story, but when she explained that she and Ghantapa now had two children, a son and a daughter, the king was delighted with the news and told her to bring Ghantapa to the city on a particular day. He then issued a proclamation disparaging Ghantapa, and ordered his subjects to assemble on the appointed day to insult and humiliate the monk.

When the day came, Ghantapa and the woman left the forest with their children, the son on Ghantapa's right and the daughter on his left. As they entered the city Ghantapa was walking as if he were drunk, holding a bowl into which the woman was pouring wine. All the people who had gathered laughed and jeered, hurling abuse and insults at him. 'Long ago', they taunted him, 'our king invited you to the city but you arrogantly refused his invitation. Now you come drunk and with a wine-seller. What a bad example of a Buddhist and a monk!' When they had finished, Ghantapa appeared to become angry and threw his bowl to the ground. The bowl sank into the earth, splitting the ground and causing a spring of water to appear. Ghantapa immediately transformed into Heruka and the woman into Vajrayogini. The boy transformed into a vajra which Ghantapa held in his right hand, and the girl into a bell which he held in his left hand. Ghantapa and his consort then embraced and flew into the sky.

The people were astonished and immediately developed deep regret for their disrespect. They prostrated to Ghantapa, begging him and the emanation of Vajrayogini to return. Ghantapa and his consort refused, but told the people that if their regret was sincere they should make confession to Mahakaruna, the embodiment of Buddha's great compassion. Through the deep remorse of the people of Odivisha and the force of their prayers a statue of Mahakaruna arose from the spring water. The people of Odivisha became very devoted Dharma practitioners and many of them gained realizations. The statue of Mahakaruna can still be seen today.

Because of Ghantapa's pure practice of Heruka and Vajrayogini in the forest, Vajrayogini saw that it was the right time for him to receive her blessings and so she manifested as the wine-seller. Through living with her Ghantapa attained the state of full enlightenment.

In this modern age, people find it difficult to believe that human beings are able to fly, but such things were very common in ancient times when people had strong potentialities for spiritual attainments. Milarepa, who was a great practitioner of

Heruka and Vajrayogini, at one time – as explained in his life story – told a large assembly of his disciples how he had gained the ability to fly. Through various methods, including his tummo meditation, he had released the central channel knots at his heart, navel and below the navel, and because of this he developed a very special physical suppleness that pervaded his body. This made his body extremely light, like a soft feather. At first he could only levitate but gradually he was able to move through space until finally he was able to fly like an eagle. One day Milarepa was flying above a small town called Longda, near where a father and son were ploughing a field. The son first saw Milarepa flying and said, 'Father, look in the sky. There's a man flying!' The father looked carefully and, realizing that it was Milarepa, told his son, 'This man is called Milarepa. He is an evil person who killed many people through his black magic.' However, the son deeply appreciated what he saw and said 'There is no sight more amazing than a human being flying through the sky.' Milarepa attained the enlightened state of Buddha Heruka through the practice of Heruka body mandala, and many of his disciples including Rechungpa attained the Pure Land of Keajra without abandoning their human body. We can understand this from his collection of songs called 'gur bum' in Tibetan. Shortly before he intended passing away, Milarepa gave advice to his assembled disciples, finally saying 'We will meet in the Pure Land of Keajra.' The actual method to attain the Pure Land of Keajra is qualified meditation on the self-generation of Heruka and Vajrayogini.

Milarepa and his root Guru Marpa, and Je Tsongkhapa and his heart disciple Khedrubje have a special connection. It is said that Marpa is one of Je Tsongkhapa's former incarnations and Milarepa is one of Khedrubje's former incarnations. Through this we can understand the great kindness of these holy beings who, by changing their physical aspect, continually benefit the people of this world from generation to generation.

The Pure Land of Keajra is the Pure Land of Heruka. It is sometimes also called 'Akanishta', which means the 'Highest' Pure Land, and 'Pure Dakini Land' indicating that it is also the Pure Land of Vajrayogini. In general, when an ordinary person takes rebirth in any of the Pure Lands of Buddha he or she is permanently freed from all sufferings and will never again take rebirth within samsara, a contaminated rebirth. Therefore taking rebirth in the Pure Land of Buddha is like attaining liberation or nirvana. For this reason, when an ordinary person takes rebirth in a Pure Land of Buddha through the practice of transference of consciousness, or powa, it is called 'attaining enlightenment in one moment'. However, this is only similar to the attainment of enlightenment and is not the actual attainment.

The Pure Land of Keajra is unequalled among all the other Pure Lands of Buddhas. Living beings who abide in other Pure Lands, such as Sukhavati and Tushita, do not have the opportunity to practise completion stage Tantra. Because their bodies have no channels, drops and inner fire (tummo), they are unable to meditate on the central channel, drops and inner fire. However, living beings who dwell in the Pure Land of Keajra have bodies that possess channels, drops and inner fire. These have the nature of light, but they function in the same way as the channels, drops and inner fire of human beings. They can therefore meditate on the central channel, indestructible drop and indestructible wind and mind, and in this way they can accomplish the realizations of meaning clear light and pure illusory body, and attain enlightenment within one single life. This is the special good fortune of living beings who dwell in the Pure Land of Keajra. This shows the special power of the instructions on the practices of Heruka and Vajrayogini. It is through practising these instructions that living beings who dwell in the Pure Land of Keajra have this special good fortune.

The extensive sadhana of Heruka body mandala lists thirty-nine lineage holder Teachers, or 'lineage Gurus', from Ghantapa to Heruka Losang Yeshe, Trijang Rinpoche. All these spiritual Teachers and many of their disciples attained the realization of Highest Yoga Tantra through practising Heruka body mandala and Vajrayogini. We should therefore engage with confidence in our practice of Heruka body mandala and Vajrayogini.

WHAT IS THE HERUKA BODY MANDALA?

In this context, 'body' refers to our subtle body – our channels and drops; and 'mandala' means an assembly of enlightened Deities. Our channels and drops are called our 'subtle body' because they are parts of our body that are not easy to recognize. The Heruka body mandala is the assembly of the imagined Heruka (ourself) with the consort Vajravarahi (who is the same as Vajrayogini) – the nature of our purified indestructible white and red drops – and our imagined retinue (the Heroes and Heroines) – the nature of our purified channels and drops – in the imagined Pure Land of Keajra. Generally, 'mandala' refers to either a 'supporting' mandala, which means the world, environment and palace of an enlightened Deity or Deities, or a 'supported' mandala, which means an assembly of enlightened Deities.

The purpose of meditating on Heruka body mandala is to receive the powerful blessings of Buddha Heruka and his retinue within our channels and drops. Through these blessings we can be freed from any obstacles within our channels and drops, and our meditation on the central channel, indestructible drop and indestructible wind and mind will be successful. Because of this we shall easily develop and make progress in the five stages of completion stage mentioned above, and through this fulfil our final goal.

The explanation of how to generate the Heruka body mandala and how to meditate on it given in this book is simple but presents the very essence. I have prepared this for those who are unable to practise the extensive sadhana of Heruka body mandala. In this practice, we need to visualize thirty-six channels of our body, which are the twenty-four channels of the twenty-four places of our body, the four channels of our heart channel wheel, and the eight channels of our eight sense doors. We also visualize the white indestructible drop and the red indestructible drop at our heart, and the twenty-four drops that are contained within the twenty-four channels of the twenty-four places of our body. We then need to receive the powerful blessings of Heruka Father and Mother and his retinue of Heroes and Heroines within these channels and drops.

The twenty-four places of our body represent the twenty-four places of Heruka in the world. The twenty-four places of our body are: (1) the hairline; (2) the crown; (3) the right ear; (4) the back of the neck; (5) the left ear; (6) the point between the eyebrows; (7) the two eyes; (8) the two shoulders; (9) the two armpits; (10) the two breasts; (11) the navel; (12) the tip of the nose; (13) the mouth; (14) the throat; (15) the heart; (16) the two testicles; (17) the tip of the sex organ; (18) the anus; (19) the two thighs; (20) the two calves; (21) the eight fingers and eight toes; (22) the tops of the feet; (23) the two thumbs and two big toes; and (24) the two knees.

When we meditate on Heruka body mandala we meditate on ourself as Heruka with our consort Vajravarahi, surrounded in concentric circles by the four Yoginis of the great bliss wheel, the eight Heroes and Heroines of the heart wheel, the eight Heroes and Heroines of the speech wheel, the eight Heroes and Heroines of the body wheel, and the eight Heroines of the commitment wheel. In this way we meditate on the assembly of sixty-two enlightened Deities. Ourself Heruka, and Vajravarahi, are included within the Deities of the great bliss wheel, and are the principal Deities.

While meditating on the assembly of sixty-two enlightened Deities we should believe that ourself Heruka is the nature of our purified indestructible white drop and Vajravarahi is the nature of our purified indestructible red drop. The four Yoginis of the great bliss wheel are the nature of our purified four channels in the cardinal directions of the heart channel wheel. The twenty-four Heroines of the heart, speech and body wheels are the nature of our purified twenty-four channels of the twenty-four places of our body. The twenty-four Heroes of the heart, speech and body wheels are the nature of our purified twenty-four drops that are contained inside the twenty-four channels of the twenty-four places of our body. The eight Heroines of the commitment wheel are the nature of our purified eight channels of the eight sense doors.

If we continually meditate in this way on this assembly of the sixty-two enlightened Deities every day with strong faith and conviction, we shall definitely receive the powerful blessings of these enlightened Deities within our channels and drops, we shall be free from obstacles of the channels and drops, and our meditations on completion stage will therefore be effective. This means that through these meditations we shall attain meaning clear light, pure illusory body and finally enlightenment in this short life.

Many completion stage practitioners experience difficulties in gathering and dissolving their inner winds into the central channel through meditation, and in developing qualified clear light and bliss. This is because their channels and drops do not function correctly, and may even give rise to physical pain. Through sincerely practising the meditations on Heruka body mandala we shall be freed from all these obstacles.

Within the sixty-two enlightened Deities, Heruka and Vajravarahi are the principal and the others are their retinue. The four Yoginis of the great bliss wheel are Dakini, Lama, Khandarohi and Rupini; and their function is to bestow upon us spontaneous great bliss. The eight Heroes and Heroines of the heart wheel are Khandakapala and Partzandi, Mahakankala and Tzändriakiya, Kankala and Parbhawatiya, Vikatadamshtri and Mahanasa, Suraberi and Biramatiya, Amitabha and Karwariya, Vajraprabha and Lamkeshöriya, Vajradeha and Drumatzaya; and their function is to bestow upon us the attainment of Buddha's holy mind. The eight Heroes and Heroines of the speech wheel are Ankuraka and Airawatiya, Vajrajatila and Mahabhairawi, Mahavira and Bayubega, Vajrahumkara and Surabhakiya, Subhadra and Shamadewi, Vajrabhadra and Suwatre, Mahabhairawa and Hayakarne, Virupaksha and Khaganane; and their function is to bestow upon us the attainment of Buddha's holy speech. The eight Heroes and Heroines of the body wheel are Mahabala and Tzatrabega, Ratnavajra and Khandarohi, Hayagriva and Shaundini, Akashagarbha and Tzatrawarmini, Shri Heruka and Subira, Pämanarteshvara and Mahabala, Vairochana and Tzatrawartini, Vajrasattva and Mahabire; and their function is to bestow upon us the attainment of Buddha's holy body. Our present body, speech and mind are contaminated by the poison of delusions, so they act as the basis of all suffering. We therefore need to attain a Buddha's holy body, speech and mind. The eight Heroines of the commitment wheel are

Kakase, Ulukase, Shönase, Shukarase, Yamadhathi, Yamaduti, Yamadangtrini and Yamamatani; and their function and commitment is to pacify our obstacles. The Heroes and Heroines of the five wheels are so called because they are victorious over the enemies of ordinary appearance and conceptions.

THE PRELIMINARY PRACTICES

The following explanation of how to practise Heruka body mandala is based on the instructions of the Ganden Oral Lineage. It is simple but very profound. Following these instructions we should practise Heruka body mandala in conjunction with the sadhana, or ritual prayer, called *The Yoga of Buddha Heruka* (see Appendix V). As this sadhana implies, there are six stages to practising Heruka body mandala: 1. training in going for refuge; 2. training in renunciation; 3. training in bodhichitta; 4. training in Guru yoga; 5. training in the generation stage of Heruka body mandala, and 6. training in completion stage.

The first four trainings are preliminary practices and the remaining two are the actual practice of Heruka body mandala. Just as a vehicle depends upon its four wheels, so the precious vehicle of Heruka body mandala practice depends upon the four wheels of training in going for refuge, renunciation, bodhichitta and Guru yoga. Training in going for refuge is the gateway through which we enter Buddhism; renunciation is the gateway through which we enter the path to liberation; bodhichitta is the gateway through which we enter the path to enlightenment; and Guru yoga is the gateway through which the blessings of all the Buddhas will enter our mind. These are the basic foundations that make the practice of Heruka body mandala effective.

TRAINING IN GOING FOR REFUGE

In this training we should remember and contemplate the following, as explained in Part One:

I want to protect and liberate myself permanently from the sufferings of this life and countless future lives. I can accomplish this only by receiving Buddha's blessings, putting Dharma into practice and receiving help from Sangha – the supreme spiritual friends.

Thinking deeply in this way, we first make the strong determination and then the promise to seek refuge sincerely in Buddha, Dharma and Sangha throughout our life. We should meditate on this determination every day and maintain our promise continually for the rest of our life. As the principal commitment of our refuge vow we should always apply effort to receive Buddha's blessings, to put Dharma into practice and to receive help from Sangha, our pure spiritual friends including our Spiritual Teacher. This is how we go for refuge to Buddha, Dharma and Sangha. Through this we shall accomplish our aim – permanent liberation from all the sufferings of this life and countless future lives, the real meaning of our human life.

To maintain our promise to go for refuge to Buddha, Dharma and Sangha throughout our life, and so that we and all living beings may receive Buddha's blessings and protection, we recite the following refuge prayer from the sadhana *The Yoga of Buddha Heruka* every day with strong faith:

I and all sentient beings, until we achieve enlightenment,
Go for refuge to Buddha, Dharma and Sangha.

TRAINING IN RENUNCIATION

In this training we remember and contemplate how we shall experience unbearable suffering in our countless future lives, as explained in detail in Part One. Then, from the depths of our heart, we should think:

> There is no benefit in denying the sufferings of future lives; when they actually descend upon me it will be too late to protect myself from them. Therefore I definitely need to prepare protection now, while I have this human life that gives me the opportunity to liberate myself permanently from the sufferings of my countless future lives. If I do not apply effort to accomplish this, but allow my human life to become empty of meaning, there is no greater deception and no greater foolishness. I must put effort now into liberating myself permanently from the sufferings of my countless future lives.

We meditate on this determination continually until we develop the spontaneous wish to liberate ourself permanently from the sufferings of countless future lives.

TRAINING IN BODHICHITTA

In this training we should maintain the practice of the five stages of training in bodhichitta that was explained in detail in Part One. In conclusion, we think:

> I should not be content with seeking merely my own liberation; I must consider the welfare of other living beings. They are all my mothers, and they are drowning in the vast and deep ocean of samsara, experiencing unbearable suffering in life after life, without end. While I am just one single person, other living

beings are countless in number; the happiness and freedom of others are therefore far more important than my own. I cannot bear that my countless mothers are experiencing unbearable physical suffering and mental pain in this life and in their countless future lives; I must permanently liberate them all from their suffering, and for this purpose I will make great effort to become an enlightened Buddha.

We should maintain this supreme good heart of bodhichitta, continually day and night. All our meditations on generation and completion stages should be motivated by this supreme good heart, and we should always remember that all our meditations on generation and completion stages are methods to fulfil our bodhichitta wishes. To generate bodhichitta we recite from the sadhana:

Through the virtues I collect by giving and other perfections,
May I become a Buddha for the benefit of all.

TRAINING IN GURU YOGA

The term 'Guru' is a Sanskrit word that means 'Spiritual Guide'. A Spiritual Guide can be eastern, western, male, female, ordained or lay. Our Spiritual Guide is any Spiritual Teacher who leads us into correct paths to liberation and enlightenment by giving teachings and showing a good example. Guru yoga is a special training in relying upon our Spiritual Guide; in this context, 'yoga' means training in spiritual paths, not physical training. The sadhana *The Yoga of Buddha Heruka* in Appendix V presents the Guru yoga of Je Tsongkhapa inseparable from our root Guru, Buddha Shakyamuni and Heruka, who is known as Guru Sumati

Buddha Heruka. In this context, 'root Guru' refers to our Spiritual Guide from whom we have received the instructions, transmission and empowerment of Heruka body mandala. The name Guru Sumati Buddha Heruka implies that our root *Guru*, Je Tsongkhapa (or *Sumati* Kirti, Sanskrit for Je Tsongkhapa's ordained name), *Buddha* Shakyamuni and *Heruka* are one person but have different aspects. We need to maintain this recognition at all times for our practice of Heruka body mandala to be effective. To benefit each and every living being directly every day, definitive Heruka emanated Buddha Shakyamuni, who in turn emanated Je Tsongkhapa, who in turn emanated our Spiritual Guide; they are like one actor showing different aspects at different times.

The purpose of this Guru yoga practice is:

(1) To accumulate a great collection of merit, or good fortune. Because of our lack of merit it is difficult for us to fulfil our wishes and we experience many obstacles to accomplishing spiritual attainments.

(2) To purify negativity, or non-virtuous actions. When we purify the countless potentialities of our non-virtuous actions we purify our mind. As mentioned above, by purifying our mind we shall attain full enlightenment.

(3) To receive the powerful blessings of all the Buddhas. We have the seed of the realizations of Highest Yoga Tantra in general and Heruka body mandala in particular, which is part of our Buddha nature. However, without receiving the powerful blessings of all Buddhas through our Spiritual Guide, who is their representative, our seed of the realization of Highest Yoga Tantra will never ripen.

(4) To generate the experience of great bliss and emptiness. This practice is a powerful method to ripen our seed of the realization of Mahamudra Tantra.

Through accomplishing these four necessary conditions we can easily make progress in the main practice of this sadhana, which is training in generation and completion stages.

Je Sherab Senge, one of Je Tsongkhapa's heart disciples, received the special instructions of the Guru yoga of Je Tsongkhapa from Je Tsongkhapa himself. This is called the 'Guru yoga of the Segyu lineage', now known as the Guru yoga of *Heart Jewel*. The instructions of the Guru yoga of *Heart Jewel* were originally only given as oral instructions. Later the great Yogi Palden Sangpo composed a sadhana based on these oral instructions, and since then it has been practised publicly. The Guru yoga of *Heart Jewel* can be practised either according to Sutra tradition or according to Highest Yoga Tantra tradition. The sadhana, *The Yoga of Buddha Heruka*, presents the practice of the Guru yoga of *Heart Jewel* according to Highest Yoga Tantra. Those who have the commitment to practise *Heart Jewel* can add prayers to Dorje Shugden just before the dedication verses of *The Yoga of Buddha Heruka*.

The practice of this Guru yoga has five stages: 1. visualization and meditation; 2. inviting the wisdom beings; 3. the practice of the seven limbs; 4. making special requests; and 5. generating the experience of great bliss and emptiness.

VISUALIZATION AND MEDITATION

We recite the following from the sadhana, while concentrating on its meaning:

Guru Sumati Buddha Heruka

In the space before me is Guru Sumati Buddha Heruka – Je Tsongkhapa inseparable from my root Guru, Buddha Shakyamuni and Heruka – surrounded by all the Buddhas of the ten directions.

While we visualize this we think and contemplate:

Je Tsongkhapa attained enlightenment to lead all living beings to the liberating path through his emanations. Who is his emanation now leading me to the liberating path? It is definitely my Spiritual Guide from whom I have received instructions, transmission and empowerment of Heruka body mandala, and who shows a qualified example.

Thinking in this way we should strongly believe that our Spiritual Guide is an emanation of Je Tsongkhapa, and then meditate on this belief single-pointedly. We should practise this meditation continually.

INVITING THE WISDOM BEINGS

We recite the following verse from the sadhana, while concentrating on its meaning:

From the heart of the Protector of the hundreds of Deities
    of the Joyful Land,
To the peak of a cloud which is like a cluster of fresh,
    white curd,
All-knowing Losang Dragpa, King of the Dharma,
Please come to this place together with your Sons.

The 'Protector of the hundreds of Deities of the Joyful Land' refers to Buddha Maitreya. We believe that wisdom being Je Tsongkhapa together with his retinue dissolves into the assembly of Guru Sumati Buddha Heruka visualized in front of us, and they become non-dual.

We also recite the following request from the sadhana:

In the space before me on a lion throne lotus and moon,
The venerable Gurus smile with delight.
O Supreme Field of Merit for my mind of faith,
Please remain for a hundred aeons to spread the doctrine.

THE PRACTICE OF THE SEVEN LIMBS

With strong faith in our Spiritual Guide, Guru Sumati Buddha Heruka, we should sincerely engage every day in the practice of the seven limbs. These are: 1. prostration; 2. offerings; 3. purification; 4. rejoicing; 5. requesting the turning of the Wheel of Dharma; 6. beseeching the Spiritual Guides to remain for a long time; and 7. dedication. In this context, the actual practice of Heruka body mandala is like the main body, and the seven limbs are like the limbs that support the main body. Just as our body is able to function in dependence upon its limbs, so the effectiveness of our training in Heruka body mandala depends upon our practice of the seven limbs.

PROSTRATION

Making prostrations to enlightened beings is a powerful method for purifying negative karma, sickness and obstacles, and for increasing our merit, our happiness and our Dharma realizations. Temporarily prostrations improve our physical health and make our mind happy, and ultimately they cause us to attain a Buddha's Form Body. Generating faith in the holy beings is mental prostration, reciting praises to them is verbal prostration, and showing respect to them with our body is physical prostration. We can make physical prostrations by respectfully prostrating our entire body on the ground; by respectfully touching our knees, palms and forehead to the ground; or by respectfully placing our palms together at the level of our heart.

To make powerful prostrations to the holy beings, we imagine that from every pore of our body we emanate another body, and from every pore of these bodies we emanate yet more bodies, until our emanated bodies fill the entire world. Then, while reciting the following verse, we strongly believe that all these countless bodies make prostrations to Guru Sumati Buddha Heruka and all the Buddhas of the ten directions:

Your mind of wisdom realizes the full extent of objects of
  knowledge,
Your eloquent speech is the ear-ornament of the fortunate,
Your beautiful body is ablaze with the glory of renown,
I prostrate to you, whom to see, to hear, and to remember
  is so meaningful.

We should do this practice of prostration every day. As a preliminary guide for our actual practice of Heruka body mandala, we can collect a hundred thousand prostrations, either throughout our daily life or in retreat.

OFFERINGS

From the depths of our heart we make the following determination:

To liberate all living beings from suffering permanently
I make excellent offerings to the supreme holy being

Guru Sumati Buddha Heruka,
And to all the other holy beings.

However many flowers and fruits there are,
And all the different types of medicine;
All the jewels there are in the world,
And all the pure, refreshing waters;

Mountains of jewels, forest groves,
And quiet and joyful places;
Heavenly trees adorned with flowers,
And trees whose branches hang with delicious fruits;

Scents that come from the celestial realms,
Incense, wish-granting trees, and jewelled trees;
Harvests that need no cultivation,
And all ornaments that are suitable to be offered;

Lakes and pools adorned with lotuses,
And the beautiful call of wild geese;
Everything that is unowned
Throughout all worlds as extensive as space –

Holding these in my mind, I offer them well
To you, the supreme beings, the Buddhas and Bodhisattvas.
O Compassionate Ones, holy objects of offering,
Think of me kindly and accept what I offer.

Eternally I will offer all my bodies
To you, the Buddhas and Bodhisattvas.
Out of respect, I will become your servant;
Please accept me, O Supreme Heroes.

While we imagine making all of these offerings, we can recite
the following short verse:

Pleasing water offerings, various flowers,
Sweet-smelling incense, lights, scented water and so forth,
A vast cloud of offerings both set out and imagined,
I offer to you, O Supreme Field of Merit.

In Buddhism an offering is anything that delights the enlightened beings. Our main offering is our practice of compassion, as this gives enlightened beings the greatest delight. Therefore, our motivation for making offerings should be compassion for all living beings – our sincere wish to liberate all living beings from suffering permanently.

In summary, we should always regard all our daily Dharma practices as unsurpassed offerings to Guru Sumati Buddha Heruka – the synthesis of our Spiritual Guide, Je Tsongkhapa, Buddha Shakyamuni and Heruka – and to all the other enlightened beings. In this way we can accumulate immeasurable merit, or good fortune.

PURIFICATION

Purification is the supreme method to prevent future suffering and to remove obstacles to our Dharma practice, especially to the practice of Heruka body mandala. It makes our actions pure so that we ourselves become pure. Since our body is not our self, cleaning our body alone is not enough; we need to clean our self through purification practice.

What is it that we need to purify? We need to purify our non-virtuous and inappropriate actions. In our countless previous lives we performed many actions that caused other living beings to experience suffering and problems and, as a result of these non-virtuous actions, we now experience suffering and many different problems. Although the actions themselves have ceased, their potential to give rise to suffering and problems still remains on our subtle consciousness, and will remain for life after life until it ripens. Therefore, on our root consciousness there are infinite negative potentials, which function to lead us into wrong paths and cause us to experience endless suffering. These are serious obstacles to our Dharma practice in general, and to our practice of Heruka body mandala in particular.

We can understand how our non-virtuous potentials are the main obstacle to our Dharma practice through contemplating the following:

In our previous lives we performed actions that rejected holy Dharma, and denied rebirth, karma and the attainment of liberation and enlightenment. As a result of this we now experience: (1) difficulties in developing the intention to practise Dharma, (2) difficulties in believing Dharma teachings, such as karma, and (3) difficulties in making progress in our Dharma practice.

Purification practice is very simple. All we need to do is contemplate the great disadvantages of the non-virtuous actions that we have performed since beginningless time. Then with strong regret we confess all these non-virtuous actions, as well as transgressions of our vows and commitments, to Guru Sumati Buddha Heruka, and to all the other holy beings, while reciting the following verse:

Whatever non-virtues of body, speech and mind
I have accumulated since time without beginning,
Especially transgressions of my three vows,
With great remorse I confess each one from the depths
    of my heart.

We should repeat this practice many times. At the end of each session we make a strong determination not to perform any non-virtuous action or to transgress any of our vows and commitments. As the great preliminary guide for our Heruka body mandala practice, we can collect a hundred thousand recitations of this verse – concentrating strongly on its meaning. Alternatively we can collect a hundred thousand recitations of Vajrasattva's mantra.

REJOICING

We should learn to rejoice in others' virtuous actions, happiness, good qualities and good fortune. Normally we do the opposite and develop jealousy. Jealousy is very harmful for individuals and society. In an instant it can destroy our own and others' happiness and harmony, and lead to fighting, or even war. In everyday life we can see how people react with jealousy in regard to relationships, business, position and religious views, causing suffering to so many people. Our problems of jealousy can be solved simply by learning to rejoice in others' happiness and goodness. This can be practised even while we are lying down, relaxing, or going about our daily activities.

With very little effort we can accumulate immeasurable good fortune simply by rejoicing in the excellent deeds of Buddhas such as Je Tsongkhapa. We can do this while reciting the following verse with strong concentration on the meaning:

In this degenerate age you strove for much learning and
    accomplishment.
Abandoning the eight worldly concerns, you made your
    freedom and endowment meaningful.

Buddha Vajradhara

O Protector, from the very depths of my heart,
I rejoice in the great wave of your deeds.

REQUESTING THE TURNING OF THE
WHEEL OF DHARMA

We begin this practice by thinking:

I have the opportunity to listen to, understand and practise
holy Dharma, and therefore the good fortune to enter, make
progress on and complete the path to enlightenment. How
wonderful it would be if all other living beings could enjoy the
same good fortune!

From the depths of our heart we then repeatedly request
Guru Sumati Buddha Heruka to emanate countless Spiritual
Teachers to teach holy Dharma and guide all living beings to
the state of ultimate happiness, enlightenment, while reciting
the following verse:

From the billowing clouds of wisdom and compassion
In the space of your Truth Body, O Venerable and holy Gurus,
Please send down a rain of vast and profound Dharma
Appropriate to the disciples of this world.

BESEECHING THE SPIRITUAL GUIDES
TO REMAIN FOR A LONG TIME

In this practice we think:

If the Spiritual Teachers who have been emanated by holy
beings remain in this world for many aeons, all living beings
will gradually have the opportunity to listen to, understand

and practise Dharma. In this way, eventually all living beings
without exception will attain enlightenment.

We then request Guru Sumati Buddha Heruka that his emanations who are teaching Dharma will remain in this world until
samsara ends, while reciting the following verse:

From your actual deathless body, born from meaning
clear light,
Please send countless emanations throughout the world
To spread the oral lineage of the Ganden doctrine;
And may they remain for a very long time.

DEDICATION

Whenever we perform any virtuous actions, we should
dedicate them to the attainment of enlightenment and to the
flourishing of Buddha's doctrine, which benefits all living
beings. The great Master Atisha said:

Dedicate your virtues throughout the day and the night,
and always watch your mind.

If we dedicate our virtuous actions in this way, their potentialities will never be destroyed by anger and wrong views but
instead will increase in strength. The practice of dedication
makes our virtuous actions effective. We can engage in this
practice while reciting the following verse:

Through the virtues I have accumulated here,
May the doctrine and all living beings receive every benefit.
Especially may the essence of the doctrine
Of Venerable Losang Dragpa shine forever.

In summary, while practising each of the seven limbs we should apply effort to making the sun of our faith shine continually on the snow mountain of our Spiritual Guide – Guru Sumati Buddha Heruka – and make strong requests. Through this, the blessing waters of all the Buddhas of the ten directions will flow down, our very subtle body will receive a special power that transforms it into an enlightened body, and our very subtle mind will receive a special power that transforms it into an enlightened mind.

MAKING SPECIAL REQUESTS

To make this special request, we first offer the entire universe, regarding it as the Pure Land of Buddha, to Guru Sumati Buddha Heruka and all the Buddhas of the ten directions. This offering is called a 'mandala offering', a detailed explanation of which can be found in *Guide to Dakini Land*. Then, while concentrating on its meaning, we recite three times the following request prayer from the sadhana:

O Guru Sumati Buddha Heruka, from now until I attain
  enlightenment,
I shall seek no refuge other than you.
Please pacify my obstacles and bestow upon me
The two attainments of liberating and ripening.
Please bless me so that I will become definitive Heruka,
In which state I shall experience all phenomena as purified
  and gathered into emptiness, inseparable from great bliss.

This prayer has the same meaning as the essence mantra of Heruka. Through completing the meditations on generation and completion stages, we abandon all our subtle mistaken appearances; this abandonment is the attainment of 'liberating'. And, due to ripening our Buddha nature completely, we experience ourself as a real Buddha, and our world, enjoyments and activities as those of a Buddha; this experience is the attainment of 'ripening'. By accomplishing these two attainments we become definitive Heruka; that is, Heruka imputed upon Buddha's Truth Body, or Dharmakaya. At the same time we experience all phenomena as purified, which means that we have purified the subtle mistaken appearance of all phenomena; and we experience all phenomena gathered into emptiness, which means we realize that all phenomena are not other than emptiness. These two experiences of 'purified' and 'gathered' imply that we have realized the union of the two truths directly and simultaneously; this realization is actual enlightenment. With this prayer we are requesting Guru Sumati Buddha Heruka to bestow all these attainments upon us.

As ordinary beings we have only one body that we can use, and this in reality is part of our parents' bodies. Buddhas, however, possess four bodies simultaneously: the two Truth Bodies, which are the Wisdom Truth Body and Nature Truth Body; and the two Form Bodies, which are the Enjoyment Body and Emanation Body. Buddha's mind is the Wisdom Truth Body and the emptiness of Buddha's mind is the Nature Truth Body; together they are called the 'Truth Body' or 'Dharmakaya'. Buddha's bodies that possess form are called Form Bodies. Buddha's subtle Form Body is called the Enjoyment Body, and Buddha's gross Form Body is called the Emanation Body. A Buddha's Truth Body is extremely subtle and therefore can be seen only by Buddhas and not by others. A Buddha's Enjoyment Body can be seen by Superior Bodhisattvas, and a Buddha's Emanation Body can be seen by ordinary beings who have a pure mind.

GENERATING THE EXPERIENCE OF GREAT BLISS
AND EMPTINESS

After we have recited the special request prayer three times sincerely from our heart, we then think and imagine:

Due to my making requests in this way, all the Buddhas of the ten directions dissolve into Je Tsongkhapa who is inseparable from my root Guru, he dissolves into Buddha Shakyamuni at his heart, and Buddha Shakyamuni dissolves into Heruka at his heart. With delight, Guru Heruka, who is the nature of the union of great bliss and emptiness, enters my body through my crown, and dissolves into my mind at my heart. Because Heruka, who is the nature of the union of great bliss and emptiness, becomes inseparable from my mind, I experience spontaneous great bliss and emptiness. I perceive nothing other than the emptiness of all phenomena, the mere absence of all phenomena that I normally see or perceive. My subtle mistaken appearance of all phenomena, including the channels and drops of my body, is purified.

Holding this belief, we meditate on the emptiness of all phenomena while experiencing great bliss.

TRAINING IN THE GENERATION STAGE OF
HERUKA BODY MANDALA

There are five stages to training in the generation stage of Heruka body mandala, the actual self-generation practice of Heruka body mandala: 1. generating the body mandala of Heruka; 2. training in clear appearance; 3. training in divine pride; 4. training in non-dual appearance and emptiness; and 5. training in mantra recitation.

Buddha Vajradharma

GENERATING THE BODY MANDALA OF HERUKA

While meditating on the emptiness of all phenomena, perceiving nothing other than emptiness, we think and imagine:

In the vast space of emptiness of all phenomena, the nature of my purified mistaken appearance of all phenomena – which is the Pure Land of Keajra – I appear as Buddha Heruka with a blue-coloured body, four faces and twelve arms, the nature of my purified white indestructible drop. I am embracing Vajravarahi, the nature of my purified red indestructible drop. I am surrounded by the Heroes and Heroines of the five wheels, who are the nature of my purified subtle body – the channels and drops. I reside in the mandala, the celestial mansion, which is the nature of my purified gross body. Although I have this appearance it is not other than the emptiness of all phenomena.

At this point, (1) while experiencing great bliss and emptiness, (2) we meditate on the clear appearance of the mandala and Deities with divine pride, while (3) recognizing that the Deities are the nature of our purified channels and drops, which are our subtle body, and that the mandala is the nature of our purified gross body.

In this way we train sincerely in one single meditation on generation stage possessing these three characteristics. Holding the third characteristic – recognizing the Deities as the nature of our purified subtle body, and the mandala as the nature of our purified gross body – makes this concentration an actual body mandala meditation.

TRAINING IN CLEAR APPEARANCE

For our meditation on the body mandala of Heruka to be qualified we need to train in clear appearance. We think and imagine deeply, as above:

In the vast space of emptiness of all phenomena, the nature of my purified mistaken appearance of all phenomena – which is the Pure Land of Keajra – I appear as Buddha Heruka with a blue-coloured body, four faces and twelve arms, the nature of my purified white indestructible drop. I am embracing Vajravarahi, the nature of my purified red indestructible drop. I am surrounded by the Heroes and Heroines of the five wheels, who are the nature of my purified subtle body – the channels and drops. I reside in the mandala, the celestial mansion, which is the nature of my purified gross body. Although I have this appearance it is not other than the emptiness of all phenomena.

We mentally repeat this contemplation again and again until we perceive clearly the object of our meditation – the Heruka body mandala, which is the assembly of imagined Heruka (ourself) with consort Vajravarahi, the nature of our purified white and red indestructible drops, and our imagined retinue of Heroes and Heroines, who are the nature of our purified channels and drops, in the imagined Pure Land of Keajra. When we perceive the assembly of this supporting mandala and supported Deities – the Heruka body mandala – we hold it without forgetting and remain on it single-pointedly for as long as possible.

We should repeat this meditation again and again, until we are able to maintain our concentration clearly for one minute every time we meditate on it. Our concentration that has this ability is called 'concentration of placing the mind'. In the second stage, with the concentration of placing the mind, we meditate on the Heruka body mandala continually until we are able to maintain our concentration clearly for five minutes every time we meditate on it. Our concentration that has this ability is called 'concentration of continual placement'. In the third stage, with the concentration of continual placement, we meditate on the Heruka body mandala continually until we are able to remember immediately our object of meditation – the Heruka body mandala – whenever we lose it during meditation. Our concentration that has this ability is called 'concentration of replacement'. In the fourth stage, with the concentration of replacement, we meditate on the Heruka body mandala continually until we are able to maintain our concentration clearly throughout our whole meditation session without forgetting every time we meditate on it. Our concentration that has this ability is called 'concentration of close placement'. At this stage we have very stable and clear concentration focused on the Heruka body mandala.

Then, with the concentration of close placement, we meditate on the Heruka body mandala continually until finally we attain the concentration of tranquil abiding focused on the Heruka body mandala, which causes us to experience special physical and mental suppleness and bliss. Through this concentration of tranquil abiding focused on the Heruka body mandala, we shall certainly attain the Pure Land of Keajra in this life or in our next life.

TRAINING IN DIVINE PRIDE

Through perceiving our imagined Heruka's body and mind we develop the thought 'I am Heruka'; this thought is divine pride. It is a correct thought or belief because it arises from wisdom that realizes correct reasons. Generally, if we improve our clear appearance of perceiving the Heruka body mandala through the practice of concentration mentioned above, this makes it easier for us to develop and increase divine pride. This is because clear appearance reduces our ordinary appearance, and this makes it easier for us to develop and increase the thought 'I am Heruka'. However, we can train in divine pride by contemplating correct reasons why it is necessary for us to change the basis of imputation for our self from a contaminated body and mind to the uncontaminated body and mind of Heruka. How we can do this has already been explained in the chapter *The Tantra of Generation Stage*.

TRAINING IN NON-DUAL APPEARANCE AND EMPTINESS

This is a very profound practice of generation stage. The explanation of this practice presented in this book is based on the instructions of the Ganden Oral Lineage. With respect to the term 'non-dual appearance and emptiness': 'appearance' refers to the Heruka body mandala, which is the assembly of the supporting mandala and supported Deities of Heruka body mandala, the nature of our purified gross and subtle bodies; 'emptiness' refers to the emptiness of all phenomena; and 'non-dual' means that the Heruka body mandala and emptiness are one object but have different names. When we perceive and realize this non-dual Heruka body mandala and emptiness we have found the object of our meditation; we should hold this object without forgetting, and remain on it single-pointedly for as long as possible. We should practise this meditation continually and sincerely, without distraction. By doing this, initially we shall realize appearance (the Heruka body mandala), which is the conventional truth, and emptiness, which is the ultimate truth, simultaneously with our gross mind. Finally we shall realize these two truths directly and simultaneously with our very subtle mind. Our very subtle mind that realizes these two truths directly and simultaneously is the state of enlightenment.

When we first meditate on Heruka body mandala we have a strong perception of the Heruka body mandala that we normally perceive. This perception is our mistaken appearance of the Heruka body mandala. It is mistaken because the Heruka body mandala that we normally perceive does not exist, even if we perceive it. The strong perception of the Heruka body mandala that we normally perceive, directly interferes with our understanding that the Heruka body mandala and the emptiness of all phenomena are non-dual. However, through meditating on the emptiness of all phenomena with strong concentration, the strong perception of the Heruka body mandala that we normally perceive will cease during meditation. Automatically we shall then realize that the Heruka body mandala and the emptiness of all phenomena are non-dual. This can be illustrated by the analogy of seeing two empty glasses in front of us. At first we would perceive the spaces inside the two glasses as different, but if we were to break the two glasses we would realize that the spaces inside them were non-dual.

In the sadhana the words 'Although I have this appearance it is not other than the emptiness of all phenomena' reveal the training in non-dual appearance and emptiness. If we understand clearly the meaning of the union of the two truths (explained in detail in the chapter on *Training in Ultimate Bodhichitta* in Part One) it will not be difficult to understand the meaning of non-dual appearance and emptiness that is explained in this section.

THE ACTUAL MEDITATION ON NON-DUAL APPEARANCE
AND EMPTINESS

Having accomplished clear appearance and divine pride through training in them as explained above, we then think and contemplate:

As all phenomena that I normally perceive do not exist, the Heruka body mandala that I normally perceive does not exist. Heruka body mandala is a mere name, which means that it is not other than the emptiness of all phenomena. The emptiness of all phenomena and Heruka body mandala are non-dual; they are not two different objects but one object with different names.

Thinking in this way, when we perceive as non-dual the assembly of the supporting mandala and supported Deities of the Heruka body mandala existing as mere name, and the emptiness of all phenomena, we meditate on this non-dual Heruka body mandala and emptiness single-pointedly with the experience of great bliss. As mentioned above, through continually practising this meditation, initially we shall realize the Heruka body mandala, which is the conventional truth, and emptiness, which is the ultimate truth, simultaneously with our gross mind. Finally we shall realize these two truths directly and simultaneously with our very subtle mind. Our very subtle mind that realizes these two truths directly and simultaneously is actual enlightenment. It is a wisdom that is permanently free from the mistaken appearance of all phenomena; such a wisdom is possessed only by fully enlightened Buddhas. Through this we can understand that this training in non-dual appearance and emptiness is a powerful method to attain enlightenment very quickly and easily. This training is the very essence practice of the instructions of the Ganden Oral Lineage. Through this training Gyalwa Ensapa and many of his disciples began, made progress on and completed the Vajrayana path; and in this way they attained enlightenment within three years.

TRAINING IN MANTRA RECITATION

The Sanskrit word 'mantra' means protection of mind. Through reciting the mantras of Heruka Father and Mother and their retinue with strong faith we can protect ourself from being harmed by inanimate objects such as earthquakes, floods, hurricanes and fire, and by animate objects such as humans and non-humans; we can pacify our sickness, untimely death and other adverse conditions; we can increase our good fortune, lifespan, and especially our internal qualities of faith, correct view, correct intention and other spiritual realizations; we are able to control our delusions such as anger; we can benefit others through performing various kinds of actions including wrathful actions; and especially we can lead ourself and others to the supreme happiness of enlightenment.

We recite the following mantras as a request to bestow these attainments upon us, while recognizing and believing that the wisdom beings of Heruka Father and Mother and their retinues are inseparable from the imagined Heruka (ourself) and consort Vajravarahi, and our retinue of Heroes and Heroines.

THE ESSENCE MANTRA OF HERUKA

We recite the following, while concentrating on the meaning:

At my heart is wisdom being Buddha Heruka, definitive Heruka.

O Glorious Vajra Heruka, you who enjoy
The divine illusory body and mind of clear light,
Please pacify my obstacles and bestow upon me
The two attainments of liberating and ripening.
Please bless me so that I will become definitive Heruka,
In which state I shall experience all phenomena as purified and
  gathered into emptiness, inseparable from great bliss.

OM SHRI VAJRA HE HE RU RU KAM HUM HUM PHAT DAKINI
   DZALA SHAMBARAM SÖHA

We can recite this mantra twenty-one times, a hundred times
or as many times as we wish.

THE THREE-OM MANTRA OF VAJRAYOGINI

We recite the following, while concentrating on the meaning:

At the heart of imagined Vajrayogini (Vajravarahi) is wisdom
being Buddha Vajrayogini, definitive Vajrayogini.

OM OM OM SARWA BUDDHA DAKINIYE VAJRA WARNANIYE
   VAJRA BEROTZANIYE HUM HUM HUM PHAT PHAT PHAT
   SÖHA

We should recite at least as many three-OM mantras as we
promised to recite when we received a Vajrayogini
empowerment.

The 'three-OM' mantra is the union of the essence and close
essence mantras of Vajravarahi. The meaning of this mantra
is as follows. With OM OM OM we are calling Vajrayogini
– the principal Deity – and her retinue of Heroines of the
three wheels (the body, speech and mind wheels). SARWA
BUDDHA DAKINIYE means that Vajrayogini is the synthesis

of the minds of all Buddhas, VAJRA WARNANIYE means that she is the synthesis of the speech of all Buddhas, and VAJRA BEROTZANIYE means that she is the synthesis of the bodies of all Buddhas. With HUM HUM HUM we are requesting Vajrayogini and her retinues to bestow upon us the attainments of the body, speech and mind of all the Buddhas. With PHAT PHAT PHAT we are requesting them to pacify our main obstacle – the subtle mistaken appearance of our body, speech and mind; and SÖHA means 'please build within me the basic foundation for all these attainments'.

As mentioned above, because our present body, speech and mind are contaminated by the poison of delusions they act as the basis of all suffering. We therefore need to attain a Buddha's holy body, speech and mind.

THE CONDENSED MANTRA OF THE SIXTY-TWO DEITIES OF HERUKA BODY MANDALA

We recite the following, while concentrating on the meaning:

At the heart of each of the sixty-two Deities is their individual wisdom being, their own definitive Deity.

OM HUM BAM RIM RIM LIM LIM, KAM KHAM GAM GHAM NGAM, TSAM TSHAM DZAM DZHAM NYAM, TrAM THrAM DrAM DHrAM NAM, TAM THAM DAM DHAM NAM, PAM PHAM BAM BHAM, YAM RAM LAM WAM, SHAM KAM SAM HAM HUM HUM PHAT

We can recite this mantra seven times, twenty-one times, one hundred times or more.

When we recite this mantra we are making requests to wisdom being Buddha Heruka with Vajravarahi, and his retinue of Heroes and Heroines of the five wheels, to pacify our obstacle of subtle mistaken appearance and to bestow upon us the attainments of outer and inner Dakini Land. Outer Dakini Land is the Pure Land of Keajra and inner Dakini Land is meaning clear light. The moment our mind is free from subtle mistaken appearance, we open the door through which we can directly see all enlightened Deities. For as long as our mind remains polluted by subtle mistaken appearance this door is closed. The meaning of subtle mistaken appearance has already been explained.

After mantra recitation, we conclude our practice of *The Yoga of Buddha Heruka* sadhana by reciting dedication and auspicious prayers.

Those who wish to perform a close retreat of Heruka body mandala can do so in conjunction with the sadhana *Blissful Journey: How to Engage in a Close Retreat of Heruka Body Mandala* found in Appendix VI.

TRAINING IN COMPLETION STAGE

Training in completion stage is the method for releasing our mind completely from subtle mistaken appearance. We shall finally attain enlightenment by completely abandoning the subtle mistaken appearance of all phenomena through our realization of completion stage. Developing the realization of completion stage depends upon the inner winds entering, abiding and dissolving within the central channel through the force of meditation. The objects of these meditations are the central channel, indestructible drop and the indestructible wind and mind. Therefore, in this context, training in completion stage means training in meditation on the central channel, indestructible drop and the indestructible wind and mind.

In the scriptures it is said that meditation on the central channel is like a wishfulfilling cow. Just as a wishfulfilling cow provides milk unceasingly, so meditation on the central channel will enable us to experience great bliss unceasingly, and the meditations on the indestructible drop and on the indestructible wind and mind will enable us to experience the fully qualified clear light of bliss, which has the function of releasing our mind permanently from subtle mistaken appearance. A detailed explanation of the channels, drops and winds, how to meditate on the central channel, indestructible drop, and indestructible wind and mind, and how to make progress in realizing the five stages of completion stage has already been given.

Venerable Vajrayogini

The Instructions of Vajrayogini

THE YOGAS OF SLEEPING, RISING AND
EXPERIENCING NECTAR

Vajrayogini is a female enlightened Deity of Highest Yoga Tantra who is the manifestation of the wisdom of all Buddhas. Her function is to guide all living beings to the Pure Land of Keajra, or Pure Dakini Land. The instructions of Vajrayogini were taught by Buddha in *Root Tantra of Heruka*. The great Yogi Naropa received these instructions directly from Vajrayogini, and passed them to Pamtingpa – one of his heart disciples. Pamtingpa then passed these instructions to the Tibetan translator Sherab Tseg, and from Sherab Tseg these instructions have been passed down in an unbroken lineage to Je Phabongkhapa, and then to the most venerable Kyabje Trijang Rinpoche, holder of the lineage. It is from this great master that I, the author of this book, received these precious instructions.

Highest Yoga Tantra can be divided into Father Tantra and Mother Tantra. Mother Tantras principally reveal the training in clear light, which is the main cause to attain Buddha's holy mind; and Father Tantras such as Guhyasamaja Tantra principally reveal the training in the illusory body, which is the main cause to attain Buddha's holy body. Because Vajrayogini Tantra is Mother Tantra, the main body of Vajrayogini practice is training in clear light. This main body has eleven limbs, which are called the 'eleven yogas'. In this context, 'yoga' means training in spiritual paths. For example, training in a spiritual path in conjunction with sleep is called the 'yoga of sleeping'.

When the eleven yogas are listed in the scriptures, the first is the yoga of sleeping. This indicates that we should begin the practice of Vajrayogini with the yoga of sleeping. As already mentioned, the main body of Vajrayogini practice is training in clear light. Clear light naturally manifests during sleep; we therefore have the opportunity to train in recognizing it during sleep. When we recognize and realize clear light directly, we shall have attained meaning clear light, the realization of the fourth of the five stages of completion stage.

What is clear light? It is the very subtle mind that manifests when the inner winds enter, abide and dissolve within the central channel. Clear light is the eighth sign of the dissolution of inner winds within the central channel, and it perceives emptiness. There are three different types of clear light: (1) the clear light of sleep, (2) the clear light of death, and (3) the realization of clear light.

During sleep our very subtle mind manifests because our inner winds naturally enter and dissolve within our central channel. This very subtle mind is the clear light of sleep. It perceives emptiness, but we cannot recognize the clear light itself or emptiness because our memory cannot function during sleep. In a similar way, during our death, our very subtle mind manifests because our inner winds enter and dissolve within the central channel. This very subtle mind is the clear light of death. It perceives emptiness, but we cannot recognize the clear light itself or emptiness because our memory cannot function during death.

During waking, if we are able to cause our inner winds to enter, abide and dissolve within the central channel through the power of meditation, we experience a deep dissolution of our inner winds into the central channel, and through this our very subtle mind will manifest. This very subtle mind is the realization of clear light. Its nature is a bliss arisen from the melting of the drops inside the central channel, and its function is to prevent mistaken appearance. It is also the realization of the clear light of bliss, which is the very essence of Highest Yoga Tantra and the actual quick path to enlightenment.

In conclusion, the main body of Vajrayogini practice is training in clear light of bliss. This can be divided into two: (1) training in bliss; and (2) training in clear light. Before training in bliss we should know what it is. This bliss is not sexual bliss; we do not need to train in sexual bliss as anyone, even an animal, can experience this without training. The bliss that we are training in is the bliss that Buddha explains in Highest Yoga Tantra. It is called 'great bliss', and possesses two special characteristics: (1) its nature is a bliss arisen from the melting of the drops inside the central channel; and (2) its function is to prevent subtle mistaken appearance. Ordinary beings cannot experience such bliss. As mentioned earlier, the sexual bliss of ordinary beings arises from the melting of the drops inside the left channel, and not the central channel.

In the *Condensed Heruka Root Tantra* Buddha says:

The supreme secret of great bliss
Arises through melting the drops inside the central
    channel;
Thus it is hard to find in the world
A person who experiences such bliss.

Such a great bliss is experienced only by someone who is able to cause their inner winds to enter, abide and dissolve within their central channel through the power of meditation. Because this great bliss prevents subtle mistaken appearance, when we experience this bliss our ignorance of self-grasping and all distracting conceptual thoughts cease, and we experience a deep inner peace, which is superior to the supreme inner peace of nirvana explained by Buddha in Sutra teachings.

HOW TO PRACTISE THE YOGA OF SLEEPING

Every night when we are about to sleep we should think:

> To benefit all living beings
> I shall become the enlightened Buddha Vajrayogini.
> For this purpose I will accomplish the realization of the clear
>   light of bliss.

We then recollect that our body, our self and all other phenomena that we normally perceive do not exist. We try to perceive the mere absence of all phenomena that we normally see, the emptiness of all phenomena, and we meditate on this emptiness. Then we think and imagine:

> In the vast space of emptiness of all phenomena – the Pure Land of Keajra – I appear as Vajrayogini surrounded by the enlightened Heroines and Heroes. Although I have this appearance it is not other than the emptiness of all phenomena.

We meditate on this self-generation.

We should train in this profound self-generation meditation while we are sleeping, but not in deep sleep. Through training in this practice each and every night with continual effort, gradually our memory will be able to function during sleep. Because of this, when our very subtle mind manifests during sleep we shall be able to recognize or realize it. Through further training we shall realize our very subtle mind directly. When this happens our mind will mix with the emptiness of all phenomena, like water mixing with water. Because of this our subtle mistaken appearance will quickly and permanently cease, and we shall become an enlightened being, a Buddha. As Buddha said: 'If you realize your own mind you will become a Buddha; you should not seek Buddhahood elsewhere'. With regard to this accomplishment our sleep has so much meaning.

HOW TO PRACTISE THE YOGA OF RISING

We should try to practise the yoga of sleeping throughout the night, and throughout the day we should try to practise the yoga of rising. Every day, in the early morning, we should first meditate on the mere absence of all phenomena that we normally see or perceive, the emptiness of all phenomena. Then we think and imagine:

In the vast space of emptiness of all phenomena – the Pure Land of Keajra – I appear as Vajrayogini surrounded by the enlightened Heroines and Heroes. Although I have this appearance it is not other than the emptiness of all phenomena.

We meditate on this self-generation.

We should repeat this meditation practice again and again, throughout the day. This is the yoga of rising. Then at night we again practise the yoga of sleeping. Through continually practising the cycle of the yogas of sleeping and rising, our ordinary appearances and conceptions, which are the root of our suffering, will cease.

HOW TO PRACTISE THE YOGA OF
EXPERIENCING NECTAR

Whenever we eat or drink, we should first understand and think:

For enlightened beings all food and drink are supreme nectar, which possesses three special qualities: (1) it is medicine nectar that cures sickness; (2) it is life nectar that prevents death; and (3) it is wisdom nectar that pacifies delusions.

With this recognition, whenever we eat or drink we should offer our pleasure in these objects of desire to ourself, the self-generated Vajrayogini. Through practising in this way we can transform our daily experience of eating and drinking into a spiritual path that accumulates a great collection of merit, or good fortune. In the same way, whenever we enjoy seeing attractive forms or beautiful things, enjoy hearing beautiful sounds such as music or songs, enjoy smelling beautiful scents and enjoy touching tangible objects, we should offer our pleasure in these objects of desire to ourself, the self-generated Vajrayogini. In this way we can transform all our daily experiences of objects of desire into a spiritual path that leads us to the attainment of the enlightened state of Vajrayogini.

In summary, we should recognize that in the vast space of emptiness of all phenomena – the Pure Land of Keajra – is ourself Vajrayogini surrounded by the enlightened Heroines and Heroes. We should maintain this recognition throughout the day and night, except when we are concentrating on common paths, such as going for refuge, training in renunciation and bodhichitta, and engaging in purification practices.

This way of practising the yogas of sleeping, rising and experiencing nectar is simple but very profound. There are also other ways of practising these yogas, an explanation of which can be found in *Guide to Dakini Land*.

THE REMAINING EIGHT YOGAS

The remaining eight yogas from the yoga of immeasurables to the yoga of daily actions should be practised in conjunction with the sadhana *Quick Path to Great Bliss* composed by Je Phabongkhapa (see Appendix VII). This sadhana is very blessed and precious. A detailed explanation of how to practise each yoga can be found in *Guide to Dakini Land*, but the following is a brief explanation of their essence.

THE YOGA OF IMMEASURABLES

Going for refuge, generating bodhichitta, and meditation and recitation of Vajrasattva are called the 'yoga of immeasurables' because they are trainings in spiritual paths that will bring us immeasurable benefit in this life and countless future lives.

The meditation and recitation of Vajrasattva gives us the great opportunity to purify our mind quickly, so that we can more quickly attain enlightenment. As mentioned above, attaining enlightenment is very simple; all we need to do is apply effort to purifying our mind.

THE YOGA OF THE GURU

In this Guru yoga practice, to receive the blessings of all the Buddhas' speech we visualize our root Guru in the aspect of Buddha Vajradharma. Vajradharma, Vajradhara, Vajrasattva and Heruka are different aspects of one enlightened being. The function of Buddha Vajradharma is to bestow the blessings of

Mandala of Vajrayogini

all the Buddhas' speech. Through receiving these blessings, our speech will be very powerful whenever we explain Dharma instructions. In this way we can fulfil the wishes of countless living beings and purify or heal their mental continuums through the nectar of our speech.

This Guru yoga contains a practice called 'kusali tsog offering', which has the same function as the 'chod' or 'cutting' practice. It also contains a practice of receiving the blessings of the four empowerments, which will give us great confidence in accomplishing the realizations of generation and completion stages.

THE YOGA OF SELF-GENERATION

This yoga includes the practices of bringing death, the intermediate state (bardo) and rebirth into the paths of the Truth Body, Enjoyment Body and Emanation Body.

In this practice, the supporting mandala is visualized in the aspect of a double tetrahedron, which symbolizes the emptiness of all phenomena; and the supported Dcities are ourself, the imagined Vajrayogini, and our retinue of Heroines.

THE YOGA OF PURIFYING MIGRATORS

In this practice, having generated ourself as the enlightened Buddha Vajrayogini, we imagine ourself giving blessings that liberate all living beings from suffering and negativities and transform them into the state of Vajrayogini – the state of ultimate happiness. This is a special practice of taking and giving according to Highest Yoga Tantra. It causes our potential to benefit directly each and every living being to ripen, and it also fulfils the commitment we made when we took the Highest

Yoga Tantra empowerment in which we promised to benefit all living beings.

THE YOGA OF BEING BLESSED BY HEROES AND HEROINES

In this practice, through meditating on the body mandala of Vajrayogini, our channels and drops will receive powerful blessings directly from the thirty-seven Heroines – the female enlightened Deities of the Vajrayogini body mandala – and indirectly from their consorts, the Heroes. Also, through inviting all Heroines and Heroes (female and male enlightened beings) from the ten directions in the aspect of Vajrayogini and dissolving them into us, we shall receive the blessings of all Heroes and Heroines.

The meditation on Vajrayogini's body mandala is very profound. Although it is a generation stage practice it functions to cause the inner winds to enter, abide and dissolve within the central channel. Je Phabongkhapa highly praised the practice of Vajrayogini body mandala.

THE YOGA OF VERBAL AND MENTAL RECITATION

By concentrating on verbal recitation of the Vajrayogini mantra (the 'three-OM mantra') we can accomplish the pacifying, increasing, controlling, wrathful and supreme attainments, which are mentioned in the section *Training in Mantra Recitation*. The practice of mental recitation presents two completion stage meditations, both of which are the very essence of Vajrayogini practice. These two meditations are clearly explained in *Guide to Dakini Land*.

THE YOGA OF INCONCEIVABILITY

As described in the sadhana *Quick Path to Great Bliss* (see Appendix VII), having dissolved everything from the formless realm to the nada into emptiness, we imagine that we experience the clear light of bliss, and with this experience we meditate on the emptiness of all phenomena – the mere absence of all phenomena that we normally perceive. This meditation is training in the clear light of bliss, the main body of Vajrayogini practice. Through continually practising this meditation, gradually we shall experience meaning clear light – the union of great bliss and emptiness – which is the actual inconceivability. In this context, 'inconceivability' means that it cannot be experienced by those who have not attained meaning clear light.

THE YOGA OF DAILY ACTIONS

The yoga of daily actions is a method for transforming all our daily actions such as eating, sleeping, working and talking into profound spiritual paths, and thus extracting great meaning from every moment of our life.

Dedication

Through the great collection of virtue that I have accumulated
by composing this book, may each and every living being have
the opportunity to listen to and practise the precious teachings
of Sutra and Tantra, and thereby experience the pure and everlasting happiness of enlightenment.

Appendix I

Liberating Prayer

PRAISE TO BUDDHA SHAKYAMUNI

O Blessed One, Shakyamuni Buddha,
Precious treasury of compassion,
Bestower of supreme inner peace,

You, who love all beings without exception,
Are the source of happiness and goodness;
And you guide us to the liberating path.

Your body is a wishfulfilling jewel,
Your speech is supreme, purifying nectar,
And your mind is refuge for all living beings.

With folded hands I turn to you,
Supreme unchanging friend,
I request from the depths of my heart:

Please give me the light of your wisdom
To dispel the darkness of my mind
And to heal my mental continuum.

Please nourish me with your goodness,
That I in turn may nourish all beings
With an unceasing banquet of delight.

Through your compassionate intention,
Your blessings and virtuous deeds,
And my strong wish to rely upon you,

May all suffering quickly cease
And all happiness and joy be fulfilled;
And may holy Dharma flourish for evermore.

Colophon: This prayer was composed by Venerable Geshe
Kelsang Gyatso and is recited at the beginning of teachings,
meditations and prayers in Kadampa Buddhist Centres
throughout the world.

Appendix II

Prayers for Meditation

BRIEF PREPARATORY PRAYERS FOR MEDITATION

Introduction

We all have the potential to gain realizations of all the stages of the path to enlightenment. These potentials are like seeds in the field of our mind, and our meditation practice is like cultivating these seeds. However, our meditation practice will be successful only if we make good preparations beforehand.

If we want to cultivate external crops, we begin by making careful preparations. First, we remove from the soil anything that might obstruct their growth, such as stones and weeds. Second, we enrich the soil with compost or fertilizer to give it the strength to sustain growth. Third, we provide warm, moist conditions to enable the seeds to germinate and the plants to grow. In the same way, to cultivate our inner crops of Dharma realizations we must also begin by making careful preparations.

First, we must purify our mind to eliminate the negative karma we have accumulated in the past, because if we do not purify this karma it will obstruct the growth of Dharma realizations. Second, we need to give our mind the strength to support the growth of Dharma realizations by accumulating merit. Third, we need to activate and sustain the growth of Dharma realizations by receiving the blessings of the holy beings.

The brief prayers that follow contain the essence of these three preparations. For more information on them, see *The New Meditation Handbook* or *Joyful Path of Good Fortune*.

Geshe Kelsang Gyatso

1987

Prayers for Meditation

Going for refuge

I and all sentient beings, until we achieve enlightenment,
Go for refuge to Buddha, Dharma and Sangha.

(3x, 7x, 100x, or more)

Generating bodhichitta

Through the virtues I collect by giving and other perfections,
May I become a Buddha for the benefit of all. (3x)

Generating the four immeasurables

May everyone be happy,
May everyone be free from misery,
May no one ever be separated from their happiness,
May everyone have equanimity, free from hatred and attachment.

Visualizing the Field for Accumulating Merit

In the space before me is the living Buddha Shakyamuni
surrounded by all the Buddhas and Bodhisattvas, like the
full moon surrounded by stars.

Prayer of seven limbs

With my body, speech and mind, humbly I prostrate,
And make offerings both set out and imagined.
I confess my wrong deeds from all time,
And rejoice in the virtues of all.
Please stay until samsara ceases,
And turn the Wheel of Dharma for us.
I dedicate all virtues to great enlightenment.

Offering the mandala

The ground sprinkled with perfume and spread with flowers,
The Great Mountain, four lands, sun and moon,
Seen as a Buddha Land and offered thus,
May all beings enjoy such Pure Lands.

I offer without any sense of loss
The objects that give rise to my attachment, hatred and
    confusion,
My friends, enemies and strangers, our bodies and
    enjoyments;
Please accept these and bless me to be released directly
    from the three poisons.

IDAM GURU RATNA MANDALAKAM NIRYATAYAMI

Prayer of the Stages of the Path

The path begins with strong reliance
On my kind Teacher, source of all good;
O Bless me with this understanding
To follow him with great devotion.

This human life with all its freedoms,
Extremely rare, with so much meaning;
O Bless me with this understanding
All day and night to seize its essence.

My body, like a water bubble,
Decays and dies so very quickly;
After death come results of karma,
Just like the shadow of a body.

With this firm knowledge and remembrance
Bless me to be extremely cautious,
Always avoiding harmful actions
And gathering abundant virtue.

Samsara's pleasures are deceptive,
Give no contentment, only torment;
So please bless me to strive sincerely
To gain the bliss of perfect freedom.

O Bless me so that from this pure thought
Come mindfulness and greatest caution,
To keep as my essential practice
The doctrine's root, the Pratimoksha.

Just like myself all my kind mothers
Are drowning in samsara's ocean;
O So that I may soon release them,
Bless me to train in bodhichitta.

But I cannot become a Buddha
By this alone without three ethics;
So bless me with the strength to practise
The Bodhisattva's ordination.

By pacifying my distractions
And analyzing perfect meanings,
Bless me to quickly gain the union
Of special insight and quiescence.

When I become a pure container
Through common paths, bless me to enter
The essence practice of good fortune,
The supreme vehicle, Vajrayana.

The two attainments both depend on
My sacred vows and my commitments;
Bless me to understand this clearly
And keep them at the cost of my life.

By constant practice in four sessions,
The way explained by holy Teachers,
O Bless me to gain both the stages,
Which are the essence of the Tantras.

May those who guide me on the good path,
And my companions all have long lives;
Bless me to pacify completely
All obstacles, outer and inner.

May I always find perfect Teachers,
And take delight in holy Dharma,
Accomplish all grounds and paths swiftly,
And gain the state of Vajradhara.

Receiving blessings and purifying

From the hearts of all the holy beings, streams of light
and nectar flow down, granting blessings and purifying.

*At this point, we begin the actual contemplation and meditation.
After the meditation, we dedicate our merit while reciting the
following prayers:*

Dedication prayers

Through the virtues I have collected
By practising the stages of the path,
May all living beings find the opportunity
To practise in the same way.

May everyone experience
The happiness of humans and gods,
And quickly attain enlightenment,
So that samsara is finally extinguished.

Prayers for the Virtuous Tradition

So that the tradition of Je Tsongkhapa,
The King of the Dharma, may flourish,
May all obstacles be pacified
And may all favourable conditions abound.

Through the two collections of myself and others
Gathered throughout the three times,
May the doctrine of Conqueror Losang Dragpa
Flourish for evermore.

The nine-line *Migtsema* prayer

Tsongkhapa, crown ornament of the scholars of the
    Land of the Snows,
You are Buddha Shakyamuni and Vajradhara, the
    source of all attainments,
Avalokiteshvara, the treasury of unobservable
    compassion,
Manjushri, the supreme stainless wisdom,
And Vajrapani, the destroyer of the hosts of maras.
O Venerable Guru-Buddha, synthesis of all Three Jewels,
With my body, speech and mind, respectfully I make
    requests:
Please grant your blessings to ripen and liberate myself
    and others,
And bestow the common and supreme attainments.

(3x)

Colophon: These prayers were compiled from traditional
sources by Venerable Geshe Kelsang Gyatso.

Naropa

Appendix III

An Explanation of Channels

There are three main channels: the central channel, the right channel and the left channel. The central channel is like the pole of an umbrella, running through the centre of each of the channel wheels, and the other two run either side of it. The central channel is pale blue and has four attributes: (1) it is very straight, like the trunk of a plantain tree; (2) inside it has an oily red colour, like pure blood; (3) it is very clear and transparent, like a candle flame; and (4) it is very soft and flexible, like a lotus petal.

The central channel is located exactly midway between the left and right halves of the body, but is closer to the back than the front. Immediately in front of the spine, there is the life channel, which is quite thick; and in front of this is the central channel. As mentioned before, it begins at the point between the eyebrows, from where it ascends in an arch to the crown of the head and then descends in a straight line to the tip of the sex organ. Although its most common name is the central channel, it is also known as the 'two abandonments' because gathering the winds into this channel causes the negative activity associated with the winds of the right and left channels to be abandoned. It is also known as the 'mind channel' and as 'Rahu'.

Either side of the central channel, with no intervening space, are the right and left channels. The right channel is red in colour and the left is white. The right channel begins at the tip of the right nostril and the left channel at the tip of the left nostril. From there they both ascend in an arch to the crown of the head, either side of the central channel. From the crown of the head down to the navel, these three major channels are straight and adjacent to one another. As the left channel continues down below the level of the navel, it curves a little to the right, separating slightly from the central channel and rejoining it at the tip of the sex organ. There it functions to hold and release sperm, blood and urine. As the right channel continues down below the level of the navel, it curves a little to the left and terminates at the tip of the anus, where it functions to hold and release faeces and so forth.

Other names for the right channel are the 'sun channel', the 'speech channel' and the 'channel of the subjective holder'. This last title indicates that the winds flowing through this channel cause the generation of conceptions developed in terms of the subjective mind. Other names for the left channel are the 'moon channel', the 'body channel' and the 'channel of the held object', with the last title indicating that the winds flowing through this channel cause the generation of conceptions developed in terms of the object.

The right and left channels coil around the central channel at various places, thereby forming the so-called 'channel knots'. The four places at which these knots occur are, in ascending order, the navel channel wheel, the heart channel wheel, the throat channel wheel and the crown channel wheel. At each of these places, except at the heart level, there is one two-fold knot formed by a single coil of the right channel and a single coil of the left. As the right and left channels ascend to these places, they coil around the central channel by crossing in front and then looping around it. They then continue upward to the level of the next knot. At the heart level, the same thing happens, except that here there is a six-fold knot formed by three overlapping loops of each of the flanking channels.

The four places where these knots occur are four of the six major channel wheels. At each of the six major channel wheels, a different number of spokes, or petals, branch off from the central channel in the same way that the ribs of an umbrella appear to branch off from the central pole. Thus, at the crown channel wheel (known as the 'great bliss wheel') there are thirty-two such petals or channel spokes, all of them white in colour. The centre is triangular with the apex facing forwards. (This refers to the shape of the coiled knot through which the spokes emanate, as seen from the top.) These thirty-two spokes arch downwards, like the ribs of an upright umbrella. A description of this and the three other major channel wheels where knots occur is given in Chart 1.

Chart 1 The Four Major Channel Wheels

location	name	shape of centre	number of spokes	colour	direction of arching
crown	great bliss wheel	triangular	thirty-two	white	downwards
throat	enjoyment wheel	circular	sixteen	red	upwards
heart	Dharma wheel	circular	eight	white	downwards
navel	emanation wheel	triangular	sixty-four	red	upwards

These four channel wheels contain a total of one hundred and twenty spokes. As for the remaining two major channel wheels, the channel wheel at the secret place has thirty-two red-coloured spokes arching downwards and the jewel channel wheel has eight white spokes arching upwards. It should also be noted that according to some texts the spokes at the crown, navel and secret place can be visualized as having various colours.

Since the heart channel wheel is of particular importance, it will now be described in more detail. Its eight spokes, or petals, are arranged in the cardinal and intermediate directions with the front being the east. In each spoke, there flows mainly the supporting wind of a particular element as indicated in Chart 2.

Chart 2 The Spokes of the Heart Channel Wheel

direction	supporting wind
east	of the earth element
north	of the wind element
west	of the fire element
south	of the water element
south-east	of the element of form
south-west	of the element of smell
north-west	of the element of taste
north-east	of the element of touch

From each of these eight petals or channel spokes of the heart, three channels split off, making twenty-four channels in all. These are the channels of the twenty-four places. They are all included in three groups of eight: the channels of the mind wheel, which are blue and contain mainly winds; the channels of the speech wheel, which are red and contain mostly red drops; and the channels of the body wheel, which are white and contain mostly white drops. Each channel goes to a different place in the body. These places are the twenty-four inner places. When we practise the extensive Heruka sadhana, we visualize the Deities of the body mandala at these places.

The outer tips of the eight channels of the mind wheel terminate at: (1) the hairline; (2) the crown; (3) the right ear; (4) the back of the neck; (5) the left ear; (6) the brow (the place between the eyebrows); (7) the two eyes; and (8) the two shoulders. Those of the speech wheel terminate at: (9) the two armpits; (10) the two breasts; (11) the navel; (12) the tip of the nose; (13) the mouth; (14) the throat; (15) the heart (the area midway between the two breasts); and (16) the two testicles or the two sides of the vagina. Finally, those of the body wheel terminate at: (17) the tip of the sex organ; (18) the anus; (19) the two thighs; (20) the two calves; (21) the eight fingers and eight lesser toes; (22) the tops of the feet; (23) the two thumbs and the two big toes; and (24) the two knees.

Each of these twenty-four channels splits into three branches, which are distinguished by the principal elements – winds, red drops and white drops – that flow through them. Each of these seventy-two channels then splits into a thousand, making seventy-two thousand channels in all. It is important for a Highest Yoga Tantric practitioner to be familiar with the arrangement of the channels since it is through gaining control over the winds and drops flowing through these channels that the union of spontaneous great bliss and emptiness is accomplished.

The winds in the body of an ordinary person flow through most of these channels except the central channel. Because these winds are impure, the various minds that they support are also impure, and so for as long as these winds continue to flow through the peripheral channels they will continue to support the various negative conceptions that keep us trapped in samsara. Through the force of meditation, however, these winds can be brought into the central channel, where they are no longer able to support the development of gross conceptions of dualistic appearance. With a mind free from dualistic appearances, we shall be able to gain a direct realization of ultimate truth, emptiness.

Corresponding to the twenty-four inner places of the Heruka body mandala are the 'twenty-four outer places', which are located at various points throughout this world. Practitioners with pure karma can see these outer places of Heruka as Pure Lands, but people with impure karma see them only as ordinary places.

Appendix IV

An Explanation of Inner Winds

The definition of wind is any of the four elements that is light in weight and moving. Winds can be divided into external and internal winds, and into gross and subtle winds. Gross external wind is the wind we experience on a windy day. Subtle external wind is much more difficult to detect. It is the energy that makes plants grow and exists even inside rocks and mountains. It is with the help of subtle winds that plants draw up water, grow new leaves, and so forth. Such winds are the life-force of plants. Indeed, in some Tantric texts wind is called 'life' or 'life-force'. Thus, although it is incorrect to say that plants are alive in the sense of being conjoined with consciousness, we can say that they are alive in this sense.

Internal winds are the winds in the continuum of a person that flow through the channels of the body. The main function of internal winds is to move the mind to its object. The function of the mind is to apprehend objects, but without a wind to act as its mount it cannot move towards, or establish connection with, its object. Mind is sometimes likened to a lame person who can see, and wind to a blind person with legs. It is only by operating together with internal winds that minds can function.

There are many different winds flowing through the channels of the body, but all are included within the five root winds and the five branch winds. The five root winds are: (1) the life-supporting wind; (2) the downward-voiding wind; (3) the upward-moving wind; (4) the equally-abiding wind; and (5) the pervading wind.

Each of the five root winds has six characteristics by which it can be recognized: (1) its colour; (2) its associated Buddha family; (3) an element for which it serves as the support; (4) its principal seat or fundamental location; (5) its function; and (6) its direction (how it leaves the nostrils upon exhalation). These are summarized in Chart 1 on page 270.

The life-supporting wind is called the 'Akshobya wind' because, when it is completely purified, it transforms into the nature of Akshobya. At the moment, our life-supporting wind is like the seed of Akshobya's Form Body, but not Akshobya himself. The main function of the life-supporting wind is to support life by maintaining the connection between body and mind. The stronger the life-supporting wind, the longer we shall live. Another function of this wind is to support the water element of our body and to cause it to increase. The life-supporting wind is white in colour and its principal location is at the heart. When we exhale, it leaves from both nostrils, flowing gently downwards.

The downward-voiding wind is the seed of Ratnasambhava's Form Body and is associated with the earth element. It is yellow in colour and it functions to release urine, faeces, sperm and menstrual blood. Its principal locations are at the anus and the sex organ, and when we exhale, it leaves horizontally from both nostrils, flowing heavily forwards.

The upward-moving wind is the seed of Amitabha's Form Body and is associated with the fire element. It is red in colour and it functions to enable us to swallow food and drink, to speak, to cough and so forth. Its principal location is at the throat, and when we exhale it leaves from the right nostril, flowing violently upwards.

The equally-abiding wind is the seed of Amoghasiddhi's Form Body and is associated with the wind element. It is greenish-yellow in colour and it functions to cause the inner fire to blaze, and to digest food and drink by separating the nutrients from waste matter. Its principal location is at the navel, and when we exhale it leaves from the left nostril, moving to the left and the right from the edge of the nostril.

The pervading wind is the seed of Vairochana's Form Body and is associated with the space element. It is pale blue in colour and, as its name suggests, it pervades the entire body, particularly the three hundred and sixty joints. It functions to enable the body to move. Without this wind we would be completely immobile, like a stone. This wind does not flow through the nostrils except at the moment of death.

Generally speaking, at any one time, one of the winds is flowing more strongly through the nostrils than the other winds. If, for example, the life-supporting wind is flowing strongly, the other winds (except the pervading wind) are flowing gently. Unless we observe our breath very carefully, it is difficult to notice the different movements of the four winds, but they definitely flow through our nostrils whenever we breathe.

The five branch winds are: (1) the moving wind; (2) the intensely-moving wind; (3) the perfectly-moving wind; (4) the strongly-moving wind; and (5) the definitely-moving wind.

Chart 1 The Root Winds

	life-supporting	downward-voiding	upward-moving	equally-abiding	pervading
colour	white	yellow	red	green/yellow	pale blue
Buddha family	Akshobya	Ratnasambhava	Amitabha	Amoghasiddhi	Vairochana
element	water	earth	fire	wind	space
seat	heart	the two lower doors: the anus and the sex organ	throat	navel	both the upper and lower parts of the body, mainly the 360 joints
function	to support and maintain life	to retain and release urine, faeces, semen, blood, etc.	to speak, swallow, etc.	to cause the inner fire to blaze, to digest food and drink, etc.	to enable the body to come and go; to allow movement, lifting and placing
direction	from both nostrils, gently downwards	from both nostrils, horizontally heavily forwards	from the right nostril, violently upwards	from the left nostril, moving to the left and the right from the edge of this nostril	this wind does not flow through the nostrils except at the moment of death

The five branch winds are so called because they branch off from the life-supporting wind, which resides in the heart centre. The main location of these winds is in the four channel spokes of the heart channel wheel, from where they flow through our channels to the five doors of the sense powers. Because they function to enable sense awarenesses to develop, the five branch winds are also called the 'five winds of the sense powers'. The colour and function of each branch wind are summarized in Chart 2.

Chart 2 The Branch Winds

name	colour	function
the moving wind	red	to enable the eye awareness to move to visual forms
the intensely-moving wind	blue	to enable the ear awareness to move to sounds
the perfectly-moving wind	yellow	to enable the nose awareness to move to smells
the strongly-moving wind	white	to enable the tongue awareness to move to tastes
the definitely-moving wind	green	to enable the body awareness to move to tactile objects

The first wind, the moving wind, flows from the heart through the door of the eyes to enable the eye awareness to move to its object, visual forms. Without the moving wind, eye awareness would be powerless to contact visual forms. The reason we cannot see when we are asleep is that the moving wind has withdrawn from the door of the eye sense power back to its seat at the heart.

The intensely-moving wind flows from the heart to the ears, enabling the ear awareness to move to sounds; the perfectly-moving wind flows from the heart to the nostrils, enabling the nose awareness to move to smells; the strongly-moving wind flows from the heart to the tongue, enabling the tongue awareness to move to tastes; and the definitely-moving wind flows from the heart all over the body, enabling the body awareness to move to tactile objects.

The downward-voiding wind, the upward-moving wind, the equally-abiding wind, the pervading wind, and the five branch winds are all gross internal winds. The life-supporting wind has three levels: gross, subtle and very subtle. Most mounted winds of conceptual thoughts are gross life-supporting winds; the mounted winds of the minds of white appearance, red increase and black near-attainment are subtle life-supporting winds; and the mounted wind of the mind of clear light is a very subtle life-supporting wind.

The life-supporting wind is very extensive. If a defiled life-supporting wind manifests, negative conceptual thoughts will develop, but if the life-supporting wind is purified, negative conceptual thoughts will be pacified. All meditations use the mental awareness, and the mounted wind of mental awareness is necessarily a life-supporting wind.

Each of the five winds of the sense powers and the gross life-supporting wind has two parts: a wind that develops the specific type of awareness, and a wind that moves the awareness towards its object. These twelve winds normally flow through the right and left channels, and are the principal objects to be purified by means of vajra recitation, as explained in *Tantric Grounds and Paths* and *Essence of Vajrayana*. If we want to overcome distractions, it is very important to cause these twelve winds to enter, abide and dissolve within the central channel.

Appendix V

The Yoga of Buddha Heruka

THE BRIEF SELF-GENERATION SADHANA OF HERUKA BODY MANDALA & CONDENSED SIX-SESSION YOGA

Tantric commitments objects:
inner offering in kapala, vajra, bell, damaru, mala

Introduction

Those who have received the empowerment of Heruka body mandala, but who are unable to practise the extensive sadhana, *Essence of Vajrayana*, can practise this short sadhana, which contains the very essence of Heruka body mandala practice.

It is very important to improve our understanding of and faith in this precious practice through sincerely studying its commentary as presented in the chapter *The Practice of Heruka Body Mandala*. Having understood the meaning clearly and with strong faith we can enter, make progress on and complete the quick path to the enlightened state of Buddha Heruka.

Geshe Kelsang Gyatso
April 2010

Je Phabongkhapa

The Yoga of Buddha Heruka

PRELIMINARIES

Going for refuge

I and all sentient beings, until we achieve enlightenment,
Go for refuge to Buddha, Dharma and Sangha.　(3x)

Generating the supreme good heart, bodhichitta

Through the virtues I collect by giving and other perfections,
May I become a Buddha for the benefit of all.　(3x)

Guru yoga

VISUALIZATION AND MEDITATION

In the space before me is Guru Sumati Buddha Heruka –
Je Tsongkhapa inseparable from my root Guru, Buddha
Shakyamuni and Heruka – surrounded by all the Buddhas
of the ten directions.

INVITING THE WISDOM BEINGS

From the heart of the Protector of the hundreds of Deities
 of the Joyful Land,
To the peak of a cloud which is like a cluster of fresh,
 white curd,
All-knowing Losang Dragpa, King of the Dharma,
Please come to this place together with your Sons.

*At this point we imagine that wisdom being Je Tsongkhapa
together with his retinue dissolves into the assembly of Guru
Sumati Buddha Heruka, and they become non-dual.*

THE PRACTICE OF THE SEVEN LIMBS

In the space before me on a lion throne, lotus and moon,
The venerable Gurus smile with delight.
O Supreme Field of Merit for my mind of faith,
Please remain for a hundred aeons to spread the doctrine.

Your mind of wisdom realizes the full extent of objects
 of knowledge,
Your eloquent speech is the ear-ornament of the fortunate,
Your beautiful body is ablaze with the glory of renown,
I prostrate to you, whom to see, to hear and to remember
 is so meaningful.

Pleasing water offerings, various flowers,
Sweet-smelling incense, lights, scented water and so forth,
A vast cloud of offerings both set out and imagined,
I offer to you, O Supreme Field of Merit.

Whatever non-virtues of body, speech and mind
I have accumulated since time without beginning,
Especially transgressions of my three vows,
With great remorse I confess each one from the depths
 of my heart.

THE YOGA OF BUDDHA HERUKA

In this degenerate age you strove for much learning and
accomplishment.
Abandoning the eight worldly concerns, you made your
freedom and endowment meaningful.
O Protector, from the very depths of my heart,
I rejoice in the great wave of your deeds.

From the billowing clouds of wisdom and compassion
In the space of your Truth Body, O Venerable and holy
Gurus,
Please send down a rain of vast and profound Dharma
Appropriate to the disciples of this world.

From your actual deathless body, born from meaning
clear light,
Please send countless emanations throughout the world
To spread the oral lineage of the Ganden doctrine;
And may they remain for a very long time.

Through the virtues I have accumulated here,
May the doctrine and all living beings receive every benefit.
Especially may the essence of the doctrine
Of Venerable Losang Dragpa shine forever.

OFFERING THE MANDALA

The ground sprinkled with perfume and spread with flowers,
The Great Mountain, four lands, sun and moon,
Seen as a Buddha Land and offered thus,
May all beings enjoy such Pure Lands.

I offer without any sense of loss
The objects that give rise to my attachment, hatred and
confusion,
My friends, enemies and strangers, our bodies and enjoyments;
Please accept these and bless me to be released directly from
the three poisons.

IDAM GURU RATNA MANDALAKAM NIRYATAYAMI

279

MAKING SPECIAL REQUESTS

O Guru Sumati Buddha Heruka, from now until I attain
  enlightenment,
I shall seek no refuge other than you.
Please pacify my obstacles and bestow upon me
The two attainments of liberating and ripening.
Please bless me so that I will become definitive Heruka,
In which state I shall experience all phenomena as purified
  and gathered into emptiness, inseparable from great bliss.

(3x)

GENERATING THE EXPERIENCE OF GREAT BLISS AND EMPTINESS

Due to my making requests in this way, all the Buddhas of the
ten directions dissolve into Je Tsongkhapa who is inseparable
from my root Guru, he dissolves into Buddha Shakyamuni at
his heart, and Buddha Shakyamuni dissolves into Heruka at
his heart. With delight, Guru Heruka, who is the nature of the
union of great bliss and emptiness, enters my body through
my crown, and dissolves into my mind at my heart. Because
Heruka, who is the nature of the union of great bliss and
emptiness, becomes inseparable from my mind, I experience
spontaneous great bliss and emptiness. I perceive nothing other
than the emptiness of all phenomena, the mere absence of all
phenomena that I normally see or perceive. My subtle mistaken
appearance of all phenomena, including the channels, winds
and drops of my body, is purified.

*At this point we meditate briefly on the emptiness of all phenomena
while experiencing great bliss.*

THE ACTUAL SELF GENERATION

In the vast space of emptiness of all phenomena, the nature of
my purified mistaken appearance of all phenomena – which
is the Pure Land of Keajra – I appear as Buddha Heruka with

a blue-coloured body, four faces and twelve arms, the nature of my purified white indestructible drop. I am embracing Vajravarahi, the nature of my purified red indestructible drop. I am surrounded by the Heroes and Heroines of the five wheels, who are the nature of my purified subtle body – the channels and drops. I reside in the mandala, the celestial mansion, which is the nature of my purified gross body. Although I have this appearance it is not other than the emptiness of all phenomena.

At this point, (1) while experiencing great bliss and emptiness, (2) we meditate on the clear appearance of the mandala and Deities with divine pride, while (3) recognizing that the Deities are the nature of our purified channels and drops, which are our subtle body, and that the mandala is the nature of our purified gross body.

In this way we train sincerely in one single meditation on generation stage possessing these three characteristics. Holding the third characteristic – recognizing the Deities as the nature of our purified subtle body, and the mandala as the nature of our purified gross body – makes this concentration an actual body mandala meditation.

If we wish to practise completion stage meditation, we should change ourself through imagination from Heruka with four faces and twelve arms into Heruka with one face and two arms. We then engage in the meditations on the central channel, indestructible drop, indestructible wind, tummo and so forth.

Then, when we need to rest from meditation, we can practise mantra recitation.

Reciting the mantras

THE ESSENCE MANTRA OF HERUKA

At my heart is wisdom being Buddha Heruka, definitive
Heruka.

O Glorious Vajra Heruka, you who enjoy
The divine illusory body and mind of clear light,
Please pacify my obstacles and bestow upon me
The two attainments of liberating and ripening.
Please bless me so that I will become definitive Heruka,
In which state I shall experience all phenomena as purified
    and gathered into emptiness, inseparable from great bliss.

OM SHRI VAJRA HE HE RU RU KAM HUM HUM PHAT DAKINI
    DZALA SHAMBARAM SÖHA

(21x, 100x, etc.)

THE THREE-OM MANTRA OF VAJRAYOGINI

At the heart of imagined Vajrayogini (Vajravarahi) is wisdom
being Buddha Vajrayogini, definitive Vajrayogini.

OM OM OM SARWA BUDDHA DAKINIYE VAJRA WARNANIYE
    VAJRA BEROTZANIYE HUM HUM HUM PHAT PHAT PHAT
    SÖHA

Recite at least as many mantras as you have promised.

*The 'three-OM' mantra is the union of the essence and close essence
mantras of Vajravarahi. The meaning of this mantra is as follows.
With OM OM OM we are calling Vajrayogini – the principal
Deity – and her retinue of Heroines of the three wheels. SARWA
BUDDHA DAKINIYE means that Vajrayogini is the synthesis of the
minds of all Buddhas, VAJRA WARNANIYE means that she is the
synthesis of the speech of all Buddhas, and VAJRA BEROTZANIYE
means that she is the synthesis of the bodies of all Buddhas. With
HUM HUM HUM we are requesting Vajrayogini and her retinues*

to bestow upon us the attainments of the body, speech and mind of
all the Buddhas. With PHAT PHAT PHAT we are requesting them
to pacify our main obstacle – the subtle mistaken appearance of our
body, speech and mind; and SÖHA means 'please build within me
the basic foundation for all these attainments'.

THE CONDENSED MANTRA OF THE SIXTY-TWO DEITIES OF HERUKA BODY MANDALA

At the heart of each of the sixty-two Deities is their individual
wisdom being, their own definitive Deity.

OM HUM BAM RIM RIM LIM LIM, KAM KHAM GAM GHAM
NGAM, TSAM TSHAM DZAM DZHAM NYAM, TrAM THrAM
DrAM DHrAM NAM, TAM THAM DAM DHAM NAM, PAM
PHAM BAM BHAM, YAM RAM LAM WAM, SHAM KAM SAM
HAM HUM HUM PHAT

(7x, 21x, 100x, etc.)

When we recite this mantra we are making requests to wisdom
being Buddha Heruka with Vajravarahi, and his retinue of Heroes
and Heroines of the five wheels, to pacify our obstacle of subtle
mistaken appearance and to bestow upon us the attainments of
outer and inner Dakini Land. Outer Dakini Land is the Pure
Land of Keajra and inner Dakini Land is meaning clear light. The
moment our mind is free from subtle mistaken appearance we open
the door through which we can directly see all enlightened Deities.
For as long as our mind remains polluted by subtle mistaken
appearance this door is closed.

Dedication

Thus, through my virtues from correctly performing
   the offerings, praises, recitations and meditations
Of the generation stage of Glorious Heruka,
May I complete all the stages
Of the common and uncommon paths.

For the sake of all living beings
May I become Heruka;
And then lead every living being
To Heruka's supreme state.

And if I do not attain this supreme state in this life,
At my deathtime may I be met by the venerable Father
   and Mother and their retinue,
With clouds of breathtaking offerings, heavenly music,
And many excellent, auspicious signs.

Then, at the end of the clear light of death,
May I be led to the Pure Land of Keajra,
The abode of the Knowledge Holders who practise the
   supreme path;
And there may I swiftly complete this profound path.

May the most profound practice and instruction of
   Heruka,
Practised by millions of powerful Yogis, greatly increase;
And may it remain for a very long time without
   degenerating,
As the main gateway for those seeking liberation.

May the Heroes, Dakinis and their retinues
Abiding in the twenty-four supreme places of this world,
Who possess unobstructed power for accomplishing
   this method,
Never waver from always assisting practitioners.

Auspicious prayers

May there be the auspiciousness of a great treasury of blessings
Arising from the excellent deeds of all the root and lineage
    Gurus,
Who have accomplished the supreme attainment of Buddha
    Heruka
By relying upon the excellent, secret path of the King of Tantras.

May there be the auspiciousness of the great excellent deeds
    of the Three Jewels –
The holy Buddha Jewel, the pervading nature Heruka,
    definitive Heruka;
The ultimate, great, secret Dharma Jewel, the scriptures and
    realizations of Heruka Tantra;
And the supreme Sangha Jewel, the assemblies of Heruka's
    retinue Deities.

Through all the great good fortune there is
In the precious, celestial mansions as extensive as the three
    thousand worlds,
Adorned with ornaments like the rays of the sun and
    the moon,
May all worlds and their beings have happiness, goodness,
    glory and prosperity.

Prayers for the Virtuous Tradition

So that the tradition of Je Tsongkhapa,
The King of the Dharma, may flourish,
May all obstacles be pacified
And may all favourable conditions abound.

Through the two collections of myself and others
Gathered throughout the three times,
May the doctrine of Conqueror Losang Dragpa
Flourish for evermore.

285

The nine-line *Migtsema* prayer

Tsongkhapa, crown ornament of the scholars of the
    Land of the Snows,
You are Buddha Shakyamuni and Vajradhara, the
    source of all attainments,
Avalokiteshvara, the treasury of unobservable
    compassion,
Manjushri, the supreme stainless wisdom,
And Vajrapani, the destroyer of the hosts of maras.
O Venerable Guru-Buddha, synthesis of all Three Jewels,
With my body, speech and mind, respectfully I make
    requests:
Please grant your blessings to ripen and liberate myself
    and others,
And bestow the common and supreme attainments.

(3x)

Condensed Six-session Yoga

Everyone who has received a Highest Yoga Tantra empowerment has a commitment to practise six-session yoga. If we are very busy, we can fulfil our six-session commitment by doing the following practice six times each day. First we recall the nineteen commitments of the five Buddha families that are listed below, and then, with a strong determination to keep these commitments purely, we recite the Condensed Six-session Yoga *that follows.*

THE NINETEEN COMMITMENTS OF THE FIVE BUDDHA FAMILIES

The six commitments of the family of Buddha Vairochana:

(1) To go for refuge to Buddha
(2) To go for refuge to Dharma
(3) To go for refuge to Sangha
(4) To refrain from non-virtue
(5) To practise virtue
(6) To benefit others

The four commitments of the family of Buddha Akshobya:

(1) To keep a vajra to remind us to emphasize the development of great bliss through meditation on the central channel
(2) To keep a bell to remind us to emphasize meditation on emptiness
(3) To generate ourself as the Deity while realizing all things that we normally see do not exist
(4) To rely sincerely upon our Spiritual Guide, who leads us to the practice of the pure moral discipline of the Pratimoksha, Bodhisattva and Tantric vows

The four commitments of the family of Buddha Ratnasambhava:

(1) To give material help
(2) To give Dharma
(3) To give fearlessness
(4) To give love

The three commitments of the family of Buddha Amitabha:

(1) To rely upon the teachings of Sutra
(2) To rely upon the teachings of the two lower classes of Tantra
(3) To rely upon the teachings of the two higher classes of Tantra

The two commitments of the family of Buddha Amoghasiddhi:

(1) To make offerings to our Spiritual Guide
(2) To strive to maintain purely all the vows we have taken

CONDENSED SIX-SESSION YOGA

I go for refuge to the Guru and Three Jewels.
Holding vajra and bell I generate as the Deity and make
    offerings.
I rely upon the Dharmas of Sutra and Tantra and refrain
    from all non-virtuous actions.
Gathering all virtuous Dharmas, I help all living beings
    through the practice of the four givings.

All nineteen commitments are referred to in this verse. The words,
'I go for refuge to the . . . Three Jewels', *refer to the first three
commitments of the family of Buddha Vairochana – to go for
refuge to Buddha, to go for refuge to Dharma and to go for refuge to
Sangha. The word,* 'Guru', *refers to the fourth commitment of the
family of Buddha Akshobya – to rely sincerely upon our Spiritual
Guide.*

The words, 'Holding vajra and bell I generate as the Deity', *
refer to the first three commitments of the family of Buddha
Akshobya – to keep a vajra to remind us of great bliss, to keep a
bell to remind us of emptiness and to generate ourself as the Deity.
The words,* 'and make offerings', *refer to the first commitment
of the family of Buddha Amoghasiddhi – to make offerings to our
Spiritual Guide.*

The words, 'I rely upon the Dharmas of Sutra and Tantra', *
refer to the three commitments of Buddha Amitabha – to rely upon
the teachings of Sutra, to rely upon the teachings of the two lower
classes of Tantra, and to rely upon the teachings of the two higher
classes of Tantra. The words,* 'and refrain from all non-virtuous
actions', *refer to the fourth commitment of the family of Buddha
Vairochana – to refrain from non-virtue.*

The words, 'Gathering all virtuous Dharmas', *refer to the fifth
commitment of the family of Buddha Vairochana – to practise
virtue. The words,* 'I help all living beings', *refer to the sixth*

289

commitment of the family of Buddha Vairochana – to benefit others. The words, 'through the practice of the four givings', refer to the four commitments of the family of Buddha Ratnasambhava – to give material help, to give Dharma, to give fearlessness and to give love.

Finally, the entire verse refers to the second commitment of the family of Buddha Amoghasiddhi – to strive to maintain purely all the vows we have taken.

More detail on the vows and commitments of Secret Mantra can be found in the book Tantric Grounds and Paths.

Colophon: This sadhana was compiled from traditional sources by Venerable Geshe Kelsang Gyatso, June 2009, and revised April 2010

Appendix VI

Blissful Journey

HOW TO ENGAGE IN A CLOSE RETREAT OF HERUKA BODY MANDALA

Kyabje Trijang Rinpoche

Introduction

Sincere practitioners of *The Yoga of Buddha Heruka* sadhana can perform a close retreat of Heruka body mandala in accordance with the following instructions.

Having set out ritual objects, and torma and other offerings, in either a traditional or simple manner, in the evening of the first day on which the retreat begins you should engage in the practice of *The Yoga of Buddha Heruka* from *Going for refuge* up to and including *Reciting the mantras*; then perform torma and tsog offerings as presented below. The session should be concluded by reciting the *Dedication* and remaining prayers from the sadhana.

Beginning on the second day, if you intend to do four sessions of retreat each day, in the first three sessions you should engage in the practice of *The Yoga of Buddha Heruka* from *Going for refuge* up to and including reciting the *Dedication* and remaining prayers, without any additions. In the fourth or last session you should engage in the practice of *The Yoga of Buddha Heruka* from *Going for refuge* up to and including *Reciting the mantras*, and then perform the torma offerings as presented below; the session should be concluded by reciting the *Dedication* and remaining prayers from the sadhana.

Having collected 100,000 recitations of the essence mantra of Heruka, 100,000 recitations of the three-OM mantra of Vajrayogini, and 10,000 recitations of the condensed mantra of the sixty-two Deities of Heruka body mandala you then need to perform a fire puja, or burning offering. This practice and its explanation can be found in the book *Essence of Vajrayana*. In this way your close retreat of Heruka body mandala will be completed. Until the fire puja is completed you should engage in at least two sessions of *The Yoga of Buddha Heruka* each day, making torma offerings in the last session.

Once you have completed the close retreat of Heruka body mandala you can engage in the practice of Heruka body mandala self-initiation, which can be found in the sadhana *Union of No More Learning*. It is most important that whenever you recite the sadhana *The Yoga of Buddha Heruka* you should strongly concentrate on its meaning, free from distraction and impure motivation. Between sessions you should carefully read the commentary to this sadhana presented in the chapter *The Practice of Heruka Body Mandala*.

Geshe Kelsang Gyatso
April 2010

Blissful Journey

TORMA OFFERING

Having engaged in the practice of The Yoga of Buddha Heruka *from* Going for refuge *up to and including* Reciting the mantras, *now perform the torma offering.*

Blessing the inner offering

OM KHANDAROHI HUM HUM PHAT
OM SÖBHAWA SHUDDHA SARWA DHARMA SÖBHAWA
    SHUDDHO HAM
Everything becomes emptiness.

From the state of emptiness, from YAM comes wind, from RAM comes fire, from AH a grate of three human heads. Upon this from AH appears a broad and expansive skullcup. Inside from OM, KHAM, AM, TRAM, HUM come the five nectars; from LAM, MAM, PAM, TAM, BAM come the five meats, each marked by these letters. The wind blows, the fire blazes, and the substances inside the skullcup melt. Above them from HUM there arises a white, upside-down khatanga, which falls into the skullcup and melts whereby the substances take on the colour of mercury. Above them three rows of vowels and consonants, standing one above the other, transform into OM AH HUM. From these, light rays draw the nectar of exalted wisdom from the hearts of all the Tathagatas, Heroes and Yoginis of the ten directions. When this is added the contents increase and become vast. OM AH HUM   (3x)

Blessing the outer offerings

OM KHANDAROHI HUM HUM PHAT
OM SÖBHAWA SHUDDHA SARWA DHARMA SÖBHAWA
    SHUDDHO HAM
Everything becomes emptiness.

From the state of emptiness, from KAMs come broad and expansive skullcups, inside which from HUMs come water for drinking, water for bathing, water for the mouth, flowers, incense, lights, perfume, food and music. By nature emptiness, they have the aspect of the individual offering substances, and function as objects of enjoyment of the six senses to bestow special, uncontaminated bliss.

OM AHRGHAM AH HUM
OM PADÄM AH HUM
OM ÄNTZAMANAM AH HUM
OM VAJRA PUPE AH HUM
OM VAJRA DHUPE AH HUM
OM VAJRA DIWE AH HUM
OM VAJRA GÄNDHE AH HUM
OM VAJRA NEWIDE AH HUM
OM VAJRA SHAPTA AH HUM

Blessing the tormas

OM KHANDAROHI HUM HUM PHAT
OM SÖBHAWA SHUDDHA SARWA DHARMA SÖBHAWA
    SHUDDHO HAM
Everything becomes emptiness.

From the state of emptiness, from YAM comes wind, from
RAM comes fire, from AH a grate of three human heads.
Upon this from AH appears a broad and expansive skullcup.
Inside from OM, KHAM, AM, TRAM, HUM come the five
nectars; from LAM, MAM, PAM, TAM, BAM come the five
meats, each marked by these letters. The wind blows, the
fire blazes, and the substances inside the skullcup melt.
Above them from HUM there arises a white, upside-down
khatanga, which falls into the skullcup and melts whereby
the substances take on the colour of mercury. Above them
three rows of vowels and consonants, standing one above
the other, transform into OM AH HUM. From these, light
rays draw the nectar of exalted wisdom from the hearts of
all the Tathagatas, Heroes and Yoginis of the ten directions.
When this is added the contents increase and become vast.
OM AH HUM   (3x)

Inviting the guests of the tormas

PHAIM
Light rays radiate from the letter HUM on the sun seat
at my heart and invite to the space before me the entire
assembly of the Deities of Chakrasambara together with
his mundane retinues, such as the directional guardians
who reside in the eight charnel grounds.

OM AHRGHAM PARTITZA SÖHA
OM PADÄM PARTITZA SÖHA
OM VAJRA PUPE AH HUM SÖHA
OM VAJRA DHUPE AH HUM SÖHA

OM VAJRA DIWE AH HUM SÖHA
OM VAJRA GÄNDHE AH HUM SÖHA
OM VAJRA NEWIDE AH HUM SÖHA
OM VAJRA SHAPTA AH HUM SÖHA

From a white HUM in the tongue of each guest, there arises a white, three-pronged vajra, through which they partake of the essence of the torma by drawing it through straws of light the thickness of only a grain of barley.

Offering the principal torma

OM VAJRA AH RA LI HO: DZA HUM BAM HO: VAJRA DAKINI
  SAMAYA TÖN TRISHAYA HO   (3x)

With the first recitation, offer the torma to the Principal Father, with the second to the Principal Mother, and with the third to the four Yoginis, beginning in the east and offering counter-clockwise.

Offering the torma to the Deities of the heart wheel, speech wheel and body wheel

OM KARA KARA, KURU KURU, BÄNDHA BÄNDHA, TRASAYA
TrASAYA, KYOMBHAYA KYOMBHAYA, HROM HROM, HRAH
HRAH, PHAIM PHAIM, PHAT PHAT, DAHA DAHA, PATSA
PATSA, BHAKYA BHAKYA BASA RUDHI ÄNTRA MALA
WALAMBINE, GRIHANA GRIHANA SAPTA PATALA GATA
BHUDZAMGAM SARWAMPA TARDZAYA TARDZAYA,
AKANDYA AKANDYA, HRIM HRIM, GYÖN GYÖN, KYAMA
KYAMA, HAM HAM, HIM HIM, HUM HUM, KILI KILI, SILI
SILI, HILI HILI, DHILI DHILI, HUM HUM PHAT

Offering the torma to the Deities of the commitment wheel

OM VAJRA AH RA LI HO: DZA HUM BAM HO: VAJRA DAKINI
SAMAYA TÖN TRISHAYA HO   (2x)

Outer offerings

OM AHRGHAM PARTITZA SÖHA
OM PADÄM PARTITZA SÖHA
OM VAJRA PUPE AH HUM SÖHA
OM VAJRA DHUPE AH HUM SÖHA
OM VAJRA DIWE AH HUM SÖHA
OM VAJRA GÄNDHE AH HUM SÖHA
OM VAJRA NEWIDE AH HUM SÖHA
OM VAJRA SHAPTA AH HUM SÖHA

OM AH VAJRA ADARSHE HUM
OM AH VAJRA WINI HUM
OM AH VAJRA GÄNDHE HUM
OM AH VAJRA RASE HUM
OM AH VAJRA PARSHE HUM
OM AH VAJRA DHARME HUM

Inner offering

OM HUM BAM RIM RIM LIM LIM, KAM KHAM GAM GHAM
NGAM, TSAM TSHAM DZAM DZHAM NYAM, TrAM THrAM
DrAM DHrAM NAM, TAM THAM DAM DHAM NAM, PAM
PHAM BAM BHAM, YAM RAM LAM WAM, SHAM KAM SAM
HAM HUM HUM PHAT OM AH HUM

Secret and thatness offerings

Through Father and Mother uniting in embrace, all the
principal and retinue Deities enjoy a special experience
of great bliss and emptiness.

Eight lines of praise to the Father

OM I prostrate to the Blessed One, Lord of the Heroes
    HUM HUM PHAT
OM To you with a brilliance equal to the fire of the great aeon
    HUM HUM PHAT
OM To you with an inexhaustible topknot HUM HUM PHAT
OM To you with a fearsome face and bared fangs HUM
    HUM PHAT
OM To you whose thousand arms blaze with light HUM
    HUM PHAT
OM To you who hold an axe, an uplifted noose, a spear
    and a khatanga HUM HUM PHAT
OM To you who wear a tiger-skin garment HUM HUM PHAT
OM I bow to you whose great smoke-coloured body dispels
    obstructions HUM HUM PHAT

Eight lines of praise to the Mother

OM I prostrate to Vajravarahi, the Blessed Mother HUM
    HUM PHAT
OM To the Superior and powerful Knowledge Lady
    unconquered by the three realms HUM HUM PHAT
OM To you who destroy all fears of evil spirits with your
    great vajra HUM HUM PHAT
OM To you with controlling eyes who remain as the vajra
    seat unconquered by others HUM HUM PHAT
OM To you whose wrathful fierce form desiccates Brahma
    HUM HUM PHAT
OM To you who terrify and dry up demons, conquering
    those in other directions HUM HUM PHAT
OM To you who conquer all those who make us dull, rigid
    and confused HUM HUM PHAT
OM I bow to Vajravarahi, the Great Mother, the Dakini
    consort who fulfils all desires HUM HUM PHAT

Requesting the fulfilment of wishes

You who have destroyed equally attachment to samsara
and solitary peace, as well as all conceptualizations,
Who see all things that exist throughout space;
O Protector endowed with strong compassion, may I be
blessed by the waters of your compassion,
And may the Dakinis take me into their loving care.

Offering the torma to the mundane Deities

The directional guardians, regional guardians, nagas and
so forth, who reside in the eight great charnel grounds,
instantly enter into the clear light, and arise in the form of
the Deities of Heruka in the aspect of Father and Mother.
From a white HUM in the tongue of each guest, there
arises a white, three-pronged vajra, through which they
partake of the essence of the torma by drawing it through
straws of light the thickness of only a grain of barley.

OM KHA KHA, KHAHI KHAHI, SARWA YAKYA RAKYASA,
BHUTA, TRETA, PISHATSA, UNATA, APAMARA, VAJRA
DAKA, DAKI NÄDAYA, IMAM BALING GRIHANTU, SAMAYA
RAKYANTU, MAMA SARWA SIDDHI METRA YATZANTU,
YATIPAM, YATETAM, BHUDZATA, PIWATA, DZITRATA,
MATI TRAMATA, MAMA SARWA KATAYA, SÄDSUKHAM
BISHUDHAYE, SAHAYEKA BHAWÄNTU, HUM HUM PHAT
PHAT SÖHA   (2x)

*With the first recitation, offer the torma to the guests in the
cardinal directions, and with the second to the guests in the
intermediate directions.*

Outer offerings

OM AHRGHAM PARTITZA SÖHA
OM PADÄM PARTITZA SÖHA
OM VAJRA PUPE AH HUM SÖHA

OM VAJRA DHUPE AH HUM SÖHA
OM VAJRA DIWE AH HUM SÖHA
OM VAJRA GÄNDHE AH HUM SÖHA
OM VAJRA NEWIDE AH HUM SÖHA
OM VAJRA SHAPTA AH HUM SÖHA

Inner offering

To the mouths of the directional guardians, regional guardians, nagas and so forth, OM AH HUM

Requests

You the entire gathering of gods,
The entire gathering of nagas,
The entire gathering of givers of harm,
The entire gathering of cannibals,
The entire gathering of evil spirits,
The entire gathering of hungry ghosts,
The entire gathering of flesh-eaters,
The entire gathering of crazy-makers,
The entire gathering of forgetful-makers,
The entire gathering of dakas,
The entire gathering of female spirits,
All of you without exception
Please come here and listen to me.
O Glorious attendants, swift as thought,
Who have taken oaths and heart commitments
To guard the doctrine and benefit living beings,
Who subdue the malevolent and destroy the dark forces
With terrifying forms and inexhaustible wrath,
Who grant results to yogic actions,
And who have inconceivable powers and blessings,
To you eight types of guest I prostrate.

I request all of you together with your consorts, children
    and servants

To grant me the fortune of all the attainments.
May I and other practitioners
Have good health, long life, power,
Glory, fame, fortune,
And extensive enjoyments.
Please grant me the attainments
Of pacifying, increasing, controlling and wrathful actions.
O Guardians, always assist me.
Eradicate all untimely death, sicknesses,
Harm from spirits and hindrances.
Eliminate bad dreams,
Ill omens and bad actions.

May there be happiness in the world, may the years be good,
May crops increase, and may Dharma flourish.
May all goodness and happiness come about,
And may all wishes be accomplished.

At this point you can, if you wish, make the tsog offering. This starts on page 305.

Purifying any mistakes made during this practice with the hundred-letter mantra of Heruka

OM VAJRA HERUKA SAMAYA, MANU PALAYA, HERUKA
TENO PATITA, DRIDHO ME BHAWA, SUTO KAYO ME BHAWA,
SUPO KAYO ME BHAWA, ANURAKTO ME BHAWA, SARWA
SIDDHI ME PRAYATZA, SARWA KARMA SUTZA ME, TZITAM
SHRIYAM KURU HUM, HA HA HA HA HO BHAGAWÄN,
VAJRA HERUKA MA ME MUNTSA, HERUKA BHAWA, MAHA
SAMAYA SATTÖ AH HUM PHAT

OM YOGA SHUDDHA SARWA DHARMA YOGA SHUDDHO HAM

VAJRA MU

The mundane beings return to their own places, and the
assembly of the Deities of the in-front-generation dissolve
into me.

Dissolution and generating the action Deities

The charnel grounds and protection circle dissolve into the celestial mansion. The celestial mansion dissolves into the Deities of the commitment wheel. They dissolve into the Deities of the body wheel. They dissolve into the Deities of the speech wheel. They dissolve into the Deities of the heart wheel. They dissolve into the four Yoginis of the great bliss wheel. They dissolve into me, the Principal Deity Father and Mother, the nature of the white and red indestructible drop. I, the Principal Deity Father and Mother, also melt into light and dissolve into the letter HUM at my heart, in nature the emptiness of the Dharmakaya.

From the state of emptiness our world arises as Heruka's Pure Land, Keajra. I and all sentient beings arise as the Blessed One Heruka, with a blue-coloured body, one face, and two arms embracing Vajravarahi.

The session should be concluded by reciting the Dedication *and remaining prayers from the sadhana* The Yoga of Buddha Heruka.

THE TSOG OFFERING TO HERUKA BODY MANDALA

Blessing the outer and inner offerings, the environment and beings, and the substances of the tsog offering

OM AH HUM   (3x)

By nature exalted wisdom, having the aspect of the inner offering and the individual offering substances, and functioning as objects of enjoyment of the six senses to generate a special, exalted wisdom of bliss and emptiness, inconceivable clouds of outer, inner and secret offerings, commitment substances and attractive offerings, cover all the ground and fill the whole of space.

EH MA HO Great manifestation of exalted wisdom.
All realms are vajra realms
And all places are great vajra palaces
Endowed with vast clouds of Samantabhadra's offerings,
An abundance of all desired enjoyments.
All beings are actual Heroes and Heroines.
Everything is immaculately pure,
Without even the name of mistaken impure appearance.

HUM All elaborations are completely pacified in the state of the Truth Body. The wind blows and the fire blazes. Above, on a grate of three human heads, AH within a qualified skullcup, OM the individual substances blaze. Above these stand OM AH HUM, each ablaze with its brilliant colour. Through the wind blowing and the fire blazing, the substances melt. Boiling, they swirl in a great vapour. Masses of light rays from the three letters radiate to the ten directions and invite the three vajras together with nectars. These dissolve separately into the three letters. Melting into nectar, they blend with the mixture. Purified, transformed and increased,

EH MA HO They become a blazing ocean of magnificent
delights.

OM AH HUM   (3x)

Inviting the guests of the tsog offering

PHAIM
From the sacred palace of the Dharmakaya,
Great Master, holder of the supreme lineage of the Vajrayana,
Who fulfil our hopes for all the attainments,
O Assembly of root and lineage Gurus, please come to this
place.

From the twenty-four holy places throughout the world,
O Glorious Heruka, whose nature is the compassion of all
the Buddhas,
And all the Heroes and Heroines of these places,
Please come here to bestow the attainments that we long for.

From the pure and impure lands of the ten directions,
O Assembly of Yidams, Buddhas, Bodhisattvas and Dharma
Protectors,
And all the beings of samsara and nirvana,
Please come here as guests of this tsog offering.

OM GURU VAJRADHARA CHAKRASAMBARA SÄMANDALA
DEWA SARWA BUDDHA BODHISATTÖ SAPARIWARA EH
HAYE HI VAJRA SAMAYA DZA DZA

PÄMA KAMALAYE TÖN

Making the tsog offering

HO This ocean of tsog offering of uncontaminated nectar,
Blessed by concentration, mantra and mudra,
I offer to please my kind root Guru, Guru Sumati Buddha
Heruka.
OM AH HUM

Delighted by enjoying these magnificent objects of desire,
EH MA HO
Please bless me so that I may attain outer and inner
Dakini Land.

HO This ocean of tsog offering of uncontaminated nectar,
Blessed by concentration, mantra and mudra,
I offer to please the four Yoginis of the great bliss wheel.
OM AH HUM
Delighted by enjoying these magnificent objects of desire,
EH MA HO
Please bless me so that I may attain spontaneous great bliss.

HO This ocean of tsog offering of uncontaminated nectar,
Blessed by concentration, mantra and mudra,
I offer to please the Heroes and Heroines of the vajra mind.
OM AH HUM
Delighted by enjoying these magnificent objects of desire,
EH MA HO
Please bless me so that I may experience delight with the
messengers of the vajra mind family.

HO This ocean of tsog offering of uncontaminated nectar,
Blessed by concentration, mantra and mudra,
I offer to please the Heroes and Heroines of the vajra speech.
OM AH HUM
Delighted by enjoying these magnificent objects of desire,
EH MA HO
Please bless me so that I may experience delight with the
messengers of the vajra speech family.

HO This ocean of tsog offering of uncontaminated nectar,
Blessed by concentration, mantra and mudra,
I offer to please the Heroes and Heroines of the vajra body.
OM AH HUM
Delighted by enjoying these magnificent objects of desire,
EH MA HO

Please bless me so that I may experience delight with the
messengers of the vajra body family.

HO This ocean of tsog offering of uncontaminated nectar,
Blessed by concentration, mantra and mudra,
I offer to please the Deities of the commitment wheel.
OM AH HUM
Delighted by enjoying these magnificent objects of desire,
EH MA HO
Please bless me so that I may pacify all obstacles.

HO This ocean of tsog offering of uncontaminated nectar,
Blessed by concentration, mantra and mudra,
I offer to please all other Yidams, Buddhas, Bodhisattvas
    and Dharma Protectors.
OM AH HUM
Delighted by enjoying these magnificent objects of desire,
EH MA HO
Please bless me so that I may attain all the realizations of
    Sutra and Tantra.

HO This ocean of tsog offering of uncontaminated nectar,
Blessed by concentration, mantra and mudra,
I offer to please the assembly of mother sentient beings.
OM AH HUM
Delighted by enjoying these magnificent objects of desire,
EH MA HO
May suffering and mistaken appearance be pacified.

Outer offerings

OM AHRGHAM PARTITZA SÖHA
OM PADÄM PARTITZA SÖHA
OM VAJRA PUPE AH HUM SÖHA
OM VAJRA DHUPE AH HUM SÖHA
OM VAJRA DIWE AH HUM SÖHA
OM VAJRA GÄNDHE AH HUM SÖHA

OM VAJRA NEWIDE AH HUM SÖHA
OM VAJRA SHAPTA AH HUM SÖHA

Inner offering

OM HUM BAM RIM RIM LIM LIM, KAM KHAM GAM GHAM
NGAM, TSAM TSHAM DZAM DZHAM NYAM, TrAM THrAM
DrAM DHrAM NAM, TAM THAM DAM DHAM NAM, PAM
PHAM BAM BHAM, YAM RAM LAM WAM, SHAM KAM SAM
HAM HUM HUM PHAT OM AH HUM

Secret and thatness offerings

Through Father and Mother uniting in embrace, all the
principal and retinue Deities enjoy a special experience
of great bliss and emptiness.

Eight lines of praise to the Father

OM I prostrate to the Blessed One, Lord of the Heroes
    HUM HUM PHAT
OM To you with a brilliance equal to the fire of the great
    aeon HUM HUM PHAT
OM To you with an inexhaustible topknot HUM HUM PHAT
OM To you with a fearsome face and bared fangs HUM
    HUM PHAT
OM To you whose thousand arms blaze with light HUM
    HUM PHAT
OM To you who hold an axe, an uplifted noose, a spear
    and a khatanga HUM HUM PHAT
OM To you who wear a tiger-skin garment HUM HUM PHAT
OM I bow to you whose great smoke-coloured body dispels
    obstructions HUM HUM PHAT

Eight lines of praise to the Mother

OM I prostrate to Vajravarahi, the Blessed Mother HUM
   HUM PHAT
OM To the Superior and powerful Knowledge Lady
   unconquered by the three realms HUM HUM PHAT
OM To you who destroy all fears of evil spirits with your
   great vajra HUM HUM PHAT
OM To you with controlling eyes who remain as the vajra
   seat unconquered by others HUM HUM PHAT
OM To you whose wrathful fierce form desiccates Brahma
   HUM HUM PHAT
OM To you who terrify and dry up demons, conquering
   those in other directions HUM HUM PHAT
OM To you who conquer all those who make us dull, rigid
   and confused HUM HUM PHAT
OM I bow to Vajravarahi, the Great Mother, the Dakini
   consort who fulfils all desires HUM HUM PHAT

Making the tsog offering to the Vajra Master

EH MA HO Great circle of tsog!
O Great Hero we understand
That, following in the path of the Sugatas of the three times,
You are the source of all attainments.
Forsaking all minds of conceptualization
Please continuously enjoy this circle of tsog.
AH LA LA HO

The Master's reply

OM With a nature inseparable from the three vajras
I generate as the Guru-Deity.
AH This nectar of uncontaminated exalted wisdom and bliss,
HUM Without stirring from bodhichitta,
I partake to delight the Deities dwelling in my body.
AH HO MAHA SUKHA

Song of the Spring Queen

HUM All you Tathagatas,
Heroes, Yoginis,
Dakas and Dakinis,
To all of you I make this request:
O Heruka who delight in great bliss,
You engage in the Union of spontaneous bliss,
By attending the Lady intoxicated with bliss
And enjoying in accordance with the rituals.
AH LA LA, LA LA HO, AH I AH, AH RA LI HO
May the assembly of stainless Dakinis
Look with loving affection and accomplish all deeds.

HUM All you Tathagatas,
Heroes, Yoginis,
Dakas and Dakinis,
To all of you I make this request:
With a mind completely aroused by great bliss
And a body in a dance of constant motion,
I offer to the hosts of Dakinis
The great bliss from enjoying the lotus of the mudra.
AH LA LA, LA LA HO, AH I AH, AH RA LI HO
May the assembly of stainless Dakinis
Look with loving affection and accomplish all deeds.

HUM All you Tathagatas,
Heroes, Yoginis,
Dakas and Dakinis,
To all of you I make this request:
You who dance with a beautiful and peaceful manner,
O Blissful Protector and the hosts of Dakinis,
Please come here before me and grant me your blessings,
And bestow upon me spontaneous great bliss.
AH LA LA, LA LA HO, AH I AH, AH RA LI HO
May the assembly of stainless Dakinis
Look with loving affection and accomplish all deeds.

HUM All you Tathagatas,
Heroes, Yoginis,
Dakas and Dakinis,
To all of you I make this request:
You who have the characteristic of the liberation of great bliss,
Do not say that deliverance can be gained in one lifetime
Through various ascetic practices having abandoned great bliss,
But that great bliss resides in the centre of the supreme lotus.
AH LA LA, LA LA HO, AH I AH, AH RA LI HO
May the assembly of stainless Dakinis
Look with loving affection and accomplish all deeds.

HUM All you Tathagatas,
Heroes, Yoginis,
Dakas and Dakinis,
To all of you I make this request:
Like a lotus born from the centre of a swamp,
This method, though born from attachment, is unstained by the
    faults of attachment.
O Supreme Dakini, through the bliss of your lotus,
Please quickly bring liberation from the bonds of samsara.
AH LA LA, LA LA HO, AH I AH, AH RA LI HO
May the assembly of stainless Dakinis
Look with loving affection and accomplish all deeds.

HUM All you Tathagatas,
Heroes, Yoginis,
Dakas and Dakinis,
To all of you I make this request:
Just as the essence of honey in the honey source
Is drunk by swarms of bees from all directions,
So through your broad lotus with six characteristics
Please bring satisfaction with the taste of great bliss.
AH LA LA, LA LA HO, AH I AH, AH RA LI HO
May the assembly of stainless Dakinis
Look with loving affection and accomplish all deeds.

Blessing the remaining tsog offering

HUM Impure mistaken appearances are purified in emptiness,
AH Great nectar accomplished from exalted wisdom,
OM It becomes a vast ocean of desired enjoyment.
OM AH HUM   (3x)

Giving the remaining tsog offering to the spirits

HO This ocean of remaining tsog offering of
     uncontaminated nectar,
Blessed by concentration, mantra and mudra,
I offer to please the assembly of oath-bound guardians.
OM AH HUM
Delighted by enjoying these magnificent objects of desire,
EH MA HO
Please perform perfect actions to help practitioners.

Send out the remainder of the tsog offering to the spirits.

HO
O Guests of the remainder together with your retinues
Please enjoy this ocean of remaining tsog offering.
May those who spread the precious doctrine,
The holders of the doctrine, their benefactors and others,
And especially I and other practitioners
Have good health, long life, power,
Glory, fame, fortune,
And extensive enjoyments.
Please grant me the attainments
Of pacifying, increasing, controlling and wrathful actions.
You who are bound by oaths please protect me
And help me to accomplish all the attainments.
Eradicate all untimely death, sicknesses,
Harm from spirits and hindrances.
Eliminate bad dreams,
Ill omens and bad actions.

May there be happiness in the world, may the years
  be good,
May crops increase, and may Dharma flourish.
May all goodness and happiness come about,
And may all wishes be accomplished.

By the force of this bountiful giving
May I become a Buddha for the sake of living beings;
And through my generosity may I liberate
All those not liberated by previous Buddhas.

Colophon: This sadhana was compiled from traditional
sources by Venerable Geshe Kelsang Gyatso, April 2010.

Appendix VII

Quick Path to Great Bliss

VAJRAYOGINI SELF-GENERATION SADHANA

by Je Phabongkhapa

Introduction

The instructions on the Highest Yoga Tantra practice of Venerable Vajrayogini were taught by Buddha Vajradhara in the forty-seventh and forty-eighth chapters of the *Condensed Root Tantra of Heruka*. This particular lineage of instructions, the Narokhacho lineage, was passed directly from Vajrayogini to Naropa, and from him through an unbroken lineage of realized practitioners to the present-day Teachers.

After Buddha Vajradharma had taught the practice he left the mandalas of Heruka and Vajrayogini intact in twenty-four auspicious places in this world. Thus even to this day there are countless manifestations of Vajrayogini in this world who help sincere practitioners to gain realizations by blessing their mental continuum.

In many respects the practice of Vajrayogini is ideally suited to the present day. By relying upon this practice sincerely, with a good heart and a mind of faith, it is definitely possible to attain full enlightenment; but to accomplish such results we must practise the extensive sadhana regularly.

This particular sadhana, *Quick Path to Great Bliss*, was composed by the great Lama Phabongkha Rinpoche. Compared to other sadhanas it is not very long, but it contains all the essential practices of Secret Mantra. To practise the sadhana successfully we should first receive the empowerment of Vajrayogini, and then study authentic instructions on the practice such as those found in the commentary *Guide to Dakini Land*. This sadhana is suitable both for our regular daily practice and for retreat; and we can practise it alone or in a group.

Geshe Kelsang Gyatso
1985

Quick Path to Great Bliss

THE YOGA OF IMMEASURABLES

Going for refuge

In the space before me appear Guru Chakrasambara Father
and Mother, surrounded by the assembly of root and lineage
Gurus, Yidams, Three Jewels, Attendants and Protectors.

*Imagining yourself and all sentient beings going for refuge, recite
three times:*

I and all sentient beings, the migrators as extensive as
    space, from this time forth until we reach the essence
    of enlightenment,
Go for refuge to the glorious, sacred Gurus,
Go for refuge to the complete Buddhas, the Blessed Ones,
Go for refuge to the sacred Dharmas,
Go for refuge to the superior Sanghas.

(3x)

Generating bodhichitta

Generate bodhichitta and the four immeasurables while reciting three times:

Once I have attained the state of a complete Buddha, I shall free all sentient beings from the ocean of samsara's suffering and lead them to the bliss of full enlightenment. For this purpose I shall practise the stages of Vajrayogini's path.　　(3x)

Receiving blessings

Now with your palms pressed together, recite:

I prostrate and go for refuge to the Gurus and Three Precious Jewels. Please bless my mental continuum.

Due to reciting this:

The objects of refuge before me melt into the form of white, red and dark blue rays of light. These dissolve into me and I receive their blessings of body, speech and mind.

Instantaneous self-generation

In an instant I become Venerable Vajrayogini.

Blessing the inner offering

Purify the inner offering either with the mantra emanating from the four mouths or with the following:

OM KHANDAROHI HUM HUM PHAT
OM SÖBHAWA SHUDDHA SARWA DHARMA SÖBHAWA
　　SHUDDHO HAM
Everything becomes emptiness.

From the state of emptiness, from YAM comes wind, from RAM comes fire, from AH a grate of three human heads. Upon this from AH appears a broad and expansive skullcup.

Inside from OM, KHAM, AM, TRAM, HUM come the five
nectars; from LAM, MAM, PAM, TAM, BAM come the five
meats, each marked by these letters. The wind blows, the
fire blazes, and the substances inside the skullcup melt.
Above them from HUM there arises a white, upside-down
khatanga, which falls into the skullcup and melts whereby
the substances take on the colour of mercury. Above them three
rows of vowels and consonants, standing one above
the other, transform into OM AH HUM. From these, light
rays draw the nectar of exalted wisdom from the hearts of
all the Tathagatas, Heroes and Yoginis of the ten directions.
When this is added the contents increase and become vast.
OM AH HUM   (3x)

Blessing the outer offerings

*Now bless the two waters, flowers, incense, lights, perfume, food
and music.*

OM KHANDAROHI HUM HUM PHAT
OM SÖBHAWA SHUDDHA SARWA DHARMA SÖBHAWA
    SHUDDHO HAM
Everything becomes emptiness.

From the state of emptiness, from KAM come skullcup
vessels inside which from HUM come offering substances.
By nature emptiness, they have the aspect of the individual
offering substances, and function as objects of enjoyment
of the six senses to bestow special, uncontaminated bliss.

OM AHRGHAM AH HUM
OM PADÄM AH HUM
OM VAJRA PUPE AH HUM
OM VAJRA DHUPE AH HUM
OM VAJRA DIWE AH HUM
OM VAJRA GÄNDHE AH HUM
OM VAJRA NEWIDE AH HUM
OM VAJRA SHAPTA AH HUM

Meditation and recitation of Vajrasattva

On my crown, on a lotus and moon seat, sit Vajrasattva
Father and Mother embracing each other. They have
white-coloured bodies, one face and two hands, and hold
vajra and bell and curved knife and skullcup. The Father
is adorned with six mudras, the Mother with five. They sit
in the vajra and lotus postures. On a moon in his heart is a
HUM encircled by the mantra rosary. From this a stream of
white nectar descends, cleansing all sickness, spirits,
negativities and obstructions.

OM VAJRA HERUKA SAMAYA, MANU PALAYA, HERUKA
TENO PATITA, DRIDHO ME BHAWA, SUTO KAYO ME BHAWA,
SUPO KAYO ME BHAWA, ANURAKTO ME BHAWA, SARWA
SIDDHI ME PRAYATZA, SARWA KARMA SUTZA ME, TZITAM
SHRIYAM KURU HUM, HA HA HA HA HO BHAGAWÄN,
VAJRA HERUKA MA ME MUNTSA, HERUKA BHAWA, MAHA
SAMAYA SATTÖ AH HUM PHAT

Recite the mantra twenty-one times and then contemplate:

Vajrasattva Father and Mother dissolve into me and my
three doors become inseparable from the body, speech
and mind of Vajrasattva.

THE YOGA OF THE GURU

Visualization

In the space before me arising from the appearance of the
exalted wisdom of non-dual purity and clarity is a celestial
mansion which is square with four doorways, ornaments
and archways, and complete with all the essential features.
In the centre on a jewelled throne supported by eight great
lions, on a seat of a lotus of various colours, a sun and a
moon, sits my kind root Guru in the aspect of Buddha
Vajradharma. He has a red-coloured body, one face, and

two hands which are crossed at his heart and hold a vajra
and bell. His hair is tied up in a topknot and he sits with
his legs crossed in the vajra posture. He assumes the form
of a sixteen-year-old in the prime of his youth, adorned
with silks and all the bone and jewelled ornaments.

Beginning in front of him and circling counter-clockwise
are all the lineage Gurus from Buddha Vajradhara to my
root Guru. They are in the aspect of Hero Vajradharma
with red-coloured bodies, one face and two hands. Their
right hands play damarus which reverberate with the
sound of bliss and emptiness. Their left hands hold at their
hearts skullcups filled with nectar, and their left elbows
hold khatangas. They sit with their legs crossed in the
vajra posture. In the prime of their youth, they are
adorned with six bone ornaments.

The Principal and all of his retinue have at their foreheads
OM, at their throats AH, and at their hearts HUM. From the
HUM at their hearts light rays radiate and invite from their
natural abodes the Gurus, Yidams, hosts of mandala Deities,
and the assembly of Buddhas, Bodhisattvas, Heroes, Dakinis,
Dharmapalas and Protectors.

OM VAJRA SAMADZA DZA HUM BAM HO
Each becomes a nature which is the synthesis of all objects
of refuge.

Prostration

With your palms pressed together, recite:

Vajra Holder, my jewel-like Guru,
Through whose kindness I can accomplish
The state of great bliss in an instant,
At your lotus feet humbly I bow.

Offering goddesses emanate from my heart and perform the offerings.

Outer offerings

OM AHRGHAM PARTITZA SÖHA
OM PADÄM PARTITZA SÖHA
OM VAJRA PUPE AH HUM SÖHA
OM VAJRA DHUPE AH HUM SÖHA
OM VAJRA DIWE AH HUM SÖHA
OM VAJRA GÄNDHE AH HUM SÖHA
OM VAJRA NEWIDE AH HUM SÖHA
OM VAJRA SHAPTA AH HUM SÖHA

OM AH VAJRA ADARSHE HUM
OM AH VAJRA WINI HUM
OM AH VAJRA GÄNDHE HUM
OM AH VAJRA RASE HUM
OM AH VAJRA PARSHE HUM
OM AH VAJRA DHARME HUM

Inner offering

OM GURU VAJRA DHARMA SAPARIWARA OM AH HUM

Secret offering

Contemplate that innumerable knowledge goddesses such as Pemachen emanate from your heart and assume the form of Vajrayogini. Guru Father and Mother embrace and experience uncontaminated bliss.

And I offer most attractive illusory mudras,
A host of messengers born from places, born from mantra
    and spontaneously born,
With slender bodies, skilled in the sixty-four arts of love,
And possessing the splendour of youthful beauty.

Thatness offering

Remember that the three circles of the offering are indivisible bliss and emptiness.

I offer you the supreme, ultimate bodhichitta,
A great, exalted wisdom of spontaneous bliss free from
    obstructions,
Inseparable from the nature of all phenomena, the sphere
    of freedom from elaboration,
Effortless, and beyond words, thoughts and expressions.

Offering our spiritual practice

I go for refuge to the Three Jewels
And confess individually all negative actions.
I rejoice in the virtues of all beings
And promise to accomplish a Buddha's enlightenment.

I go for refuge until I am enlightened
To Buddha, Dharma and the Supreme Assembly,
And to accomplish the aims of myself and others
I shall generate the mind of enlightenment.

Having generated the mind of supreme enlightenment,
I shall invite all sentient beings to be my guests
And engage in the pleasing, supreme practices of
    enlightenment.
May I attain Buddhahood to benefit migrators.

Kusali tsog offering

My own mind, the powerful Lady of Dakini Land, the size
of only a thumb, leaves through the crown of my head and
comes face to face with my root Guru. Once again I return
and, slicing the skull from my old body, place it upon a grate
of three human heads which has arisen instantaneously. I
chop up the rest of my flesh, blood and bones, and heap it

inside. By staring with wide open eyes I purify, transform
and increase it into an ocean of nectar.
OM AH HUM HA HO HRIH   (3x)

Innumerable offering goddesses holding skullcups emanate
from my heart. With the skullcups they scoop up nectar
and offer it to the guests, who partake by drawing it
through their tongues which are straws of vajra-light.

I offer this nectar of commitment substance
To my root Guru, the nature of the four [Buddha] bodies;
May you be pleased.
OM AH HUM   (7x)

I offer this nectar of commitment substance
To the lineage Gurus, the source of attainments;
May you be pleased.
OM AH HUM

I offer this nectar of commitment substance
To the assembly of Gurus, Yidams, Three Jewels and
    Protectors;
May you be pleased.
OM AH HUM

I offer this nectar of commitment substance
To the guardians who reside in the local places and
    in the regions;
May you assist me.
OM AH HUM

I offer this nectar of commitment substance
To all sentient beings in the six realms and the
    intermediate state;
May you be freed.
OM AH HUM

Through this offering all the guests are satiated with an
   uncontaminated bliss
And the sentient beings attain the Truth Body free from
   obstructions.
The three circles of the offering are the nature of non-dual
   bliss and emptiness,
Beyond words, thoughts and expressions.

Offering the mandala

OM VAJRA BHUMI AH HUM
Great and powerful golden ground,
OM VAJRA REKHE AH HUM
At the edge the iron fence stands around the outer circle.
In the centre Mount Meru the king of mountains,
Around which are four continents:
In the east, Purvavideha, in the south, Jambudipa,
In the west, Aparagodaniya, in the north, Uttarakuru.
Each has two sub-continents:
Deha and Videha, Tsamara and Abatsamara,
Satha and Uttaramantrina, Kurava and Kaurava.
The mountain of jewels, the wish-granting tree,
The wish-granting cow, and the harvest unsown.
The precious wheel, the precious jewel,
The precious queen, the precious minister,
The precious elephant, the precious supreme horse,
The precious general, and the great treasure vase.
The goddess of beauty, the goddess of garlands,
The goddess of music, the goddess of dance,
The goddess of flowers, the goddess of incense,
The goddess of light, and the goddess of scent.
The sun and the moon, the precious umbrella,
The banner of victory in every direction.
In the centre all treasures of both gods and men,
An excellent collection with nothing left out.
I offer this to you my kind root Guru and lineage Gurus,

To all of you sacred and glorious Gurus;
Please accept with compassion for migrating beings,
And having accepted please grant us your blessings.

O Treasure of Compassion, my Refuge and Protector,
I offer you the mountain, continents, precious objects,
    treasure vase, sun and moon,
Which have arisen from my aggregates, sources and
    elements
As aspects of the exalted wisdom of spontaneous bliss
    and emptiness.

I offer without any sense of loss
The objects that give rise to my attachment, hatred and
    confusion,
My friends, enemies and strangers, our bodies and
    enjoyments;
Please accept these and bless me to be released directly
    from the three poisons.

IDAM GURU RATNA MANDALAKAM NIRYATAYAMI

Requesting the lineage Gurus

Vajradharma, Lord of the family of the ocean of
    Conquerors,
Vajrayogini, supreme Mother of the Conquerors,
Naropa, powerful Son of the Conquerors,
I request you, please bestow the spontaneously born
    exalted wisdom.

Pamtingpa, holder of the explanations of the great secrets
    for disciples,
Sherab Tseg, you are a treasure of all the precious secrets,
Malgyur Lotsawa, lord of the ocean of Secret Mantra,
I request you, please bestow the spontaneously born
    exalted wisdom.

Great Sakya Lama, you are powerful Vajradhara,
Venerable Sonam Tsemo, supreme vajra son,
Dragpa Gyaltsen, crown ornament of the vajra holders,
I request you, please bestow the spontaneously born
  exalted wisdom.

Great Sakya Pandita, master scholar of the Land of the
  Snows,
Drogon Chogyal Pagpa, crown ornament of all beings of
  the three grounds,
Shangton Choje, holder of the Sakya doctrine,
I request you, please bestow the spontaneously born
  exalted wisdom.

Nasa Dragpugpa, powerful accomplished one,
Sonam Gyaltsen, navigator of scholars and supremely
  accomplished ones,
Yarlungpa, lord of the whispered lineage of the family of
  accomplished ones,
I request you, please bestow the spontaneously born
  exalted wisdom.

Gyalwa Chog, refuge and protector of all migrators, both
  myself and others,
Jamyang Namka, you are a great being,
Lodro Gyaltsen, great being and lord of the Dharma,
I request you, please bestow the spontaneously born
  exalted wisdom.

Jetsun Doringpa, you are unequalled in kindness,
Tenzin Losel, you have practised in accordance with the [Guru's]
  words,
Kyentse, the expounder of the great, secret lineage of
  words,
I request you, please bestow the spontaneously born
  exalted wisdom.

Labsum Gyaltsen, holder of the mantra families,
Glorious Wangchug Rabten, all-pervading lord of the
　　hundred families,
Jetsun Kangyurpa, principal of the families,
I request you, please bestow the spontaneously born
　　exalted wisdom.

Shaluwa, all-pervading lord of the ocean of mandalas,
Kyenrabje, principal of all the mandalas,
Morchenpa, lord of the circle of mandalas,
I request you, please bestow the spontaneously born
　　exalted wisdom.

Nesarpa, navigator of the ocean of whispered lineages,
Losel Phuntsog, lord of the whispered lineages,
Tenzin Trinlay, scholar who furthered the whispered
　　lineages,
I request you, please bestow the spontaneously born
　　exalted wisdom.

Kangyurpa, all-pervading lord upholding the Ganden
　　doctrine,
Ganden Dargyay, friend of migrators in degenerate
　　times,
Dharmabhadra, holder of the Ganden tradition,
I request you, please bestow the spontaneously born
　　exalted wisdom.

Losang Chopel, lord of the Sutras and Tantras,
You have completed the essence of the paths of all the
　　Sutras and Tantras.
Jigme Wangpo, scholar who furthered the Sutras and
　　Tantras,
I request you, please bestow the spontaneously born
　　exalted wisdom.

Dechen Nyingpo, you have the blessings of Naropa
To explain perfectly in accordance with Naropa

The essence of the excellent ripening and liberating paths
  of the Naro Dakini,
I request you, please bestow the spontaneously born
  exalted wisdom.

Losang Yeshe, Vajradhara,
You are a treasury of instructions on the ripening and
  liberating [paths] of the Vajra Queen,
The supreme, quick path for attaining the vajra state,
I request you, please bestow the spontaneously born
  exalted wisdom.

Kelsang Gyatso, you have completed all the profound
  and essential exalted states,
You are the compassionate Refuge and Protector of
  mother sentient beings,
You reveal the unmistaken path,
I request you, please bestow the spontaneously born
  exalted wisdom.

My kind root Guru, Vajradharma,
You are the embodiment of all the Conquerors,
Who grant the blessings of all Buddhas' speech,
I request you, please bestow the spontaneously born
  exalted wisdom.

Please bless me so that through the force of meditation
On the Dakini yoga of the profound generation stage,
And the central channel yoga of completion stage,
I may generate the exalted wisdom of spontaneous
  great bliss and attain the enlightened Dakini state.

Receiving the blessings of the four empowerments

I request you O Guru incorporating all objects of refuge,
Please grant me your blessings,
Please grant me the four empowerments completely,
And bestow on me, please, the state of the four bodies.   (3x)

Contemplate that as a result of your requests:

White light rays and nectars radiate from the OM at the
 forehead of my Guru.
They dissolve into my forehead, purifying the negativities
 and obstructions of my body.
I receive the vase empowerment, and the blessings of my
 Guru's body enter my body.

Red light rays and nectars radiate from the AH at the
 throat of my Guru.
They dissolve into my throat, purifying the negativities
 and obstructions of my speech.
I receive the secret empowerment, and the blessings of my
 Guru's speech enter my speech.

Blue light rays and nectars radiate from the HUM at the
 heart of my Guru.
They dissolve into my heart, purifying the negativities
 and obstructions of my mind.
I receive the wisdom-mudra empowerment, and the
 blessings of my Guru's mind enter my mind.

White, red and blue light rays and nectars radiate from
 the letters at my Guru's three places.
They dissolve into my three places, purifying the
 negativities and obstructions of my body, speech
 and mind.
I receive the fourth empowerment, the precious word
 empowerment, and the blessings of my Guru's body,
 speech and mind enter my body, speech and mind.

Brief request

I request you my precious Guru, the essence of all Buddhas
of the three times, please bless my mental continuum.

(3x)

Absorbing the Gurus

Requested in this way, the encircling lineage Gurus
dissolve into my root Guru in the centre. My root Guru
too, out of affection for me, melts into the form of red
light and, entering through the crown of my head, mixes
inseparably with my mind in the aspect of a red letter
BAM at my heart.

THE YOGA OF SELF-GENERATION

Bringing death into the path of the Truth Body

This very letter BAM expands and spreads to the ends
of space whereby all worlds and their beings become the
nature of bliss and emptiness. Once again, contracting
gradually from the edges, it becomes an extremely minute
letter BAM which dissolves in stages from the bottom up
into the nada. Then even the nada disappears and becomes
the Truth Body of inseparable bliss and emptiness.
OM SHUNYATA GYANA VAJRA SÖBHAWA ÄMAKO HAM

Bringing the intermediate state into the path of the Enjoyment Body

From the state of emptiness where all appearance has
gathered like this there appears a red letter BAM standing
upright in space, in essence an aspect of my own mind,
the exalted wisdom of non-dual bliss and emptiness.

Bringing rebirth into the path of the Emanation Body

From the state of emptiness, from EH EH comes a red
phenomena source, a double tetrahedron. Inside from AH
comes a moon mandala, white with a shade of red. Upon
this standing in a circle counter-clockwise rests the mantra
OM OM OM SARWA BUDDHA DAKINIYE VAJRA WARNANIYE
VAJRA BEROTZANIYE HUM HUM HUM PHAT PHAT PHAT SÖHA.

I, the letter BAM in space, see the moon and, motivated to take rebirth in its centre, enter the centre of the moon.

Light rays radiate from the moon, letter BAM, and mantra rosary making all worlds and beings of samsara and nirvana into the nature of Venerable Vajrayogini. These gather back and dissolve into the letter BAM and mantra rosary which change completely into the supported and supporting mandala, fully and all at once.

Checking meditation on the mandala and the beings within it

Furthermore, there is the vajra ground, fence, tent and canopy, outside of which a mass of five-coloured fires blaze, swirling counter-clockwise. Inside these is the circle of the eight great charnel grounds, the Ferocious One and so forth. In the centre of these is a red phenomena source, a double tetrahedron, with its broad neck facing upwards and its fine tip pointing downwards. Except for the front and back, each of the other four corners is marked by a pink joy swirl whirling counter-clockwise.

Inside the phenomena source, in the centre of an eight-petalled lotus of various colours, is a sun mandala. Upon this I arise in the form of Venerable Vajrayogini. My outstretched right leg treads on the breast of red Kalarati. My bent left leg treads on the head of black Bhairawa, which is bent backwards. I have a red-coloured body which shines with a brilliance like that of the fire of the aeon. I have one face, two hands and three eyes looking towards the Pure Land of the Dakinis. My right hand, outstretched and pointing downwards, holds a curved knife marked with a vajra. My left holds up a skullcup filled with blood which I partake of with my upturned mouth. My left shoulder holds a khatanga marked with a vajra from which hang a damaru, bell and triple banner. My black

hair hanging straight covers my back down to my waist.
In the prime of my youth, my desirous breasts are full and
I show the manner of generating bliss. My head is adorned
with five human skulls and I wear a necklace of fifty
human skulls. Naked, I am adorned with five mudras
and stand in the centre of a blazing fire of exalted wisdom.

THE YOGA OF PURIFYING MIGRATORS

At my heart inside a red phenomena source, a double
tetrahedron, is a moon mandala. In the centre of this is
a letter BAM encircled by a mantra rosary. From these
light rays radiate, leaving through the pores of my skin.
Touching all sentient beings of the six realms, they purify
their negativities and obstructions together with their
imprints and transform them all into the form of
Vajrayogini.

THE YOGA OF BEING BLESSED BY
HEROES AND HEROINES

Meditation on the body mandala

At my heart, in the centre of a phenomena source and moon
seat, is a letter BAM which is the nature of the four elements.
By splitting it changes into the four letters YA, RA, LA, WA
which are the seeds of the four elements. They are the nature
of the heart channel petals of the four directions such as the
Desirous One. These transform starting from the left into
Lama, Khandarohi, Rupini and Dakini. In the centre, the
crescent moon, drop, and nada of the letter BAM, whose
nature is the union of my very subtle red and white drops,
transform into Venerable Vajrayogini.

Outside these in sequence are the channels such as the
Unchanging One of the twenty-four places of the body,
such as the hairline and crown, and the twenty-four

elements from which come the nails, teeth, and so forth. These channels and elements, which are by nature inseparable, become the nature of the twenty-four letters of the mantra, OM OM and so forth, standing in a circle counter-clockwise from the east. These transform into the eight Heroines of the heart family: Partzandi, Tzändriakiya, Parbhawatiya, Mahanasa, Biramatiya, Karwariya, Lamkeshöriya and Drumatzaya; the eight Heroines of the speech family: Airawatiya, Mahabhairawi, Bayubega, Surabhakiya, Shamadewi, Suwatre, Hayakarne and Khaganane; and the eight Heroines of the body family: Tzatrabega, Khandarohi, Shaundini, Tzatrawarmini, Subira, Mahabala, Tzatrawartini and Mahabire. These are the actual Yoginis who are non-dual with the Heroes of the twenty-four external places such as Puliramalaya. The channels and elements of the eight doors such as the mouth, by nature inseparable from the eight letters HUM HUM and so forth, transform into Kakase, Ulukase, Shönase, Shukarase, Yamadhathi, Yamaduti, Yamadangtrini and Yamamatani. They all have the bodily form of the Venerable Lady, complete with ornaments and details.

Absorbing the wisdom beings and mixing the three messengers

Perform the blazing mudra and recite:

PHAIM
Light rays radiate from the letter BAM at my heart and, leaving from between my eyebrows, go to the ten directions. They invite all the Tathagatas, Heroes and Yoginis of the ten directions in the aspect of Vajrayogini.
DZA HUM BAM HO

The wisdom beings are summoned, dissolve, remain firm and are delighted. Now with the lotus-turning mudra followed by the embracing mudra, recite:

OM YOGA SHUDDHA SARWA DHARMA YOGA SHUDDHO HAM
I am the nature of the yoga of the complete purity of all
phenomena.

Contemplate divine pride.

Putting on the armour

At places in my body arise moon mandalas upon which
at my navel is red OM BAM, Vajravarahi; at my heart blue
HAM YOM, Yamani; at my throat white HRIM MOM, Mohani;
at my forehead yellow HRIM HRIM, Sachalani; at my crown
green HUM HUM, Samtrasani; at all my limbs smoke-coloured
PHAT PHAT, essence of Chandika.

Granting empowerment and adorning the crown

PHAIM
Light rays radiate from the letter BAM at my heart and invite
the empowering Deities, the supported and supporting
mandala of Glorious Chakrasambara.

O, all you Tathagatas, please grant the empowerment.

Requested in this way, the eight Goddesses of the doorways
drive away hindrances, the Heroes recite auspicious verses,
the Heroines sing vajra songs, and the Rupavajras and so
forth make offerings. The Principal mentally resolves to
grant the empowerment and the four Mothers together with
Varahi, holding jewelled vases filled with the five nectars,
confer the empowerment through the crown of my head.

'Just as all the Tathagatas granted ablution
At the moment of [Buddha's] birth,
Likewise do we now grant ablution
With the pure water of the gods.

OM SARWA TATHAGATA ABHIKEKATA SAMAYA SHRIYE HUM'

Saying this, they grant the empowerment. My whole body is filled, all stains are purified, and the excess water remaining on my crown changes into Vairochana-Heruka, together with the Mother, who adorn my crown.

Offerings to the self-generation

If you are doing self-generation in conjunction with self-initiation it is necessary to bless the outer offerings at this point.

Offering goddesses emanate from my heart and perform the offerings.

Outer offerings

OM AHRGHAM PARTITZA SÖHA
OM PADÄM PARTITZA SÖHA
OM VAJRA PUPE AH HUM SÖHA
OM VAJRA DHUPE AH HUM SÖHA
OM VAJRA DIWE AH HUM SÖHA
OM VAJRA GÄNDHE AH HUM SÖHA
OM VAJRA NEWIDE AH HUM SÖHA
OM VAJRA SHAPTA AH HUM SÖHA

OM AH VAJRA ADARSHE HUM
OM AH VAJRA WINI HUM
OM AH VAJRA GÄNDHE HUM
OM AH VAJRA RASE HUM
OM AH VAJRA PARSHE HUM
OM AH VAJRA DHARME HUM

Inner offering

OM OM OM SARWA BUDDHA DAKINIYE VAJRA WARNANIYE VAJRA BEROTZANIYE HUM HUM HUM PHAT PHAT PHAT SÖHA OM AH HUM

Secret and thatness offerings

To perform the secret and thatness offerings either imagine:

I, Vajrayogini, stand in union with Chakrasambara, who has transformed from my khatanga, and generate spontaneous bliss and emptiness.

or imagine that as Vajrayogini you transform into Heruka and with divine pride perform the secret and thatness offerings:

With the clarity of Vajrayogini I give up my breasts and develop a penis. In the perfect place in the centre of my vagina the two walls transform into two bell-like testicles and the stamen into the penis itself. Thus I take on the form of Great Joy Heruka together with the Secret Mother Vajrayogini who is by nature the synthesis of all Dakinis.

From the sphere of the unobservability of the secret place of the Father, from a white HUM there arises a white, five-pronged vajra, and from a red BÄ there arises a red jewel with a yellow BÄ marking its tip.

From the sphere of the unobservability of the secret place of the Mother, from an AH there arises a red, three-petalled lotus, and from a white DÄ there arises a white stamen, signifying white bodhichitta, with a yellow DÄ marking its tip.

OM SHRI MAHA SUKHA VAJRA HE HE RU RU KAM AH
    HUM HUM PHAT SÖHA

Through Father and Mother being absorbed in union, the bodhichitta melts. When from my crown it reaches my throat [I experience] joy. When from my throat it reaches my heart [I experience] supreme joy. When from my heart it reaches my navel [I experience] extraordinary joy. When from my navel it reaches the tip of my jewel I generate a spontaneous exalted wisdom whereby I remain absorbed

in the concentration of inseparable bliss and emptiness.
Thus, through this bliss inseparably joined with emptiness
remaining in single-pointed absorption on the thatness
that is the lack of inherent existence of the three circles of
the offering, I delight in the secret and thatness offerings.

Then contemplate:

Once again I become Venerable Vajrayogini.

Eight lines of praise to the Mother

OM NAMO BHAGAWATI VAJRA VARAHI BAM HUM HUM PHAT
OM NAMO ARYA APARADZITE TRE LOKYA MATI BIYE SHÖRI
    HUM HUM PHAT
OM NAMA SARWA BUTA BHAYA WAHI MAHA VAJRE HUM
    HUM PHAT
OM NAMO VAJRA SANI ADZITE APARADZITE WASHAM
    KARANITRA HUM HUM PHAT
OM NAMO BHRAMANI SHOKANI ROKANI KROTE KARALENI
    HUM HUM PHAT
OM NAMA DRASANI MARANI PRABHE DANI PARADZAYE
    HUM HUM PHAT
OM NAMO BIDZAYE DZAMBHANI TAMBHANI MOHANI
    HUM HUM PHAT
OM NAMO VAJRA VARAHI MAHA YOGINI KAME SHÖRI KHAGE
    HUM HUM PHAT

THE YOGA OF VERBAL AND MENTAL RECITATION

Verbal recitation

At my heart inside a red phenomena source, a double
tetrahedron, in the centre of a moon mandala, is a letter
BAM encircled by a red-coloured mantra rosary standing
counter-clockwise. From these, immeasurable rays of red
light radiate. They purify the negativities and obstructions

of all sentient beings and make offerings to all the Buddhas. All the power and force of their blessings is invoked in the form of rays of red light, which dissolve into the letter BAM and mantra rosary, blessing my mental continuum.

OM OM OM SARWA BUDDHA DAKINIYE VAJRA WARNANIYE VAJRA BEROTZANIYE HUM HUM HUM PHAT PHAT PHAT SÖHA

Recite at least as many mantras as you have promised to.

Mental recitation

(1) Sit in the sevenfold posture and bring the phenomena source, moon and mantra letters from the heart down to the secret place if you want to generate bliss, or to the navel if you want to generate a non-conceptual mind, and enclose them with the winds. As if mentally reading the mantra rosary, which stands counter-clockwise in a circle, collect just three, five, or seven recitations. Then, while holding your breath, focus your mind on the pink joy swirls spinning counter-clockwise in the four corners of the phenomena source other than the front and the back, and especially on the nada of the BAM in the centre, which is about to blaze.

(2) The red joy swirl at the upper tip of the central channel and the white joy swirl at the lower tip, each the size of only a grain of barley, travel to the heart while spinning furiously counter-clockwise. At the heart they mix and gradually diminish into emptiness. Place your mind in absorption on bliss and emptiness.

THE YOGA OF INCONCEIVABILITY

From the letter BAM and the mantra rosary at my heart, light rays radiate and pervade all three realms. The formless realm dissolves into the upper part of my body in the aspect of rays of blue light. The form realm dissolves into the middle part of my body in the aspect of rays of red light. The desire

realm dissolves into the lower part of my body in the aspect
of rays of white light. I, in turn, gradually melt into light
from below and above and dissolve into the phenomena
source. That dissolves into the moon. That dissolves into the
thirty-two Yoginis. They dissolve into the four Yoginis, and
they dissolve into the Principal Lady of the body mandala.
The Principal Lady, in turn, gradually melts into light from
below and above and dissolves into the phenomena source.
That dissolves into the moon. That dissolves into the mantra
rosary. That dissolves into the letter BAM. That dissolves into
the head of the BAM. That dissolves into the crescent moon.
That dissolves into the drop. That dissolves into the nada,
and that, becoming smaller and smaller, dissolves into clear
light emptiness.

THE YOGA OF DAILY ACTIONS

From the state of emptiness in an instant I become Venerable
Vajrayogini. At places in my body arise moon mandalas upon
which at my navel is red OM BAM, Vajravarahi; at my heart
blue HAM YOM, Yamani; at my throat white HRIM MOM,
Mohani; at my forehead yellow HRIM HRIM, Sachalani; at my
crown green HUM HUM, Samtrasani; at all my limbs smoke-
coloured PHAT PHAT, essence of Chandika.

*To protect the main directions and intermediate directions recite
twice:*

OM SUMBHANI SUMBHA HUM HUM PHAT
OM GRIHANA GRIHANA HUM HUM PHAT
OM GRIHANA PAYA GRIHANA PAYA HUM HUM PHAT
OM ANAYA HO BHAGAWÄN VAJRA HUM HUM PHAT

The yoga of the tormas

Set up offerings in the traditional manner and then purify them in the following way:

OM KHANDAROHI HUM HUM PHAT
OM SÖBHAWA SHUDDHA SARWA DHARMA SÖBHAWA
   SHUDDHO HAM
Everything becomes emptiness.

From the state of emptiness, from KAM come skullcup vessels inside which from HUM come offering substances. By nature emptiness, they have the aspect of the individual offering substances and function as objects of enjoyment of the six senses to bestow special, uncontaminated bliss.

OM AHRGHAM AH HUM
OM PADÄM AH HUM
OM VAJRA PUPE AH HUM
OM VAJRA DHUPE AH HUM
OM VAJRA DIWE AH HUM
OM VAJRA GÄNDHE AH HUM
OM VAJRA NEWIDE AH HUM
OM VAJRA SHAPTA AH HUM

Blessing the tormas

OM KHANDAROHI HUM HUM PHAT
OM SÖBHAWA SHUDDHA SARWA DHARMA SÖBHAWA
   SHUDDHO HAM
Everything becomes emptiness.

From the state of emptiness, from YAM comes wind, from RAM comes fire, from AH a grate of three human heads. Upon this from AH appears a broad and expansive skullcup. Inside from OM, KHAM, AM, TRAM, HUM come the five nectars; from LAM, MAM, PAM, TAM, BAM come the five meats, each marked by these letters. The wind blows, the fire blazes, and the substances inside the skullcup melt. Above them from HUM there arises a white, upside-down khatanga, which falls into the skullcup and melts whereby the substances take on the colour of mercury. Above them three rows of vowels and consonants, standing one above the other, transform into OM AH HUM. From these, light rays draw the nectar of exalted wisdom from the hearts of all the Tathagatas, Heroes and Yoginis of the ten directions. When this is added the contents increase and become vast.

OM AH HUM (3x)

Inviting the guests of the torma

PHAIM

Light rays radiate from the letter BAM at my heart and invite Venerable Vajrayogini surrounded by the assembly of Gurus, Yidams, Buddhas, Bodhisattvas, Heroes, Dakinis, and both Dharma and mundane Protectors to come from Akanishta to the space before me. From a HUM in the tongue of each guest there arises a three-pronged vajra through which they partake of the essence of the torma by drawing it through straws of light the thickness of only a grain of barley.

Offering the principal torma

Offer the torma while reciting three or seven times:

OM VAJRA AH RA LI HO: DZA HUM BAM HO: VAJRA DAKINI SAMAYA TÖN TRISHAYA HO

Offering the torma to the mundane Dakinis

Offer the torma while reciting twice:

OM KHA KHA, KHAHI KHAHI, SARWA YAKYA RAKYASA, BHUTA, TRETA, PISHATSA, UNATA, APAMARA, VAJRA DAKA, DAKI NÄDAYA, IMAM BALING GRIHANTU, SAMAYA RAKYANTU, MAMA SARWA SIDDHI METRA YATZANTU, YATIPAM, YATETAM,

BHUDZATA, PIWATA, DZITRATA, MATI TRAMATA, MAMA SARWA
KATAYA, SÄDSUKHAM BISHUDHAYE, SAHAYEKA BHAWÄNTU,
HUM HUM PHAT PHAT SÖHA

Outer offerings

OM VAJRA YOGINI SAPARIWARA AHRGHAM, PADÄM, PUPE,
    DHUPE, ALOKE, GÄNDHE, NEWIDE, SHAPTA AH HUM

Inner offering

OM VAJRA YOGINI SAPARIWARA OM AH HUM

Praise

O Glorious Vajrayogini,
Chakravatin Dakini Queen,
Who have five wisdoms and three bodies,
To you Saviour of all I prostrate.

To the many Vajra Dakinis,
Who as Ladies of worldly actions,
Cut our bondage to preconceptions,
To all of you Ladies I prostrate.

Prayer to Behold the Beautiful Face of Vajrayogini

Bliss and emptiness of infinite Conquerors who, as if in
    a drama,
Appear as so many different visions in samsara and nirvana;
From among these you are now the beautiful, powerful
    Lady of Dakini Land,
I remember you from my heart, please care for me with
    your playful embrace.

You are the spontaneously born Mother of the Conquerors
    in the land of Akanishta,
You are the field-born Dakinis in the twenty-four places,

You are the action mudras covering the whole earth,
O Venerable Lady, you are the supreme refuge of myself,
    the Yogi.

You who are the manifestation of the emptiness of the mind itself,
Are the actual BAM, the sphere of EH, in the city of the vajra.
In the land of illusion you show yourself as a fearsome cannibal
And as a smiling, vibrant, fair young maiden.

But no matter how much I searched, O Noble Lady,
I could find no certainty of your being truly existent.
Then the youth of my mind, exhausted by its elaborations,
Came to rest in the forest hut which is beyond expression.

How wonderful, please arise from the sphere of the
    Dharmakaya
And care for me by the truth of what it says
In the Glorious Heruka, King of Tantras,
That attainments come from reciting the supreme close
    essence mantra of the Vajra Queen.

In the isolated forest of Odivisha
You cared for Vajra Ghantapa, the powerful Siddha,
With the bliss of your kiss and embrace and he came to
    enjoy the supreme embrace;
O, please care for me in the same way.

Just as the venerable Kusali was led directly
From an island in the Ganges to the sphere of space,
And just as you cared for the glorious Naropa,
Please lead me also to the city of the joyful Dakini.

Through the force of the compassion of my supreme root
    and lineage Gurus,
The especially profound and quick path of the ultimate,
    secret, great Tantra,
And the pure superior intention of myself, the Yogi,
May I soon behold your smiling face, O Joyful Dakini Lady.

Requesting fulfilment of wishes

O Venerable Vajrayogini, please lead me and all sentient
beings to the Pure Land of the Dakinis. Please bestow on
us every single mundane and supramundane attainment.   (3x)

*If you wish to make a tsog offering you should include it at this
point. The tsog offering starts on page 355.*

Offering the torma to the general Dharma Protectors

OM AH HUM HA HO HRIH   (3x)

HUM
From your pure palace of great bliss in Akanishta,
Great powerful one emanating from Vairochana's heart,
Dorje Gur, chief of all the Protectors of the doctrine,
O Glorious Mahakala come here please and partake of this
    offering and torma.

From Yongdui Tsel and Yama's palace
And from the supreme place of Devikoti in Jambudipa,
Namdru Remati, chief Lady of the desire realm,
O Palden Lhamo come here please and partake of this
    offering and torma.

From the mandala of the bhaga sphere of appearance and
    existence,
Mother Yingchugma, principal Lady of all samsara and nirvana,
Chief of Dakinis and demons, fierce female protector of the
    mantras,
O Great Mother Ralchigma come here please and partake of
    this offering and torma.

From Silwa Tsel and Haha Gopa,
From Singaling and the Ti Se snow mountain,
And from Darlungnay and Kaui Dragdzong,
O Zhingkyong Wangpo come here please and partake of
    this offering and torma.

From the eight charnel grounds and Risul in the south,
From Bodhgaya and glorious Samye,
And from Nalatse and glorious Sakya,
O Legon Pomo come here please and partake of this
    offering and torma.

From the charnel grounds of Marutse in the north-east,
From the red, rocky hills of Bangso in India,
And from the supreme places of Darlung Dagram and so forth,
O Yakya Chamdrel come here please and partake of this
    offering and torma.

Especially from Odiyana, Land of the Dakinis,
And from your natural abode,
Completely encircled by mundane and supramundane Dakinis,
O Father-Mother Lord of the Charnel Grounds come here
    please and partake of this offering and torma.

From the supreme places such as Tushita, Keajra, and so forth,
Great Protector of the doctrine of the second Conqueror,
Dorje Shugden, five lineages, together with your retinues,
Come here please and partake of this offering and torma.

I request you, I make offerings to you, O Host of Protectors
    of the Conqueror's doctrine,
I propitiate you and rely upon you, O Great Protectors of
    the Guru's words,
I cry out to you and beseech you, O Host of Destroyers of
    the obstructors of Yogis,
Please come here quickly and partake of this offering
    and torma.

I offer a torma adorned with red flesh and blood.
I offer drinks of alcohol, medicine nectars, and blood.
I offer the sound of large drums, thigh-bone trumpets,
    and cymbals.
I offer large, black silk pennants that billow like clouds.

I offer breath-taking attractions equal to space.
I offer loud chants that are powerful and melodious.
I offer an ocean of outer, inner, and secret commitment
substances.
I offer the play of the exalted wisdom of inseparable bliss
and emptiness.

May you protect the precious doctrine of Buddha.
May you increase the renown of the Three Jewels.
May you further the deeds of the glorious Gurus,
And may you fulfil whatever requests I make of you.

Requesting forbearance

Now recite the hundred-letter mantra of Heruka:

OM VAJRA HERUKA SAMAYA, MANU PALAYA, HERUKA
TENO PATITA, DRIDHO ME BHAWA, SUTO KAYO ME BHAWA,
SUPO KAYO ME BHAWA, ANURAKTO ME BHAWA, SARWA
SIDDHI ME PRAYATZA, SARWA KARMA SUTZA ME, TZITAM
SHRIYAM KURU HUM, HA HA HA HA HO BHAGAWÄN,
VAJRA HERUKA MA ME MUNTSA, HERUKA BHAWA, MAHA
SAMAYA SATTÖ AH HUM PHAT

Request forbearance by reciting:

Whatever mistakes I have made
Through not finding, not understanding,
Or not having the ability,
Please, O Protector, be patient with all of these.

OM VAJRA MU The wisdom beings, guests of the torma,
dissolve into me and the worldly beings return to their
own places.

Dedication prayers

By this virtue may I quickly
Accomplish the actual Dakini,

And then lead every living being
Without exception to that ground.

At my deathtime may the Protectors, Heroes, Heroines
and so forth,
Bearing flowers, parasols and victory banners,
And offering the sweet music of cymbals and so forth,
Lead me to the Land of the Dakinis.

By the truth of the valid Goddesses,
Their valid commitments,
And the supremely valid words they have spoken,
May [my virtues] be the cause for me to be cared for by
the Goddesses.

Extensive dedication

If you have the time and the wish you can finish with these prayers,
which were composed by Tsarpa Dorjechang:

In the great ship of freedom and endowment,
Flying the white sail of mindfulness of impermanence,
And blown by the favourable wind of accepting and
abandoning actions and effects,
May I be delivered from the fearsome ocean of samsara.

Relying upon the crown-jewel of the non-deceptive objects
of refuge,
Taking to heart the great purpose of migrators, my mothers,
And cleansing my stains and faults with the nectar of
Vajrasattva,
May I be cared for by the compassionate, venerable Gurus.

The beautiful Mother of the Conquerors is the outer Yogini,
The letter BAM is the supreme inner Vajra Queen,
The clarity and emptiness of the mind itself is the secret
Dakini Mother;
May I enjoy the sport of seeing the self-nature of each.

The worldly environment is the celestial mansion of the
    letter EH,
And its inhabitants, the sentient beings, are the Yoginis of
    the letter BAM;
Through the concentration of the great bliss of their union,
May whatever appearance arises be pure appearance.

Thus, through the yogas [numbering] the directions and
    the moon,
May I eventually be led directly to the city of Knowledge
    Holders
By the coral-coloured Lady of joy
With freely hanging vermilion hair and orange, darting
    eyes.

Having practised in a place of corpses with sindhura and
    a langali stem,
And having wandered throughout the land,
May the beautiful Lady to whom the swirl at my forehead
    transfers
Lead me to the Land of the Dakinis.

When the inner Varahi has destroyed the creeping vine of
    apprehender and apprehended,
And the dancing Lady residing in my supreme central
    channel
Has emerged through the door of Brahma into the sphere
    of the pathway of clouds,
May she embrace and sport with the Hero, Drinker of
    Blood.

Through the yoga of unifying [the two winds], meditating
    single-pointedly
On the tiny seed of the five winds at the lotus of my navel,
May my mental continuum be satiated by a supreme bliss
From the fragrant drops pervading the channels of my
    body-mind.

When, through the laughing and smiling play of the
    beautiful Lady
Of blazing light tummo within my central channel,
The youthful letter HAM has been completely softened,
May I attain the ground of the great bliss of union.

When the reddish-black RAM residing in the centre of the
    three channels at my navel
Has been set ablaze by my upper and lower winds,
And its cleansing fire has burned away the seventy-two
    thousand impure elements,
May my central channel be completely filled with pure
    drops.

When the five-coloured drop between my eyebrows has
    gone to my crown,
And the stream of moon-liquid originating from it
Has reached the stamen of my secret lotus,
May I be satiated by the four joys of descending and
    ascending.

When, through being struck by the rays of five lights
    radiating from that drop,
All stable and moving phenomena, my body and so forth,
Have been transformed into a mass of brilliant, clear
    rainbows,
May I once again enter the natural abode, the sphere of
    bliss and emptiness.

When the Yogini of my own mind, the union beyond intellect,
The primordial state of inexpressible emptiness and clarity,
The original nature free from arising, ceasing and abiding,
Recognizes its own entity, may I be forever nourished.

When my channels, winds and drops have dissolved into
    the sphere of EVAM,
And the mind itself has attained the glory of the Truth Body
    of great bliss,

May I care for these migrators as extensive as space
With immeasurable manifestations of countless Form Bodies.

Through the blessings of the Conquerors and their
marvellous Sons,
The truth of non-deceptive dependent relationship,
And the power and force of my pure, superior intention,
May all the points of my sincere prayers be fulfilled.

Auspicious prayers

May there be the auspiciousness of swiftly receiving the
blessings
Of the hosts of glorious, sacred Gurus,
Vajradhara, Pandit Naropa, and so forth,
The glorious Lords of all virtue and excellence.

May there be the auspiciousness of the Dakini Truth Body,
Perfection of wisdom, the supreme Mother of the Conquerors,
The natural clear light, free from elaboration from the
beginning,
The Lady who emanates and gathers all things stable and
moving.

May there be the auspiciousness of the Complete Enjoyment
Body, spontaneously born,
A body, radiant and beautiful, ablaze with the glory of the
major and minor marks,
A speech proclaiming the supreme vehicle with sixty
melodies,
And a mind of non-conceptual bliss and clarity possessing
the five exalted wisdoms.

May there be the auspiciousness of the Emanation Body,
born from the places,
Ladies who with various Form Bodies, in various places,
Fulfil by various means the aims of various ones to be tamed
In accordance with their various wishes.

May there be the auspiciousness of the supreme Dakini,
    mantra-born,
A venerable Lady with a colour similar to that of a ruby,
With a smiling, wrathful manner, one face, two hands
    holding curved knife and skullcup,
And two legs in bent and outstretched positions.

May there be the auspiciousness of your countless
    millions of emanations
And the hosts of the seventy-two thousand [Dakinis]
Eliminating all the obstructions of practitioners
And bestowing the attainments that are longed for.

THE TSOG OFFERING

Blessing the tsog offering

OM KHANDAROHI HUM HUM PHAT
OM SÖBHAWA SHUDDHA SARWA DHARMA SÖBHAWA
SHUDDHO HAM
Everything becomes emptiness.

From the state of emptiness, from AH comes a broad and
expansive skullcup inside which the five meats, the five
nectars, and the five exalted wisdoms melt and there
arises a vast ocean of the nectar of exalted wisdom.
OM AH HUM HA HO HRIH   (3x)

*Contemplate that it becomes an inexhaustible ocean of exalted
wisdom nectar.*

Offering medicine nectars

I offer this supreme nectar
That far transcends vulgar objects;
The supreme commitment of all the Conquerors,
And the foundation of all attainments.

May you be pleased with the great bliss
Of the unsurpassed bodhichitta,
Purified of all stains of obstructions,
And completely free from all conceptions.

Making the tsog offering

HO This ocean of tsog offering of uncontaminated nectar,
Blessed by concentration, mantra and mudra,
I offer to please the assembly of root and lineage Gurus.
OM AH HUM
Delighted by enjoying these magnificent objects of desire,

EH MA HO
Please bestow a great rain of blessings.

HO This ocean of tsog offering of uncontaminated nectar,
Blessed by concentration, mantra and mudra,
I offer to please the divine assembly of powerful Dakinis.
OM AH HUM
Delighted by enjoying these magnificent objects of desire,
EH MA HO
Please bestow the Dakini attainment.

HO This ocean of tsog offering of uncontaminated nectar,
Blessed by concentration, mantra and mudra,
I offer to please the divine assembly of Yidams and their
    retinues.
OM AH HUM
Delighted by enjoying these magnificent objects of desire,
EH MA HO
Please bestow a great rain of attainments.

HO This ocean of tsog offering of uncontaminated nectar,
Blessed by concentration, mantra and mudra,
I offer to please the assembly of Three Precious Jewels.
OM AH HUM
Delighted by enjoying these magnificent objects of desire,
EH MA HO
Please bestow a great rain of sacred Dharmas.

HO This ocean of tsog offering of uncontaminated nectar,
Blessed by concentration, mantra and mudra,
I offer to please the assembly of Dakinis and Dharma
    Protectors.
OM AH HUM
Delighted by enjoying these magnificent objects of desire,
EH MA HO
Please bestow a great rain of virtuous deeds.

HO This ocean of tsog offering of uncontaminated nectar,
Blessed by concentration, mantra and mudra,
I offer to please the assembly of mother sentient beings.
OM AH HUM
Delighted by enjoying these magnificent objects of desire,
EH MA HO
May suffering and mistaken appearance be pacified.

Outer offerings

OM VAJRA YOGINI SAPARIWARA AHRGHAM, PADÄM, PUPE,
DHUPE, ALOKE, GÄNDHE, NEWIDE, SHAPTA AH HUM

Inner offering

OM VAJRA YOGINI SAPARIWARA OM AH HUM

Eight lines of praise to the Mother

OM I prostrate to Vajravarahi, the Blessed Mother HUM
HUM PHAT
OM To the Superior and powerful Knowledge Lady
unconquered by the three realms HUM HUM PHAT
OM To you who destroy all fears of evil spirits with your
great vajra HUM HUM PHAT
OM To you with controlling eyes who remain as the vajra
seat unconquered by others HUM HUM PHAT
OM To you whose wrathful fierce form desiccates Brahma
HUM HUM PHAT
OM To you who terrify and dry up demons, conquering
those in other directions HUM HUM PHAT
OM To you who conquer all those who make us dull,
rigid and confused HUM HUM PHAT
OM I bow to Vajravarahi, the Great Mother, the Dakini
consort who fulfils all desires HUM HUM PHAT

Making the tsog offering to the Vajra Master

Vajra Holder please listen to me,
This special tsog offering of mine,
I offer to you with a mind of faith;
Please partake as is your pleasure.

EH MA, great peace.
This great, blazing tsog offering burns up delusions
And in that way brings great bliss.
AH HO Everything is great bliss.
AH HO MAHA SUKHA HO

Concerning this, all phenomena are seen as pure,
Of this the assembly should have no doubt.
Since brahmins, outcasts, pigs and dogs
Are of one nature, please enjoy.

The Dharma of the Sugatas is priceless,
Free from the stains of attachment and so forth,
The abandonment of apprehender and apprehended;
Respectfully I prostrate to thatness.
AH HO MAHA SUKHA HO

Song of the Spring Queen

HUM All you Tathagatas,
Heroes, Yoginis,
Dakas and Dakinis,
To all of you I make this request:
O Heruka who delight in great bliss,
You engage in the Union of spontaneous bliss,
By attending the Lady intoxicated with bliss
And enjoying in accordance with the rituals.
AH LA LA, LA LA HO, AH I AH, AH RA LI HO
May the assembly of stainless Dakinis
Look with loving affection and accomplish all deeds.

HUM All you Tathagatas,
Heroes, Yoginis,
Dakas and Dakinis,
To all of you I make this request:
With a mind completely aroused by great bliss
And a body in a dance of constant motion,
I offer to the hosts of Dakinis
The great bliss from enjoying the lotus of the mudra.
AH LA LA, LA LA HO, AH I AH, AH RA LI HO
May the assembly of stainless Dakinis
Look with loving affection and accomplish all deeds.

HUM All you Tathagatas,
Heroes, Yoginis,
Dakas and Dakinis,
To all of you I make this request:
You who dance with a beautiful and peaceful manner,
O Blissful Protector and the hosts of Dakinis,
Please come here before me and grant me your blessings,
And bestow upon me spontaneous great bliss.
AH LA LA, LA LA HO, AH I AH, AH RA LI HO
May the assembly of stainless Dakinis
Look with loving affection and accomplish all deeds.

HUM All you Tathagatas,
Heroes, Yoginis,
Dakas and Dakinis,
To all of you I make this request:
You who have the characteristic of the liberation of great bliss,
Do not say that deliverance can be gained in one lifetime
Through various ascetic practices having abandoned great
    bliss,
But that great bliss resides in the centre of the supreme lotus.
AH LA LA, LA LA HO, AH I AH, AH RA LI HO
May the assembly of stainless Dakinis
Look with loving affection and accomplish all deeds.

HUM All you Tathagatas,
Heroes, Yoginis,
Dakas and Dakinis,
To all of you I make this request:
Like a lotus born from the centre of a swamp,
This method, though born from attachment, is unstained
   by the faults of attachment.
O Supreme Dakini, through the bliss of your lotus,
Please quickly bring liberation from the bonds of samsara.
AH LA LA, LA LA HO, AH I AH, AH RA LI HO
May the assembly of stainless Dakinis
Look with loving affection and accomplish all deeds.

HUM All you Tathagatas,
Heroes, Yoginis,
Dakas and Dakinis,
To all of you I make this request:
Just as the essence of honey in the honey source
Is drunk by swarms of bees from all directions,
So through your broad lotus with six characteristics
Please bring satisfaction with the taste of great bliss.
AH LA LA, LA LA HO, AH I AH, AH RA LI HO
May the assembly of stainless Dakinis
Look with loving affection and accomplish all deeds.

Blessing the offerings to the spirits

OM KHANDAROHI HUM HUM PHAT
OM SÖBHAWA SHUDDHA SARWA DHARMA SÖBHAWA
   SHUDDHO HAM
Everything becomes emptiness.

From the state of emptiness, from AH comes a broad and
expansive skullcup inside which the five meats, the five
nectars, and the five exalted wisdoms melt and there
arises a vast ocean of the nectar of exalted wisdom.
OM AH HUM HA HO HRIH   (3x)

Actual offering to the spirits

PHAIM
UTSIKTRA BALINGTA BHAKYÄSI SÖHA

HO This ocean of remaining tsog offering of
 uncontaminated nectar,
Blessed by concentration, mantra and mudra,
I offer to please the assembly of oath-bound guardians.
OM AH HUM
Delighted by enjoying these magnificent objects of desire,
EH MA HO
Please perform perfect actions to help practitioners.

*Send out the remainder of the tsog offering to the accompaniment
of music.*

May I and other practitioners
Have good health, long life, power,
Glory, fame, fortune,
And extensive enjoyments.
Please grant me the attainments
Of pacifying, increasing, controlling and wrathful actions.
You who are bound by oaths please protect me
And help me to accomplish all the attainments.
Eradicate all untimely death, sicknesses,
Harm from spirits and hindrances.
Eliminate bad dreams,
Ill omens and bad actions.

May there be happiness in the world, may the years be good,
May crops increase, and may Dharma flourish.
May all goodness and happiness come about,
And may all wishes be accomplished.

By the force of this bountiful giving
May I become a Buddha for the sake of living beings;
And through my generosity may I liberate
All those not liberated by previous Buddhas.

Prayers for the Virtuous Tradition

So that the tradition of Je Tsongkhapa,
The King of the Dharma, may flourish,
May all obstacles be pacified
And may all favourable conditions abound.

Through the two collections of myself and others
Gathered throughout the three times,
May the doctrine of Conqueror Losang Dragpa
Flourish for evermore.

The nine-line *Migtsema* prayer

Tsongkhapa, crown ornament of the scholars of the
    Land of the Snows,
You are Buddha Shakyamuni and Vajradhara, the
    source of all attainments,
Avalokiteshvara, the treasury of unobservable
    compassion,
Manjushri, the supreme stainless wisdom,
And Vajrapani, the destroyer of the hosts of maras.
O Venerable Guru-Buddha, synthesis of all Three Jewels,
With my body, speech, and mind, respectfully I make
    requests:
Please grant your blessings to ripen and liberate myself
    and others,
And bestow the common and supreme attainments. (3x)

Colophon: This sadhana was translated under the
compassionate guidance of Venerable Geshe Kelsang Gyatso.
The verse to Venerable Geshe Kelsang Gyatso in *Requesting the
lineage Gurus* was composed by the glorious Dharma Protector,
Duldzin Dorje Shugden, and included in the sadhana at the
request of Geshe Kelsang's faithful disciples. The verse to Dorje
Shugden in *Offering the torma to the general Dharma Protectors* was
composed by Venerable Geshe Kelsang Gyatso and included in
the sadhana at the request of his faithful disciples.

Appendix VIII

The nada
(Please note that the nada should be visualized
to the size of a small pea)

Glossary

Absorption of cessation An uncontaminated wisdom focused single-pointedly on emptiness in dependence upon the actual absorption of peak of samsara. See *Ocean of Nectar*.

Action mudra A Highest Yoga Tantra consort who assists in developing great bliss. See *Clear Light of Bliss* and *Tantric Grounds and Paths*.

Affirming negative See *Negative phenomenon*.

Aggregate In general, all functioning things are aggregates because they are an aggregation of their parts. In particular, a person of the desire realm or form realm has five aggregates: the aggregates of form, feeling, discrimination, compositional factors and consciousness. A being of the formless realm lacks the aggregate of form but has the other four. A person's form aggregate is his or her body. The remaining four aggregates are aspects of his mind. See also *Contaminated aggregate*. See *Heart of Wisdom*.

Akshobya The manifestation of the aggregate of consciousness of all Buddhas. He has a blue-coloured body.

Alertness A mental factor that is a type of wisdom which examines our activity of body, speech and mind, and knows whether or not faults are developing. See *Understanding the Mind* and *Meaningful to Behold*.

Amitabha The manifestation of the aggregate of discrimination of all Buddhas. He has a red-coloured body. See *Eight Steps to Happiness*.

Amoghasiddhi The manifestation of the aggregate of compositional factors of all Buddhas. He has a green-coloured body.

Arya Tara/Tara A female Buddha who is a manifestation of the ultimate wisdom of all the Buddhas. 'Arya' means 'Superior' and 'Tara' means 'Liberator'. Because she is a wisdom Buddha, and a manifestation of the completely purified wind element, Tara is able to help us very quickly.

Aryadeva A third century AD Indian Buddhist scholar and meditation master, who was a disciple of Nagarjuna.

Attachment A deluded mental factor that observes its contaminated object, regards it as a cause of happiness and wishes for it. See *Understanding the Mind* and *Joyful Path of Good Fortune*.

Attention A mental factor that functions to focus the mind on a particular attribute of an object. See *Understanding the Mind*.

Bardo See *Intermediate state*.

Basis of imputation All phenomena are imputed upon their parts, therefore any of the individual parts, or the entire collection of the parts, of any phenomenon is its basis of imputation. A phenomenon is imputed by mind in dependence upon its basis of imputation appearing to that mind. See *Heart of Wisdom* and *Ocean of Nectar*.

Beginningless time According to the Buddhist world view, there is no beginning to mind, and so no beginning to time. Therefore, all living beings have taken countless previous rebirths.

Blessing The transformation of our mind from a negative state to a positive state, from an unhappy state to a happy state, or from a state of weakness to a state of strength, through the inspiration of holy beings such as our Spiritual Guide, Buddhas and Bodhisattvas.

Bodh Gaya The place where Buddha Shakyamuni showed the manner of attaining enlightenment; near the modern city of Gaya in the north Indian state of Bihar.

Brahma A worldly god who resides in the first form realm. See *Ocean of Nectar*.

Changing suffering For beings within samsara every experience of happiness or pleasure that arises from samsara's enjoyments is changing suffering. This is because these experiences are contaminated and have the nature of suffering.

Commitments Promises and pledges taken when engaging in certain spiritual practices.

Compositional factors The aggregate of compositional factors comprises all mental factors except feeling and discrimination, as well as non-associated compounded phenomena. See *Heart of Wisdom* and *Understanding the Mind*.

Concentration A mental factor that makes its primary mind remain on its object single-pointedly. See *Joyful Path of Good Fortune*, *Understanding the Mind* and *Meaningful to Behold*.

Consciousness The six consciousnesses, or primary minds, are the eye consciousness, ear consciousness, nose consciousness, tongue consciousness, body consciousness and mental consciousness. See *Understanding the Mind*.

Conqueror Buddha Buddhas are called 'Conquerors' because they have conquered all the obstructions to attaining liberation and enlightenment, or maras. See also *Mara*.

Conscientiousness A mental factor that, in dependence upon effort, cherishes what is virtuous and guards the mind from delusion and non-virtue. See *Meaningful to Behold* and *Understanding the Mind*.

Contact A mental factor that functions to perceive its object as pleasant, unpleasant or neutral. See *Understanding the Mind*.

Contaminated aggregate Any of the aggregates of form, feeling, discrimination, compositional factors and consciousness of a samsaric being. See also *Aggregate*. See *Heart of Wisdom*.

Dakini Land The Pure Land of Heruka and Vajrayogini. In Sanskrit it is called 'Keajra' and in Tibetan 'Dagpa Khacho'. See *Guide to Dakini Land*.

Dakinis Female Tantric Buddhas and those women who have attained the realization of meaning clear light. Dakas are the male equivalent. See *Guide to Dakini Land*.

Damaru A small hand-drum used in Tantric rituals. Playing the damaru symbolizes the gathering of the outer Dakinis into our body, and the manifestation of the inner Dakini (the mind of clear light) within our mind through the blazing of inner fire. It is also used as a music offering to the Buddhas.

Deity 'Yidam' in Tibetan. A Tantric enlightened being.

Delusion A mental factor that arises from inappropriate attention and functions to make the mind unpeaceful and uncontrolled. There are three main delusions: ignorance, desirous attachment and anger. From these arise all the other delusions, such as jealousy, pride and deluded doubt. See also *Innate delusions* and *Intellectually-formed delusions*. See *Joyful Path of Good Fortune* and *Understanding the Mind*.

Demi-god A being of the demi-god realm, the second highest of the six realms of samsara. Demi-gods are similar to gods but their bodies, possessions and environments are inferior. See *Joyful Path of Good Fortune*.

Desire realm The environment of hell beings, hungry ghosts, animals, human beings and demi-gods, and the gods who enjoy the five objects of desire.

Dharma Protector An emanation of a Buddha or a Bodhisattva whose main functions are to avert the inner and outer obstacles that prevent Dharma practitioners from gaining spiritual realizations, and to arrange all the necessary conditions for their practice. Also called 'Dharmapala' in Sanskrit. See *Heart Jewel*.

Discrimination A mental factor that functions to apprehend the uncommon sign of an object. See *Understanding the Mind*.

Dorje Shugden A Dharma Protector who is an emanation of the Wisdom Buddha Manjushri. His main functions are to avert the inner and outer obstacles that prevent practitioners from gaining spiritual realizations, and to arrange all the necessary conditions for their spiritual development. See *Heart Jewel.*

Dromtonpa (AD 1004-1064) Atisha's foremost disciple. See *Joyful Path of Good Fortune.*

Elements, four Earth, water, fire and wind. These elements are not the same as the earth of a field, the water of a river, and so forth. Rather, the elements of earth, water, fire and wind in broad terms are the properties of solidity, liquidity, heat and movement respectively.

Example clear light A mind of clear light that realizes emptiness by means of a generic image. See *Clear Light of Bliss* and *Tantric Grounds and Paths.*

Faith A naturally virtuous mind that functions mainly to oppose the perception of faults in its observed object. There are three types of faith: believing faith, admiring faith and wishing faith. See *Transform Your Life, Joyful Path of Good Fortune* and *Understanding the Mind.*

Feeling A mental factor that functions to experience pleasant, unpleasant or neutral objects. See *Understanding the Mind.*

Field of Merit Generally, this refers to the Three Jewels. Just as external seeds grow in a field of soil, so the virtuous internal seeds produced by virtuous actions grow in dependence upon Buddha Jewel, Dharma Jewel and Sangha Jewel. Also known as 'Field for Accumulating Merit'.

Form aggregate Includes all the objects of the five sense awarenesses – all colours and shapes (visual form), sounds, smells, tastes and tactile objects. A person's form aggregate is his or her body.

Form realm The environment of the gods who possess form and who are superior to desire realm gods. So-called because the gods who inhabit it have subtle form. See *Ocean of Nectar.*

Functioning thing A phenomenon that is produced and disintegrates within a moment. Synonymous with impermanent phenomenon, thing and product.

Gelug The tradition established by Je Tsongkhapa. The name 'Gelug' means 'Virtuous Tradition'. A Gelugpa is a practitioner who follows this tradition. The Gelugpas are sometimes referred to as the 'new Kadampas'. See *Heart Jewel*.

Generic image The appearing object of a conceptual mind. A generic image, or mental image, of an object is like a reflection of that object. Conceptual minds know their object through the appearance of a generic image of that object, not by seeing the object directly. See *Heart of Wisdom* and *Understanding the Mind*.

Geshe A title given by Kadampa monasteries to accomplished Buddhist scholars. Contracted form of the Tibetan 'ge wai she nyen', literally meaning 'virtuous friend'.

Geshe Chekhawa (AD 1102-1176) A great Kadampa Bodhisattva who composed the text *Training the Mind in Seven Points*, a commentary to Bodhisattva Langri Tangpa's *Eight Verses of Training the Mind*. He spread the study and practice of training the mind throughout Tibet. See *Universal Compassion*.

Ghantapa A great Indian Mahasiddha and a lineage Guru in the Highest Yoga Tantra practices of Heruka and Vajrayogini. See *Guide to Dakini Land*.

Gods Beings of the god realm, the highest of the six realms of samsara. There are many different types of god. Some are desire realm gods, while others are form or formless realm gods. See *Joyful Path of Good Fortune*.

Gungtang Gungtang Konchog Tenpai Dronme (AD 1762-1823), a Gelug scholar and meditator famous for his spiritual poems and philosophical writings.

Guru Sanskrit word for 'Spiritual Guide'.

Heroes and Heroines A Hero is a male Tantric Deity embodying method. A Heroine is a female Tantric Deity embodying wisdom. See *Guide to Dakini Land*.

Hevajra A principal Deity of Mother Tantra. See *Great Treasury of Merit*.

Hinayana Sanskrit term for 'Lesser Vehicle'. The Hinayana goal is to attain merely one's own liberation from suffering by completely abandoning delusions. See *Joyful Path of Good Fortune*.

Hungry ghosts Beings of the hungry ghost realm, the second lowest of the six realms of samsara. Also known as 'hungry spirits'. See *Joyful Path of Good Fortune*.

Imprint/s There are two types of imprint: imprints of actions and imprints of delusions. Every action we perform leaves an imprint on the mental consciousness, and these imprints are karmic potentialities to experience certain effects in the future. The imprints left by delusions remain even after the delusions themselves have been abandoned, like the smell of garlic lingers in a container after the garlic has been removed. Imprints of delusions are obstructions to omniscience, and are completely abandoned only by Buddhas.

Imputation, mere According to the highest school of Buddhist philosophy, the Madhyamika-Prasangika school, all phenomena are merely imputed by conception in dependence upon their basis of imputation. Therefore, they are mere imputations and do not exist from their own side in the least. See *Heart of Wisdom* and *Ocean of Nectar*.

Imputed object An object imputed by the mind in dependence upon its basis of imputation. See *Heart of Wisdom* and *Ocean of Nectar*.

Indra A worldly god. See *Heart of Wisdom*.

Inferential cognizer A completely reliable cognizer whose object is realized in direct dependence upon a conclusive reason. See *Understanding the Mind*.

Inner fire 'Tummo' in Tibetan. An inner heat located at the centre of the navel channel wheel. See *Clear Light of Bliss*.

Intellectually-formed delusions Delusions that arise as a result of relying upon incorrect reasoning or mistaken tenets. See *Understanding the Mind*.

Intention A mental factor that functions to move its primary mind to the object. It functions to engage the mind in virtuous, non-virtuous and neutral objects. All bodily and verbal actions are initiated by the mental factor intention. See *Understanding the Mind*.

Intermediate state 'Bardo' in Tibetan. The state between death and rebirth. It begins the moment the consciousness leaves the body, and ceases the moment the consciousness enters the body of the next life. See *Joyful Path of Good Fortune* and *Clear Light of Bliss*.

Je Phabongkhapa (AD 1878-1941) A great Tibetan Lama who was an emanation of Heruka. Phabongkha Rinpoche was the holder of many lineages of Sutra and Secret Mantra. He was the root Guru of Kyabje Trijang Dorjechang (Kyabje Trijang Rinpoche).

Je Tsongkhapa (AD 1357-1419) An emanation of the Wisdom Buddha Manjushri, whose appearance in fourteenth-century Tibet as a monk, and the holder of the lineage of pure view and pure deeds, was prophesied by Buddha. He spread a very pure Buddhadharma throughout Tibet, showing how to combine the practices of Sutra and Tantra, and how to practise pure Dharma during degenerate times. His tradition later became known as the 'Gelug', or 'Ganden Tradition'. See *Heart Jewel* and *Great Treasury of Merit*.

Kapala A skullcup used or visualized in Tantric meditation, symbolizing the indivisible union of great bliss and emptiness.

Kyabje Trijang Rinpoche (AD 1901-1981) A special Tibetan Lama of the twentieth century who was an emanation of Buddha Shakyamuni, Heruka, Atisha, Amitabha and Je Tsongkhapa. Also known as 'Trijang Dorjechang' and 'Losang Yeshe'.

Lineage A line of instruction that has been passed down from Spiritual Guide to disciple, with each Spiritual Guide in the line having gained personal experience of the instruction before passing it on to others.

Living being Synonymous with sentient being. Any being who possesses a mind that is contaminated by delusions or their imprints. Both 'living being' and 'sentient being' are terms used to distinguish beings whose minds are contaminated by either of these two obstructions from Buddhas, whose minds are completely free from these obstructions.

Lord of Death Although the mara, or demon, of uncontrolled death is not a sentient being, it is personified as the Lord of Death, or 'Yama'. The Lord of Death is depicted in the diagram of the Wheel of Life clutching the wheel between his claws and teeth. See *Joyful Path of Good Fortune.*

Losang Dragpa 'Sumati Kirti' in Sanskrit. The ordained name of Je Tsongkhapa. See *Great Treasury of Merit.*

Mahamudra A Sanskrit term, literally meaning 'great seal'. According to Sutra, this refers to the profound view of emptiness. Since emptiness is the nature of all phenomena, it is called a 'seal', and since a direct realization of emptiness enables us to accomplish the great purpose – complete liberation from the sufferings of samsara – it is also called 'great'. According to Tantra, or Vajrayana, Mahamudra is the union of spontaneous great bliss and emptiness. See *Mahamudra Tantra, Great Treasury of Merit* and *Clear Light of Bliss.*

Mahayana Sanskrit term for 'Great Vehicle', the spiritual path to great enlightenment. The Mahayana goal is to attain Buddhahood for the benefit of all sentient beings by completely abandoning delusions and their imprints. See *Joyful Path of Good Fortune* and *Meaningful to Behold.*

Maitreya The embodiment of the loving kindness of all the Buddhas. At the time of Buddha Shakyamuni he manifested as a Bodhisattva disciple in order to show Buddha's disciples how to be perfect Mahayana disciples. In the future, he will manifest as the fifth founding Buddha.

Mala A set of prayer beads used to count recitations of prayers or mantras, usually with one hundred and eight beads. See *Guide to Dakini Land*.

Mandala offering An offering of the entire universe visualized as a Pure Land, with all its inhabitants as pure beings. See *Guide to Dakini Land* and *Great Treasury of Merit*.

Mara A Sanskrit term for 'demon', and referring to anything that obstructs the attainment of liberation or enlightenment. There are four principal types of mara: the mara of the delusions, the mara of contaminated aggregates, the mara of uncontrolled death, and the Devaputra maras. Of these, only the last are actual sentient beings. The principal Devaputra mara is wrathful Ishvara, the highest of the desire realm gods, who inhabits the Land of Controlling Emanations. A Buddha is called a 'Conqueror' because he or she has conquered all four types of mara. See *Heart of Wisdom*.

Marpa (AD 1012-1096) Marpa Lotsawa, or Marpa the translator, was a great lay Tantric Yogi and the Spiritual Guide of Milarepa. See *Joyful Path of Good Fortune*.

Meaning clear light A mind of clear light that realizes emptiness directly without a generic image. Synonymous with inner Dakini Land and with Mahamudra Tantra. See *Clear Light of Bliss*.

Meditation A mind that concentrates on a virtuous object, and is a mental action that is the main cause of mental peace. There are two types of meditation – analytical meditation and placement meditation. When we use our imagination, mindfulness and powers of reasoning to find our object of meditation, this is analytical meditation. When we find our object and hold it single-pointedly, this is placement meditation. There are different types of object. Some, such as impermanence or emptiness, are objects apprehended by the mind. Others, such as love, compassion and renunciation, are actual states of mind. We engage in analytical meditation until the specific object that we seek appears clearly to our mind or until the particular state of mind that we wish to generate arises. This object or state of mind is our object of placement meditation. See *The New Meditation Handbook*.

Meditation break See *Subsequent attainment.*

Mental continuum The continuum of a person's mind that has no beginning and no end.

Mental factor A cognizer that principally apprehends a particular attribute of an object. There are fifty-one specific mental factors. Each moment of mind comprises a primary mind and various mental factors. See *Understanding the Mind.*

Mental image See *Generic image.*

Mere appearance All phenomena are mere appearance because they are imputed by mind in dependence upon a suitable basis of imputation appearing to mind. The word 'mere' excludes any possibility of inherent existence. See *Ocean of Nectar.*

Merit The good fortune created by virtuous actions. It is the potential power to increase our good qualities and produce happiness.

Migrator A being within samsara who migrates from one uncontrolled rebirth to another. See also *Living being.*

Milarepa (AD 1040-1123) A great Tibetan Buddhist meditator and disciple of Marpa, celebrated for his beautiful songs of realization.

Mindfulness A mental factor that functions not to forget the object realized by the primary mind. See *Understanding the Mind, Meaningful to Behold* and *Clear Light of Bliss.*

Nagarjuna A great Indian Buddhist scholar and meditation master who revived the Mahayana in the first century AD by bringing to light the teachings on the *Perfection of Wisdom Sutras.* See *Ocean of Nectar.*

Nalanda Monastery A great seat of Buddhist learning and practice in ancient India.

Naropa (AD 1016-1100) An Indian Mahasiddha and a lineage Guru in the Highest Yoga Tantra practice of Vajrayogini. See *Guide to Dakini Land.*

Negative phenomenon An object that is realized through the mind explicitly eliminating a negated object. There are two types of negative phenomenon: affirming negatives and non-affirming negatives. An affirming negative is a negative phenomenon realized by a mind that eliminates its negated object while realizing another phenomenon. A non-affirming negative is a negative phenomenon realized by a mind that merely eliminates its negated object without realizing another phenomenon. See *Ocean of Nectar*.

Non-affirming negative See *Negative phenomenon*.

Object of negation An object explicitly negated by a mind realizing a negative phenomenon. In meditation on emptiness, or lack of inherent existence, it refers to inherent existence. Also known as 'negated object'.

Obstructions to liberation Obstructions that prevent the attainment of liberation. All delusions, such as ignorance, attachment and anger, together with their seeds, are obstructions to liberation. Also called 'delusion-obstructions'.

Obstructions to enlightenment The imprints of delusions, which prevent simultaneous and direct realization of all phenomena. Also known as 'obstructions to omniscience'. Only Buddhas have overcome these obstructions.

Offering That which delights the holy beings.

Phabongkha Rinpoche See *Je Phabongkhapa*.

Perfection of Wisdom Sutras Sutras of the second turning of the Wheel of Dharma, in which Buddha revealed his final view of the ultimate nature of all phenomena – emptiness of inherent existence. See *Heart of Wisdom* and *Ocean of Nectar*.

Pratimoksha vow 'Pratimoksha' is the Sanskrit term for 'personal liberation', and so a Pratimoksha vow is a vow that is motivated mainly by the wish to attain personal liberation. There are eight types of Pratimoksha vow. See *The Bodhisattva Vow*.

Primary mind A cognizer that principally apprehends the mere entity of an object. Synonymous with consciousness. There are six primary minds: eye consciousness, ear consciousness, nose consciousness, tongue consciousness, body consciousness and mental consciousness. Each moment of mind comprises a primary mind and various mental factors. A primary mind and its accompanying mental factors are the same entity but have different functions. See *Understanding the Mind*.

Pure Land A pure environment in which there are no true sufferings. There are many Pure Lands. For example, Tushita is the Pure Land of Buddha Maitreya, Sukhavati is the Pure Land of Buddha Amitabha, and Dakini Land, or Keajra, is the Pure Land of Buddha Vajrayogini and Buddha Heruka. See *Living Meaningfully, Dying Joyfully*.

Ratnasambhava The manifestation of the aggregate of feeling of all Buddhas. He has a yellow-coloured body.

Realization A stable and non-mistaken experience of a virtuous object that directly protects us from suffering.

Sadhana A ritual prayer that is a special method for attaining spiritual realizations, usually associated with a Tantric Deity.

Saraha One of the first Mahasiddhas, and the Teacher of Nagarjuna. See *Essence of Vajrayana*.

Shantideva (AD 687-763) A great Indian Buddhist scholar and meditation master. He composed *Guide to the Bodhisattva's Way of Life*. See *Meaningful to Behold* and *Guide to the Bodhisattva's Way of Life*.

Shepherd-like bodhichitta The wish to lead all living beings to Buddhahood in the way that a shepherd leads his sheep to safety. Just as shepherds first supply all the needs of their flock and attend to their own needs last of all, so some Bodhisattvas want to lead all living beings to Buddhahood first and then attain enlightenment for themselves last of all. See *Joyful Path of Good Fortune*.

Stupa A symbolic representation of Buddha's mind.

Subsequent attainment The period between meditation sessions; also known as 'meditation break'. See *Joyful Path of Good Fortune*.

Superior being 'Arya' in Sanskrit. A being who has a direct realization of emptiness. There are Hinayana Superiors and Mahayana Superiors.

Sutra The teachings of Buddha that are open to everyone to practise without the need for empowerment. These include Buddha's teachings of the three turnings of the Wheel of Dharma.

Torma offering A special food offering made according to either Sutra or Tantra. See *Essence of Vajrayana* and *Guide to Dakini Land*.

Tranquil abiding A concentration that possesses the special bliss of physical and mental suppleness that is attained in dependence upon completing the nine mental abidings. See *Joyful Path of Good Fortune* and *Meaningful to Behold*.

Transference of consciousness 'Powa' in Tibetan. A practice for transferring the consciousness to a Pure Land at the time of death. See *Living Meaningfully, Dying Joyfully* and *Great Treasury of Merit*.

Tsog offering An offering made by an assembly of Heroes and Heroines. See *Essence of Vajrayana* and *Guide to Dakini Land*.

Vaibhashika The lower of the two schools of Hinayana tenets. This school does not accept self-cognizers and asserts external objects to be truly existent. See *Meaningful to Behold* and *Ocean of Nectar*.

Vairochana The manifestation of the aggregate of form of all Buddhas. He has a white-coloured body.

Vajra and bell A vajra is a ritual object resembling a sceptre and symbolizing great bliss, and a bell is a ritual hand-bell symbolizing emptiness. See *Guide to Dakini Land* and *Tantric Grounds and Paths*.

Vajradhara The founder of Vajrayana, or Tantra. He appears directly only to highly realized Bodhisattvas to whom he gives Tantric teachings. To benefit other living beings with less merit, he manifested in the more visible form of Buddha Shakyamuni.

He also said that in degenerate times he would appear in an ordinary form as a Spiritual Guide. See *Great Treasury of Merit*.

Vajradharma The manifestation of the speech of all Buddhas. He looks like Conqueror Vajradhara, except that his body is red. There are three ways in which we can visualize him: in his outer aspect as Hero Vajradharma, in his inner aspect as Buddha Vajradharma, or in his secret aspect as Buddha Vajradharma with consort. See *Guide to Dakini Land*.

Vajrasattva Buddha Vajrasattva is the aggregate of consciousness of all the Buddhas, appearing in the aspect of a white-coloured Deity specifically in order to purify the negativity of living beings. He is the same nature as Buddha Vajradhara, differing only in aspect. The practice of meditation and recitation of Vajrasattva is a very powerful method for purifying our impure mind and actions. See *Guide to Dakini Land*.

Vinaya The moral discipline of the Pratimoksha, and in particular the moral discipline of the ordained Sangha.

Vow A virtuous determination to abandon particular faults that is generated in conjunction with a traditional ritual. The three sets of vows are the Pratimoksha vows of individual liberation, the Bodhisattva vows, and the Secret Mantra or Tantric vows. See *The Bodhisattva Vow* and *Tantric Grounds and Paths*.

Wheel of Dharma A collection of Buddha's teachings. Dharma is compared to the precious wheel, one of the possessions of a legendary chakravatin king. This wheel could transport the king across great distances in a very short time, and it is said that wherever the precious wheel travelled the king reigned. In a similar way, when Buddha revealed the path to enlightenment he was said to have 'turned the Wheel of Dharma' because, wherever these teachings are present, deluded minds are brought under control.

Wisdom A virtuous, intelligent mind that makes its primary mind realize its object thoroughly. A wisdom is a spiritual path that functions to release our mind from delusions or their imprints. An example of wisdom is the correct view of emptiness. See *Heart of Wisdom*, *Ocean of Nectar* and *Understanding the Mind*.

Wisdom being An actual Buddha, especially one who is invited to unite with a visualized commitment being.

Wrong awareness A cognizer that is mistaken with respect to its engaged, or apprehended, object. See *Understanding the Mind*.

Yidam See *Deity*.

Yoga A term used for various spiritual practices that entail maintaining a special view, such as Guru yoga and the yogas of sleeping, rising and experiencing nectar. 'Yoga' also refers to 'union', such as the union of tranquil abiding and superior seeing. See *Guide to Dakini Land*.

Yogi/Yogini Sanskrit terms usually referring to a male or a female meditator who has attained the union of tranquil abiding and superior seeing.

Bibliography

Geshe Kelsang Gyatso is a highly respected meditation master and scholar of the Mahayana Buddhist tradition founded by Je Tsongkhapa. Since arriving in the West in 1977, Geshe Kelsang has worked tirelessly to establish pure Buddhadharma throughout the world. Over this period he has given extensive teachings on the major scriptures of the Mahayana. These teachings are currently being published and provide a comprehensive presentation of the essential Sutra and Tantra practices of Mahayana Buddhism.

Books

The following books by Geshe Kelsang are all published by Tharpa Publications:

The Bodhisattva Vow A practical guide to helping others. (2nd. edn., 1995)

Clear Light of Bliss A Tantric meditation manual. (2nd. edn., 1992)

Eight Steps to Happiness The Buddhist way of loving kindness. (2000)

Essence of Vajrayana The Highest Yoga Tantra practice of Heruka body mandala. (1997)

Great Treasury of Merit How to rely upon a Spiritual Guide. (1992)

Guide to Dakini Land The Highest Yoga Tantra practice of Buddha Vajrayogini. (2nd. edn., 1996)

Guide to the Bodhisattva's Way of Life How to enjoy a life of great meaning and altruism. (A translation of Shantideva's famous verse masterpiece.) (2002)

Heart Jewel The essential practices of Kadampa Buddhism. (2nd. edn., 1997)

Heart of Wisdom An explanation of the Heart Sutra. (4th. edn., 2001)

How to Solve Our Human Problems The four noble truths. (2005)

Introduction to Buddhism An explanation of the Buddhist way of life. (2nd. edn., 2001)

Joyful Path of Good Fortune The complete Buddhist path to enlightenment. (2nd. edn., 1995)

Living Meaningfully, Dying Joyfully The profound practice of transference of consciousness. (1999)

Mahamudra Tantra The supreme Heart Jewel nectar. (2005)

Meaningful to Behold Becoming a friend of the world. (5th. edn., 2007)

Modern Buddhism The Path of Compassion and Wisdom. (2011)

The New Meditation Handbook Meditations to make our life happy and meaningful. (4th. edn., 2003)

Ocean of Nectar The true nature of all things. (1995)

Tantric Grounds and Paths How to enter, progress on and complete the Vajrayana path. (1994)

Transform Your Life A blissful journey. (2001)

Understanding the Mind The nature and power of the mind. (3rd. edn., 2002)

Universal Compassion Inspiring solutions for difficult times. (4th. edn., 2002)

Sadhanas and Other Booklets

Geshe Kelsang has also supervised the translation of a collection of essential sadhanas, or prayer booklets.

Avalokiteshvara Sadhana Prayers and requests to the Buddha of Compassion.

The Bodhisattva's Confession of Moral Downfalls The purification practice of the *Mahayana Sutra of the Three Superior Heaps*.

Condensed Essence of Vajrayana Condensed Heruka body mandala self-generation sadhana.

Dakini Yoga Six-session Guru yoga combined with self-generation as Vajrayogini.

Drop of Essential Nectar A special fasting and purification practice in conjunction with Eleven-faced Avalokiteshvara.

Essence of Good Fortune Prayers for the six preparatory practices for meditation on the stages of the path to enlightenment.

Essence of Vajrayana Heruka body mandala self-generation sadhana according to the system of Mahasiddha Ghantapa.

Feast of Great Bliss Vajrayogini self-initiation sadhana.

Great Liberation of the Father Preliminary prayers for Mahamudra meditation in conjunction with Heruka practice.

Great Liberation of the Mother Preliminary prayers for Mahamudra meditation in conjunction with Vajrayogini practice.

The Great Mother A method to overcome hindrances and obstacles by reciting the *Essence of Wisdom Sutra* (the *Heart Sutra*).

A Handbook for the Daily Practice of Bodhisattva and Tantric Vows.

Heartfelt Prayers Funeral service for cremations and burials.

Heart Jewel The Guru yoga of Je Tsongkhapa combined with the condensed sadhana of his Dharma Protector.

The Kadampa Way of Life The essential practice of Kadam Lamrim.

Liberation from Sorrow Praises and requests to the Twenty-one Taras.

Mahayana Refuge Ceremony and Bodhisattva Vow Ceremony.

Medicine Buddha Prayer A method for benefiting others.

Medicine Buddha Sadhana A method for accomplishing the attainments of Medicine Buddha.

Meditation and Recitation of Solitary Vajrasattva.

Melodious Drum Victorious in all Directions The extensive fulfilling and restoring ritual of the Dharma Protector, the great king Dorje Shugden, in conjunction with Mahakala, Kalarupa, Kalindewi and other Dharma Protectors.

Offering to the Spiritual Guide (Lama Chopa) A special way of relying upon a Spiritual Guide.

Path of Compassion for the Deceased Powa sadhana for the benefit of the deceased.

Pathway to the Pure Land Training in powa – the transference of consciousness.

Powa Ceremony Transference of consciousness for the deceased.

Prayers for Meditation Brief preparatory prayers for meditation.

Prayers for World Peace.

A Pure Life The practice of taking and keeping the eight Mahayana precepts.

Quick Path to Great Bliss Vajrayogini self-generation sadhana.

The Root Tantra of Heruka and Vajrayogini.

Treasury of Wisdom The sadhana of Venerable Manjushri.

Union of No More Learning Heruka body mandala self-initiation sadhana.

Vajra Hero Yoga A brief practice of Heruka body mandala self-generation.

The Vows and Commitments of Kadampa Buddhism.

Wishfulfilling Jewel The Guru yoga of Je Tsongkhapa combined with the sadhana of his Dharma Protector.

The Yoga of Buddha Amitayus A special method for increasing lifespan, wisdom and merit.

The Yoga of Buddha Heruka The brief self-generation sadhana of Heruka body mandala & Condensed six-session yoga.

The Yoga of Buddha Maitreya Self-generation sadhana.

The Yoga of Buddha Vajrapani Self-generation sadhana.

The Yoga of Enlightened Mother Arya Tara Self-generation sadhana.

The Yoga of Great Mother Prajnaparumita Self-generation sadhana.

The Yoga of Thousand-armed Avalokiteshvara Self-generation sadhana.

The Yoga of White Tara, Buddha of Long Life.

To order any of our publications, or to request a catalogue, please visit www.tharpa.com or contact your nearest Tharpa office listed on page 391.

NKT – IKBU

Study Programmes of
Kadampa Buddhism

Kadampa Buddhism is a Mahayana Buddhist school founded by the great Indian Buddhist Master Atisha (AD 982-1054). His followers are known as 'Kadampas'. 'Ka' means 'word' and refers to Buddha's teachings, and 'dam' refers to Atisha's special Lamrim instructions known as 'the stages of the path to enlightenment'. By integrating their knowledge of all Buddha's teachings into their practice of Lamrim, and by integrating this into their everyday lives, Kadampa Buddhists are encouraged to use Buddha's teachings as practical methods for transforming daily activities into the path to enlightenment. The great Kadampa Teachers are famous not only for being great scholars but also for being spiritual practitioners of immense purity and sincerity.

The lineage of these teachings, both their oral transmission and blessings, was then passed from Teacher to disciple, spreading throughout much of Asia, and now to many countries throughout the modern world. Buddha's teachings, which are known as 'Dharma', are likened to a wheel that moves from country to country in accordance with changing conditions and people's karmic inclinations. The external forms of presenting Buddhism may change as it meets with different cultures and societies, but its essential authenticity is ensured through the continuation of an unbroken lineage of realized practitioners.

Kadampa Buddhism was first introduced into the West in 1977 by the renowned Buddhist Master, Venerable Geshe Kelsang Gyatso. Since that time, he has worked tirelessly to spread Kadampa Buddhism throughout the world by giving extensive teachings, writing many profound texts on Kadampa Buddhism, and founding the New Kadampa Tradition – International Kadampa Buddhist Union (NKT-IKBU), which now has over a thousand Kadampa Buddhist Centres and groups worldwide. Each Centre offers study programmes on Buddhist psychology, philosophy and meditation instruction, as well as retreats for all levels of practitioner. The emphasis is on integrating Buddha's teachings into daily life to solve our human problems and to spread lasting peace and happiness throughout the world.

The Kadampa Buddhism of the NKT-IKBU is an entirely independent Buddhist tradition and has no political affiliations. It is an association of Buddhist Centres and practitioners that derive their inspiration and guidance from the example of the ancient Kadampa Buddhist Masters and their teachings, as presented by Geshe Kelsang.

There are three reasons why we need to study and practise the teachings of Buddha: to develop our wisdom, to cultivate a good heart and to maintain a peaceful state of mind. If we do not strive to develop our wisdom, we will always remain ignorant of ultimate truth – the true nature of reality. Although we wish for happiness, our ignorance leads us to engage in non-virtuous actions, which are the main cause of all our suffering. If we do not cultivate a good heart, our selfish motivation destroys harmony and good relationships with others. We have no peace, and no chance to gain pure happiness. Without inner peace, outer peace is impossible. If we do not maintain a peaceful state of mind, we are not happy even if we have ideal conditions. On the other hand, when our mind is peaceful, we are happy, even if our external conditions are unpleasant. Therefore, the development of these qualities is of utmost importance for our daily happiness.

Geshe Kelsang Gyatso, or 'Geshe-la' as he is affectionately called by his students, has designed three special spiritual programmes for the systematic study and practice of Kadampa Buddhism that are especially suited to the modern world: the General Programme (GP), the Foundation Programme (FP) and the Teacher Training Programme (TTP).

GENERAL PROGRAMME

The General Programme provides a basic introduction to Buddhist view, meditation and practice that is suitable for beginners. It also includes advanced teachings and practice from both Sutra and Tantra.

FOUNDATION PROGRAMME

The Foundation Programme provides an opportunity to deepen our understanding and experience of Buddhism through a systematic study of six texts:

1 *Joyful Path of Good Fortune* – a commentary to Atisha's Lamrim instructions, the stages of the path to enlightenment.
2 *Universal Compassion* – a commentary to Bodhisattva Chekhawa's *Training the Mind in Seven Points*.
3 *Eight Steps to Happiness* – a commentary to Bodhisattva Langri Tangpa's *Eight Verses of Training the Mind*.
4 *Heart of Wisdom* – a commentary to the *Heart Sutra*.
5 *Meaningful to Behold* – a commentary to Venerable Shantideva's *Guide to the Bodhisattva's Way of Life*.
6 *Understanding the Mind* – a detailed explanation of the mind, based on the works of the Buddhist scholars Dharmakirti and Dignaga.

The benefits of studying and practising these texts are as follows:

(1) *Joyful Path of Good Fortune* – we gain the ability to put all Buddha's teachings of both Sutra and Tantra into practice. We can easily make progress on, and complete, the stages of the path to the supreme happiness of enlightenment. From a practical point of view, Lamrim is the main body of Buddha's teachings, and the other teachings are like its limbs.

(2) and (3) *Universal Compassion* and *Eight Steps to Happiness* – we gain the ability to integrate Buddha's teachings into our daily life and solve all our human problems.

(4) *Heart of Wisdom* – we gain a realization of the ultimate nature of reality. By gaining this realization, we can eliminate the ignorance of self-grasping, which is the root of all our suffering.

(5) *Meaningful to Behold* – we transform our daily activities into the Bodhisattva's way of life, thereby making every moment of our human life meaningful.

(6) *Understanding the Mind* – we understand the relationship between our mind and its external objects. If we understand that objects depend upon the subjective mind, we can change the way objects appear to us by changing our own mind. Gradually, we will gain the ability to control our mind and in this way solve all our problems.

TEACHER TRAINING PROGRAMME

The Teacher Training Programme is designed for people who wish to train as authentic Dharma Teachers. In addition to completing the study of fourteen texts of Sutra and Tantra, which include the six texts mentioned above, the student is required to observe certain commitments with regard to behaviour and way of life, and to complete a number of meditation retreats.

All Kadampa Buddhist Centres are open to the public. Every year we celebrate Festivals in many countries throughout the world, including two in England, where people gather from around the world to receive special teachings and empowerments and to enjoy a spiritual holiday. Please feel free to visit us at any time!

For further information about NKT-IKBU study programmes or to find your nearest centre, visit www.kadampa.org, or contact:

NKT–IKBU Central Office
Conishead Priory,
Ulverston, Cumbria,
LA12 9QQ, UK
Tel: +44 (0)1229 588533
Fax: +44 (0)1229 580080
Email: info@kadampa.org
Website: www.kadampa.org

US NKT–IKBU Office
Kadampa Meditation Center
47 Sweeney Road
Glen Spey, NY 12737, USA
Tel: +1 845-856-9000
Fax: +1 845-856-2110
Email: info@nkt-kmc-newyork.org
Website: www.nkt-kmc-newyork.org

Tharpa Offices Worldwide

Tharpa books are currently published in English (UK and US), Chinese, French, German, Italian, Japanese, Portuguese and Spanish. Most languages are available from any Tharpa office listed below.

UK Office
Tharpa Publications UK
Conishead Priory
ULVERSTON
Cumbria, LA12 9QQ, UK
Tel: +44 (0)1229 588 599
Fax: +44 (0)1229 483 919
Web: www.tharpa.com/uk/
E-mail: info.uk@tharpa.com

US Office
Tharpa Publications US
47 Sweeney Road
GLEN SPEY, NY 12737, USA
Tel: +1 845-856-5102
Toll-free: 888-741-3475
Fax: +1 845-856-2110
Web: www.tharpa.com/us/
E-mail: info.us@tharpa.com

Australian Office
Tharpa Publications Australia
25 McCarthy Road,
MONBULK VIC 3793

AUSTRALIA
Tel: +61 (0)3 9752-0277
Web: www.tharpa.com/au/
E-mail: info.au@tharpa.com

Brazilian Office
Editora Tharpa Brasil
Rua Fradique Coutinho 701
VILA MADALENA
05416-011 São Paulo - SP
BRAZIL
Tel/Fax: +55 (11) 3812 7509
Web: www.budismo.org.br
E-mail: contato@tharpa.com.br

Canadian Office
Tharpa Publications Canada
631 Crawford St., TORONTO
ON M6G 3K1, CANADA
Tel: +1 (416) 762-8710
Toll-free: 866-523-2672
Fax: +1 (416) 762-2267
Web: www.tharpa.com/ca/
E-mail: info.ca@tharpa.com

French Office
Editions Tharpa,
Château de Segrais
72220 SAINT-MARS-
D'OUTILLÉ, FRANCE
Tel : +33 (0)2 43 87 71 02
Fax : +33 (0)2 76 01 34 10
Web: www.tharpa.com/fr/
E-mail: info.fr@tharpa.com

German Office
Tharpa Verlag Deutschland,
Sommerswalde 8,
16727, OBERKRÄMER,
OT Schwante, GERMANY
Tel: +49 (033055) 222135
Fax : +49 (033055) 222139
Web: www.tharpa.com/de/
E-mail: info.de@tharpa.com

Hong Kong Office
Tharpa Asia
2nd Floor, 21 Tai Wong St. East,
Wanchai, HONG KONG
Tel: +852 25205137
Fax: +852 25072208
Web: www.tharpa.com/hk-cht/
E-mail: info.hk@tharpa.com

Japanese Office
Tharpa Japan
Dai 5 Nakamura Kosan Biru #501,
Shinmachi 1-29-16, Nishi-ku
OSAKA, 550-0013, JAPAN
Tel/Fax : +81 6-6532-7632
Web: www.meditationinjapan.com
E-mail: info.jp@tharpa.com

Mexican Office
Enrique Rébsamen No 406,
Col. Narvate, entre Xola y
Diagonal de San Antonio, C.P.
03020, MÉXICO D.F., MÉXICO
Tel: +01 (55) 56 39 61 86
Tel/Fax: +01 (55) 56 39 61 80
Web: www.tharpa.com/mx/
Email: tharpa@kadampa.org/mx

South African Office
c/o Mahasiddha Kadampa
Buddhist Centre
2 Hollings Road, Malvern
DURBAN
4093 REP. OF SOUTH AFRICA
Tel : +27 (0)31 464 0984
Web: www.tharpa.com/za/
E-mail: info.za@tharpa.com

Spanish Office
Editorial Tharpa España
Camino Fuente del Perro s/n
29120 ALHAURÍN EL GRANDE
(Málaga), SPAIN
Tel.: +34 952 596808
Fax: +34 952 490175
Web: www.tharpa.com/es/
E-mail: info.es@tharpa.com

Swiss Office
Tharpa Verlag AG
Mirabellenstrasse 1
CH-8048 ZÜRICH
SWITZERLAND
Tel: +41 44 401 02 20
Fax: +41 44 461 36 88
Web: www.tharpa.com/ch/
E-mail: info.ch@tharpa.com

Index

A

action mudra 14, 189
actions 40. *See also* inappro-
     priate actions; non-virtuous
     actions; virtuous actions
   bad/good 73
   contaminated 120
   impure 22
   pure 58–59, 91
adverse conditions
   accepting 88, 94
   pacifying 231
   transforming 23
Advice from Atisha's Heart 138
affectionate love 66–67, 146
   eight benefits of 78
affirmative phenomenon 132
ageing. *See also* suffering, of
     ageing
   freedom from 185
aggregates
   contaminated/uncontam-
     inated 155–157

Akanishta. *See* Pure Land
Akshobya 268
Ambhidana Tantra 192
Amitabha 91, 269
Amoghasiddhi 269
analogies
   actor 133
   bird leaving nest 30
   blind turtle 26
   cutting down tree 60
   eagles soaring 126
   fire in house 45
   magician's illusion 9, 99,
     107, 132–133, 150
   poisonous tree 57
   seeing two moons 139
   sky and clouds 130
   sun shining on snow
     mountain 221
   thorn bush 52
   two empty glasses 229
   two wings of a bird 138, 147
Ananda 26

anger 4, 57, 66, 146, 231
 controlling 22, 231
 destroying merit 85
 overcoming through medi-
  tating on emptiness 108, 129
 solving daily problems of 5,
  76
animals 8, 10, 32, 42, 60, 76,
  239
 rebirth as 32, 35, 55, 62
 suffering of 8, 42, 79
appearance 67. *See also*
  mistaken appearance; mere
  appearance; clear appearance
 deceptive 98, 100, 121, 132
 dream 117, 145
 illusory 132
 nature of mind 145
 of waking world 117
 to mind 98, 123
Aryadeva 92
Arya Tara 13, 19, 140
 emanations of 14
 reliance upon 11
Atisha 4, 24, 386
 life story of 11–20
 quotes by 138, 220
attachment 57, 66, 100, 141
 as root of suffering 6
 controlling 5–7, 22
 laziness of 28, 29
 overcoming through medi-
  tating on emptiness 108,
  117, 120, 129, 133
 root of 5
 transforming into spiritual
  path 147–149, 182

attainments 246
 common/uncommon 16
 five 231, 246
 non-deceptive 28
 of liberating/ripening 221–222
 request to bestow 231, 233
 worldly 28, 146
attention 109
Avadhutipa 12, 13, 14
Avalokiteshvara 11, 128

B

basis of imputation
 for car 123, 155
 for Heruka 154, 156–157, 228
 for I 154–156, 164, 187
 for mind 109
 meaning of 155
Baso Chokyi Gyaltsen 191
beginningless time 4, 26, 72,
  113, 154, 164, 185, 216
beseeching the Spiritual Guides
 to remain 219–220
birth 45. *See also* rebirth;
  suffering, of birth
black near-attainment.
  See subtle minds, black
  near-attainment
blessings 10, 35, 36, 37, 38, 81,
  138, 149
 applying effort to receive 35,
  37, 205
 Guru yoga as gateway to
  receiving 204
 of all Buddhas 208, 221
 of all Heroes and Heroines
  246

receiving in degenerate times
195
receiving within our channels
and drops 200, 202
bliss. *See also* clear light, of bliss;
great bliss; spontaneous
great bliss; union of great
bliss and emptiness
sexual 149, 239
types of 181
Blissful Journey 234, 291–314
Bodh Gaya 3, 14
Bodhibhadra 12
bodhichitta 12, 14, 15, 187,
207, 242. *See also* ultimate
bodhichitta
as gateway to enlightenment
204
conventional 97, 138, 188
definition of 65
etymology of 65
five stages of training 66–82
meditation on 206–207
part of clear light 176
qualified 141
shepherd-like 94
training in actual 80–82
training in the path of 83–96
Bodhisattva 80, 94, 115, 150,
181
meaning of 65–66
Superior 86, 138, 222
Bodhisattva's path 65, 83
Bodhisattva's vow 15, 83–85
body. *See also* emptiness, of
body; inherent existence, of
body; vajra body; very subtle
body

at the time of death 51
continuously residing 93,
164, 179, 180, 185, 188
obscured by delusions 188
conventionally existent 107
deceptive nature of 105–106
divine 179
from parents 185
gross 185, 187, 188
impure 22, 53
manifestation of emptiness
128
parts of 103
pure 188
true/ultimate nature of
105–107
body wheel 202
brain 30
Buddha 27, 61, 76, 83, 209. *See
also* refuge; Shakyamuni,
Buddha
attainments of ripening and
liberating 222
awakened one 36
compassion of 9
existing by convention 108
faith in 7, 9, 10
function of 10, 36
kindness of 9
quotes by 81, 146, 241
all phenomena are like
dreams 99
blind turtle 26
from *Sutra of the Four Noble
Truths* 41, 56, 58, 61
magician's creations 9, 132
rarity of experiencing great
bliss 239

searching for body with
wisdom 101
source of all happiness 10, 36
uncommon quality of 125
Buddhadharma 20, 22, 26, 27,
97, 146. *See also* Buddha's
teachings
meeting 27
Buddha nature 88, 149, 154,
185
according to Highest Yoga
Tantra 208
complete ripening of 222
our real 165
very subtle body 93
Buddha of Compassion 96
Buddha's body 188, 203
seed of 186
Buddha's mind 203
emptiness of 222
seed of 186
Buddha's speech 203, 245
seed of 186
Buddha's teachings 3–7, 8,
10, 20, 28, 73, 177. *See also*
Buddhadharma; Dharma
method to solve human
problems 4
scientific method 7
supreme medicine 21
three sets of 15
two stages of 4
Buddhism 116, 215
entering 27, 35, 204
founder of 3
What is 3–7
Buddhist 6, 21
Buddhist faith 7–10. *See also*
faith

Buddhist path 35

C

cancer 87
car 6, 28, 54, 117, 123, 155
emptiness of 101
central channel 149, 159–161,
162, 163, 173, 183, 184, 186,
246, 261–263, 266. *See also*
channels
four attributes of 160, 261
meditation on 165–166
like a wishfulfilling cow
235
penetrating
of another's body 189
of our own body 189, 191
ten doors 189–190
cessation 61
Chakrasambara 193. *See also*
Heruka
Chandragarbha. *See* Atisha
channel knots 160, 262
at heart 162, 167
channels 200, 201, 202. *See also*
central channel
explanation of 261–266
free from obstacles 200, 202
life 160, 261
right and left 160, 161, 163,
169, 182, 262–263, 272
ordinary inner heat increasing in 183
other names for 262
channel spokes 263
channel wheel/s 160–161, 263
chart of four major 263
crown 184, 190, 262

heart 184, 189, 190, 201, 202, 262, 263, 271
  chart of spokes of 264
  dissolving winds into 173, 176
  importance of 167, 191, 264
  jewel 190, 264
  navel 176, 184, 190, 262
  secret place 190, 264
  throat 184, 190, 262
  wheel of fire 190
  wheel of wind 190
cherishing love 66
  training in 70–78
cherishing others 79, 84
  advantages of 75–76
  two levels of 71
clairvoyance 16, 33
clear appearance 150, 153, 154, 156, 228
  training in 226–227
clear light 173, 174–175, 186, 189, 191, 237, 238, 239. See also example clear light; meaning clear light; ultimate example clear light
  foundation of all other minds 176
  fully qualified 177, 180
  levels of experience of 179
  mounted wind of 272
  nature of 175
  of bliss 167, 180, 184, 239, 247
  of death 238
  of sleep 238
  realization of 239
  three types of 238
  training in 239
  what is 238

Clear Light of Bliss 172, 190, 191
compassion 4, 11, 23, 66, 74, 94
  as gateway to path to enlightenment 69
  as main offering 215
  as nature of conventional bodhichitta 97
  dying with mind of 91
  Heruka, manifestation of 154
  meditation on taking with 88–92
  of Buddha 9
  part of clear light 176
  training in universal 23, 79–80
completion stage 15, 151, 153, 199
  completing 221
  definition of 159
  effective meditation on 202, 207
  five stages of 163, 179–180, 201
  of Mahamudra 177–192
  principal objects of 159
  The Tantra of 159–176
  training in 234–235
concentration 49, 175. See also three higher trainings
  bliss of suppleness of 181
  nature of 59
  of absorption of cessation 181
  of close placement 137, 227
  of continual placement 137, 227
  of placing the mind 137, 226
  of replacement 137, 227

penetrating central channel
with 184
perfection of 84, 85–86, 88, 94
conceptual minds 115, 120, 171
conceptual thought 115–116
imprints of 124
mounted winds of 272
Condensed Heruka Root Tantra
146, 239
*Condensed Perfection of Wisdom
Sutra* 101
Condensed Root Tantra 194
Condensed Six-session Yoga
287–290
conscientiousness 16, 34
consciousness 109, 216, 267
at birth 43
at death 51, 162
consort 189. *See also* action
mudra
contact 109
continuously residing body.
See body, continuously
residing
continuously residing mind.
See mind, continuously
residing
continuously residing speech
185
conventional nature 130. *See
also* conventional truth
of I 114
conventional search 101
conventional truth 107, 228.
See also union of the two
truths
and ultimate truth 121–127
deceptive phenomena 122
gross and subtle 123

conventional world 133
convention, existing by way
of 108
correct belief 91–92, 157, 227
covetousness 39
creative yoga 153, 159
cycle of impure life 23, 26, 56.
See also samsara

D

daily life 67, 75
Dakini Land, Pure 199
outer/inner 234
Dakinis 13
death 29–32, 36, 87, 89, 164, 186.
See also suffering, of death
meditation on 31
permanent separation of
body and mind 187
realization of 29
state of mind at 39
deathless body 164, 185, 188.
See also body, continuously
residing; vajra body
deathless person 164, 185, 187
deceptive phenomena 122
dedication 220–221, 248
Deity/Deities 153, 154, 179,
193, 200, 237
of Heruka's body mandala
202–203
deluded views 62
delusions 22, 60, 74, 100, 116,
150, 188
abandonment of 180, 185
conceptions of eight extremes
root of 120
controlling 5, 142, 231

function of 57
innate 185
intellectually-formed 185
meditate on emptiness to overcome 108
reducing 90, 133
root of 148
sickness of 21
source of daily problems 4
suffering from 6
demi-gods
rebirth as 8
suffering of 43, 79
depression 5, 73
desire/s 53–54
transforming experience of objects of 242
Dharma 3, 4, 26, 386. See also Buddhadharma; Buddha's teachings; Kadam Dharma; refuge
actual protection 37
giving 85
great mirror of 23
method to solve daily problems 6–7
Dharmakaya 194, 222. See also Truth Body
Dharma practice 7, 26, 28, 29, 30, 31, 52, 59, 68
as offering 215
eliminating main obstacle to 32
obstacles to 216
Dharmarakshita 14
Dhipamkara Shrijana. See Atisha
discrimination 109
dissatisfaction 54, 55, 92

distractions 88, 184
overcoming 272
prevention of 59
divine pride 150, 153–157
training in 227–228
doctor 21, 36, 46, 87
Dorje Shugden 209
dream/s 4, 30, 43, 117
appearances 117
elephant 98
mere appearance to mind 133, 134
of samsara 36
phenomena as like 99
relative validity of 122
world 99, 145
Dromtonpa 22
drops 161, 189. See also indestructible drop
flowing in central channel 181, 184
flowing in left and right channels 183
free from obstacles 202
melting of 181, 183, 184
red and white 161, 183, 200, 201, 265
dualistic appearance 127, 266

E

effort 7, 29, 31
perfection of 84, 85, 88, 94
to receive Buddha's blessings 35, 37, 205
eighteen root downfalls 16
eight extremes 120, 124, 129
emptiness of 116–121, 125
eighty indicative conceptions 172

elements 267
  earth 169, 268
  fire 169, 269
  six, needed to experience bliss 182
  space 269
  water 170, 268
  wind 169, 269
Emanation Body 149, 154, 222, 245
emanations 81, 91, 138
  of Arya Tara 14
  of definitive Heruka 208
  of Guru Sumati Buddha Heruka 220
  of Heruka 194
  of Heruka and Vajrayogini 195
empowerment/s 149
  four 245
  of Heruka body mandala 208
  of Highest Yoga Tantra commitment of 245–246
emptiness/es 98–99, 107, 183
  all same nature 128–130
    application in meditation break 129
  and clear light 177–180
  basis for training in ultimate bodhichitta 97
  conventional bases of 129
  correct view of, qualified 141
  direct realization of 86, 97, 107, 114, 125, 138, 177, 179, 266
  existing by convention 108
  generic image of 113, 114, 179
  manifestations of 117, 129, 130

non-deceptive 177
non-mistaken awareness of 114
object of negation of 111, 132
of all phenomena 86, 98, 109, 125, 136, 193, 229, 240, 241, 242, 247
of body 100–108, 110, 118, 128, 135
of book 108
of car 101
of coming and going 118–119
of eight extremes 116–121
of emptiness 118, 124
of I 110–116, 126, 136
of impermanent phenomena 118
of mind 109–110
of obstructive contact 131
of permanent phenomena 118
of produced phenomena
  how to meditate on 126–127
of production and disintegration 116–117
of singularity and plurality 119–120
phenomena not other than 102, 222
practice of, in our daily activities 132–135
profound view of 28
real nature of phenomena 60
signs of correct meditation on 113
space-like 106, 113, 126
space-like meditative equipoise on 126

studying 127
synonyms of 123
universal solution to
  problems 135
yoga of equalizing samsara
  and nirvana 130
Enjoyment Body 149, 154, 194,
  222, 245
enlightened beings 176, 215.
  See also Buddha; Shakyamuni, Buddha
enlightenment 32, 87, 93
  actual 230
  as realization of union of two
    truths 222
  attaining within one single
    life 199
  attaining within three years
    231
  attainment of 180, 234
  bodhichitta wish to attain
    65, 81, 82, 83
  definition of 26, 80
  depending upon great bliss
    182
  depending upon kindness of
    others 69
  depending upon receiving
    blessings 138
  led to by Spiritual Guide 207
  meaning and goal of human
    life 25, 26, 28, 138
  path to 83
  principal method to attain 14
  pure and everlasting happi-
    ness of 27, 61, 82
  quick path to 71, 76, 94, 145,
    194, 239

showing the manner of
  accomplishing 3
state of 146, 229
environment
  impure 22, 53
equalizing self and others 70–71
Essence of Vajrayana 193, 272,
  275
example clear light 16. *See also*
  ultimate example clear light
exchanging self with others
  72–78
existence from its own side/
  side of the object 102, 110,
  115, 122, 124, 129, 133, 134.
  See also inherent existence
extremes of existence/non-
  existence 114–115, 139

F

faith 37, 90, 138, 212, 221, 231.
  See also Buddhist faith
  as spiritual life 7
false objects 121, 123
fear 44, 46, 51, 56, 99, 113, 150
  of death 164
  of lower rebirth 34
feelings 5, 6, 109
five impurities 22
Form Body 85, 188, 189, 212,
  222. *See also* Emanation
  Body; Enjoyment Body
  cause of 187
  subtle/gross 222
former lives 66, 215
  wasted 29, 74
fortunate rebirth 39. *See also*
  rebirth

forty-six secondary downfalls
16
four complete purities 146,
147, 148
four empties 174–175, 176
Four Hundred Verses 92
Four Kadampa Guru Deities
11
functioning thing 118
Fundamental Wisdom 121
future lives 243
countless 35
preparing for 29
showing the existence of 30
happiness and freedom of 42
suffering of 8, 36, 38, 41, 206
cessation of 121
liberation from 7, 56, 58, 60

G

Ganden Oral Lineage 191,
204, 228, 231
essence practice of 231
Gelug tradition 194
generation stage 15, 150, 151,
153–158, 165, 187
completing 221
definition of 153
function of 154
motivated by bodhichitta
158, 207
principal objects of 159
The Tantra of 153–158
training in non-dual appearance and emptiness of
228–229
generic image 113, 114, 115,
179

Geshe Chekhawa 91, 109, 133
Ghantapa 166, 178, 194, 200
story of 195–197
giving 76. *See also* taking and
giving
benefits of meditation on 94
in conjunction with six
perfections 92–95
perfection of 84–85
gods
rebirth as 8, 56
suffering of 43, 79
great bliss 177, 193. *See also*
spontaneous great bliss
training in 239
two characteristics of 181,
184, 189, 239
great bliss and emptiness 209
generating experience of 223
great bliss wheel 201–202
great scope 21, 63, 141
path of a person of 65–247
Guhyasamaja 195
Guhyasamaja Tantra 237
Guide to Dakini Land 221, 243,
246
*Guide to the Bodhisattva's Way
of Life* 73, 74, 75, 93, 100,
102, 124, 187
Gungtang 47, 177
Guru 191. *See also* Guru yoga;
lineage Gurus; Spiritual
Guide
meaning of 207
root 207–208, 211
Guru Sumati Buddha Heruka
207–208, 212, 215, 216, 219,
220, 223, 306

making requests to 221–222
visualization and meditation
  on 209–211
Guru yoga
  gateway to receiving bless-
    ings 204
  of *Heart Jewel* according to
    Highest Yoga Tantra 209
  of Segyu lineage 209
  training in 207–223
Gyalwa Ensapa 231

H

happiness
  cause of 39
  depends upon 10, 36, 75
  from virtuous actions 38
  in samsara, no real 57, 92
  of future lives 42
  pure and everlasting 23, 56,
    81, 93
hatred. *See also* anger
  overcoming through medi-
    tating on emptiness 120
heart 89, 90
  good 66, 91, 207
  warm 66, 67, 70
heart channel wheel.
  See channel wheel/s, heart
Heart Jewel 209
Heart of Wisdom 104, 132
Heart Sutra 128
hell beings 91
  rebirth as 32, 35, 91
  suffering of 8, 43, 55, 79
Heroes and Heroines 156,
  200–204, 226

of the heart, speech and body
  wheels 202
Heroines of the commitment
  wheel 202
Heruka 14, 152, 179, 207, 243,
  266
  basis of imputation for 194
  definitive 194, 208, 222
  etymology of 193
  generation stage of 150,
    153–157
  interpretative 194
  meaning of 193
  Pure Land of 195, 199
Heruka body mandala
  193–235, 266
  close retreat of 234
  lineage of these instructions
    193–200
  mistaken appearance of 229
  obstacles to 216
  preliminary practices of
    204–223
  training in completion stage
    of 234–235
  training in generation stage
    of 223–234
    five stages of 223
    three characteristics of 225
  what is the 200–204
Heruka Losang Yeshe. *See*
  Kyabje Trijang Rinpoche
Hevajra 13
Hevajra and *Heruka Tantras* 13
Hevajra Root Tantra 190
Highest Yoga Tantra 146, 148,
  164, 177, 181, 183, 188
  division of 237

explanation of Buddha
nature 186
path of seeing of 185
realization of 200
seed of realizations of 208
two stages of 153
very essence of 153, 239
Hinayana 16
human beings
basis of suffering of 45
rebirth as 8, 55, 74, 79
causes of 32
opportunity of 27
suffering of 8, 25, 43, 79
human life 68
accomplish real meaning of
4, 25, 26, 31, 38, 60
as result of virtuous actions
75
freedoms and endowments
of 32, 62
inconceivable meaning of
181
preciousness of our 25–29,
32, 62
meditation on 27
solving problems of 60
ultimate goal and meaning
of 9, 42, 61, 138
obstacle to realizing 72
wasting 42
hungry ghosts
rebirth as 8, 32, 35
suffering of 43, 55, 79

I

I. See also emptiness, of I;
inherent existence, of I
basis of imputation of 119
conventional nature of 114
self that we normally see
111, 114, 157, 158
ultimate nature of 114
ignorance 79, 81, 104. See also
self-grasping
controlling 22
sleep of 36
illusions, magician's. See
analogies
illusory body 163, 179, 186,
191, 238
of the third stage 180
pure 180, 185, 187, 188, 199
imagination 92, 149, 153, 157,
159
impermanence, subtle 118
impermanent phenomena 131
emptiness of 118
imprints 39
karmic 117
of conceptual thoughts 124
imputation 108, 123. See also
basis of imputation
of our I 114
upon our subtle body 187
inappropriate actions 39, 85,
157
abandoning 58
purification of 215
indestructible drop 159,
161–162, 176, 191
attributes of 162

inside indestructible wind
and mind 164, 173, 186
meditation on 166–167
red and white 200, 202
indestructible mind 186
indestructible red drop 202
indestructible white drop 202
indestructible wind 179, 186,
191
indestructible wind and mind
159, 162–165, 186
meditation on 167–168
Indra and Brahma 3
inferential cognizer 115
inherent existence 102, 108,
133, 134
appearance of 121, 132
eight extremes of 120
object of negation of 111, 132
of body 102, 107, 127
of body we normally see 128
of I 113, 150, 154
identifying 110–111
self-cherishing, relationship
to 72
we normally see 111
synonyms of 98
initial scope 21, 141
path of a person of 25–40
inner fire/heat. See tummo
inner peace 72, 240
intention 4, 90, 109, 117, 121, 231
isolated body 191
isolated body and speech of
completion stage 163, 179
isolated mind 179, 191
isolated speech 191

J

Jangchub Ö 11, 17, 18, 19, 20
jealousy 43, 76, 100
controlling 22
problems of 217
Je Phabongkhapa 194, 237,
243, 246, 276
Je Sherab Senge 209
Jetari 12
Je Tsongkhapa 4, 20, 21, 64,
191, 198
founder of Gelug tradition
194
founder of new Kadampa
tradition 10
instructions on Mahamudra
Tantra given by 177
ordained name of 177
quotes by 66, 97, 182, 183
Joyful Path of Good Fortune 139

K

Kadam Dharma 22–23, 27. See
also Buddhadharma;
Buddha's teachings; Dharma;
Kadam Lamrim 10, 71
as great mirror 23
as scientific method 23
as supreme medicine 23
preciousness of 20–23
Kadampa Buddhism 386–387
Kadampas 10–20
Kadampa Teachers/Geshes
386
Kadampa tradition 3
Kagyu tradition 194

karma 38–40, 59, 73, 116–117
  collective 116
  meaning of 38
  meditation on 40
  pure/impure 266
  purifying 212
karmic connection 195
karmic imprints 117
Keajra. *See* Pure Land
Kharak Gomchen 87
Khedrubje 198
killing 39, 75
kindness 13, 78
  of Buddha 9
  of living beings 68–70, 72
  meditation on 70
King of Concentration Sutra 9,
  132
kusali tsog offering 245
Kyabje Trijang Rinpoche 195,
  200, 237, 292

L

*Lamp for the Path to Enlighten-
  ment* 20
Lamrim 87, 386. *See also*
  Kadam Lamrim
  Examination of our practice
  141–142
  pre-eminent attributes of 21
laziness 31, 85, 88, 94
  of attachment 28–29, 30
leprosy 87
Liberating Prayer 249–250
liberation 56
  attainment of 185
  how to attain 8–9

path to 56, 58. *See also* three
  higher trainings
  permanent 7, 21, 32, 38, 60, 91
  temporary 8, 61
  why we need to attain 7–8
lineage Gurus 191, 200
listening to Dharma instructions
  22, 138
living beings 10, 23, 26, 36, 65,
  77, 80
  as our mothers 67
  cherishing love for 75
  countless 19
  in Pure Land Keajra 199
  kindness of 23
  repaying kindness of 13
love 76, 84. *See also* affectionate
  love; cherishing others;
  wishing love
lower rebirth. *See also* rebirth;
  three lower realms
  cause of 32
  dangers of 32–34
  fear of 34
  prevention of 91
  protection from 35

M

magician's illusions. *See*
  analogies
Mahakaruna 197
Mahamudra 14, 147, 151, 181.
  See also meaning clear light;
  union of great bliss and
  emptiness
  as collection of merit and
  wisdom 180

completion stage of 177–192
definition of 177
etymology 177
meaning of 180
nature of 179
ripening seed of the realization
of 209
Sutra 177
synonyms of 180
uncommon 191
Mahasiddha Dharmavajra 191
Mahayana 16
Maitreya 20, 211
malice 39
mandala 200. *See also* Heruka
body mandala; Vajrayogini,
body mandala of
mandala offering 221
Manjushri 191
mantra
meaning of 231
of Heruka, essence 231–232
of sixty-two Deities of
Heruka body mandala,
condensed 233–234
of Vajrayogini, three-OM
232–233, 246
recitation, training in 231
Marpa 194, 198
meaning clear light 16, 163,
179–180, 185, 191, 199. *See
also* Mahamudra
as actual inconceivability
247
inner Dakini Land 234
of the fourth stage 180
synonyms of 180

meditation 149, 272
definition of 40
preparing for 253–254
meditative equipoise 125
mental awareness 272
mental pain 8, 41, 52, 55, 73,
79, 85
mental peace 26, 36, 40, 57,
59, 80
happiness depends upon 10
mental recitation 246
mere absence 108, 118, 124,
128, 131. *See also* emptiness
of all phenomena we normally
see 136, 241, 247
of the body we normally see
105, 106, 135
of the self we normally see
113, 126, 136
mere appearance 101, 105, 150
existing conventionally as
107, 115
part of conventional truth
122
to waking/dreaming mind
99, 133, 145
using to solve problems 117,
133
mere imputation 116, 155. *See
also* basis of imputation;
imputation
of singularity/plurality 119
mere name 88, 94, 105, 107, 115
merit 39, 78, 87, 157, 212, 215
cause of Form Body 85
collection of 94, 180, 208, 242
destroying 85
middling scope 21, 141

path of a person of 41–62
Milarepa 42, 47, 190, 197–199
empty cave 81
quote from 145
teaching on emptiness 130
mind 65, 117, 130, 162, 184, 185.
See also emptiness, of mind;
peace of mind; subtle minds;
very subtle mind
appearances as nature of 145
appearances to 98, 107, 108,
123
at death 30, 39
basis of imputation of 109
conceptual/non-conceptual
115
continuously residing 164,
180, 185
creator of world 116–117
deceptive 72
depending upon 99
existing by convention 108
gross 176
impure 22, 117, 145–146
depending upon impure
winds 265
imputed by 108
like a field 39
mistaken 67
nature and function of 30, 267
projections of 98, 102, 108,
145–146
pure 145–146
uncontaminated, definition
of 124
valid 67, 115
mindfulness 16, 34, 163, 172
subtle 172
very subtle 173

miracle powers 16
mirage 99, 100, 107, 122
mirror of Dharma 23
mistaken appearance 26, 80,
86, 122, 239
Buddhas free from 36, 125
subtle 127, 146, 181, 184, 233
abandoning 221, 234, 241
preventing 239
root of self-grasping 148
two moons reminding us of
139
wisdom free from 230
mistaken awareness 122
due to imprints of self-
grasping 114
mistaken view 155, 157
modern technology 4, 62
modern world 4
monk 14, 15, 197
moral discipline 39, 59. See
also three higher trainings
nature of 58
necessary to progress in
spiritual training 59
perfection of 84, 85, 88, 94
three types of 15
three types of higher 15
mother 9, 79
kindness of 68
recognizing livings beings as
66–67

N

nada 167, 168, 247, 363
Nagarjuna 78, 121, 188
Naropa 194, 237, 260

negated object. *See* object of
    negation
new Kadampa tradition 10
New Kadampa Tradition 387
nirvana 9, 28, 56, 61, 135, 199,
    240. *See also* liberation
    attainment of 60
    meaning and nature of 183
non-affirming negative
    phenomenon 132
non-Buddhist 6, 18, 21
non-conceptual direct
    perceiver 124
non-conceptual mind 115
non-dual appearance and
    emptiness 228–231
non-virtuous actions 4, 23,
    38–39, 51, 79
    arising from ignorance 4, 57
    avoiding 34, 76
    main cause of lower rebirth
    32
    purification of 87, 208,
    215–217
nothingness 60, 112, 113, 134

O

object of negation 111, 132
obstructions to enlightenment
    150
obstructions to liberation 150
Ocean of Great Explanation 14
Ocean of Nectar 104, 132
offerings 213–215
    definition of 215
Offering to the Spiritual Guide
    191
omniscient wisdom 86, 87

ordinary appearances 94, 147,
    204, 228, 241
    freedom from gross 179
    meaning of 149–151
ordinary beings 102, 123, 149,
    172, 194
    appearances to 124
    experiencing only ordinary
    bliss 239
    very subtle body, speech and
    mind manifesting at sleep/
    death for 186
ordinary conceptions 94, 147,
    204, 241
    abandoning of 180
    gross 179
    meaning of 149–151
ordinary death, intermediate
    state and rebirth 154
ordination 14
origins 56
    meaning of 57
Ornament of Clear Realization 20

P

Padmasambhava 16
Palden Sangpo 209
Pamtingpa 237
past lives. *See* former lives
path of accumulation 80, 86, 87
path of bodhichitta
    training in 83–95
path of meditation 80, 86, 87,
    150
path of No More Learning 80,
    86, 87
path of preparation 80, 86, 87

path of seeing 80, 86, 87
  of Highest Yoga Tantra 185
path/s. *See also* spiritual path
  bringing future result into 94
  correct 60, 207
  liberating 62
  meaning of 58
  Vajrayana 231
  vast and profound 12
  wrong 216
path to enlightenment 27, 69,
    80, 84, 94, 97
patience 75
  perfection of 84, 85, 88, 94
peace of mind 40
  depends upon 10, 36
  destroying 57, 100
  dying with 39
  happiness depends upon 10,
    36
  method to experience 135
  permanent 9, 56, 60, 65
Perfection of Wisdom Sutras 15,
    20, 121
permanent phenomena 118,
    131
  emptiness of 118
person 102, 267. *See also* initial
    scope; middling scope;
    great scope
phenomena. *See also* emptiness,
    of all phenomena
  existing as mere imputations
    155
  existing conventionally 108,
    115
  gathered into emptiness 222
  like dreams 43, 99, 133
  like illusions 99

like rainbows 134
  not other than emptiness 102
  real nature of all 60
poison 57
police 36
potential 92, 164, 216, 220
  for taking rebirth in a Pure
    Land 91
  to benefit livings beings 87,
    88, 94, 245
poverty 52, 55, 61, 84
powa 199. *See also* transference
    of consciousness
Pratimoksha vows 15
*Prayer for the Flourishing of the
    Doctrine of Je Tsongkhapa* 177
prayers 37, 197
Prayers for Meditation 251–259
preliminary guides 213, 217
preliminary practices 204–223.
    See also Prayers for
    Meditation
  uncommon 191
pride 14
primary mind 109
problems 4–7, 22, 55
  inner and outer 6
  solving 23, 70
  source of 4, 66
  universal solution to 135
produced phenomena 116–117
  emptiness of 126
produced space 131
promise 35, 37, 38, 83
prostration 212–213
puja 37
Pure Land 30, 91, 181, 221
  Akanishta 188, 199

Keajra 195, 198, 199–200, 242
    attainment of 227
    outer Dakini Land 234
    outer places of Heruka as
        266
    Pure Dakini Land 199
    rebirth in 91, 199
    Sukhavati 91, 199
    Tushita 199
purification 39, 87, 208, 212,
    215–217, 242, 243
    of our world 145
    signs of 89

Q

Quick Path to Great Bliss 243,
    247, 315–362

R

Rahulagupta 13
rainbow 99, 117, 119, 134, 193
Ratnasambhava 268
realizations 7, 58, 59, 69, 88,
    212, 231
    common/uncommon 16
    development of 23
    Tantric 92, 157
real nature of things 4
rebirth 176, 245. *See also* lower
    rebirth; suffering, of rebirth
    contaminated 45, 55, 79
    freedom from 185
    fortunate/unfortunate 39
    in a Pure Land 91, 199
    various realms of 8
    what determines our 39

red increase. *See* subtle minds,
    red increase
refuge 12, 27, 32, 34, 36, 242
    gateway to entering
        Buddhism 35, 204
    going for 35–38
    meditation on 37–38, 205
    vow, commitments of 35, 37,
        205
regret 46, 50
    for non-virtuous actions 216
rejoicing 217–219
relative truths and relative
    falsities 123
renunciation 7, 28, 41, 61, 138,
    242
    development of 23, 56
    gateway to liberation 65, 204
    motivation for three higher
        trainings 59
    qualified 141
    realization of 56
    solving problems of attach-
        ment 5
    training in 56, 206
requesting the turning of the
    Wheel of Dharma 219
Rinchen Sangpo 16, 17
Root Tantra of Heruka 237
Rupakaya 85. *See also* Form
    Body

S

samsara 6, 8, 27, 45, 53, 65,
    105, 116, 130, 266
    free from 86, 199
    no real happiness in 57, 81
    root of 120, 148, 155

Sangha 35, 37, 205. *See also*
     refuge
Saraha 58
satisfaction 54
scientific method 7, 23
Secret Mantra 145. *See also*
     Tantra
self-cherishing 100, 141, 164
  abandoning 88
  and self-grasping 72
  destroying 89, 90
  disadvantages of 72–75, 77
  what is 72
self-generation 187, 198, 240,
     241, 242, 245
self-grasping 45, 57, 89, 90,
     114, 141, 154, 155.
  abandonment of 9
     profound bliss of 181
  and self-cherishing 72
  cessation of 183
  dependent on mounted wind
     182
  different aspects of 120
  imprints of 110, 114, 125
  inner poison 57
  poisonous tree of 60
  reducing 128
  root of 148
  source of all delusions and
     suffering 5, 7, 9, 57, 61
sense awareness 271
sense powers 271
Serlingpa 15
seven limbs 212–222
Seven Sets of Abhidharma 14
sexual intercourse 183, 189
sexual misconduct 39

Shakyamuni, Buddha 2, 7, 14,
     20, 188, 207
  founder of Buddhism 3
  reliance upon 10
Shantideva 74, 102, 105, 106,
     107, 187, 188, 189. *See also*
     Guide to the Bodhisattva's
     Way of Life
Sherab Tseg 237
Shilarakshita 14
sickness 22, 36, 90, 231. *See
     also* suffering, of sickness
  freedom from 185
six perfections 15
  as our daily practice 84
  training in 83–95
Six-session Yoga, Condensed
     287–290
Six Yogas of Naropa 190
Song of the Spring Queen 182
special request prayer 221–222
speech wheel 202
spiritual experience 46, 51
Spiritual Guide 12, 17, 19, 83,
     191, 194, 221. *See also* Guru
  as Buddha 151
  as emanation of Buddha 138
  as emanation of Heruka 194
  inner 60, 81
  reliance upon 138–139, 207.
     See also Guru yoga
  who is our 207
spiritual path 23, 29, 37, 69, 243
  necessary conditions for 62
  training in 238
  transforming daily actions
     into 247
  transforming daily
     experiences into 242

transforming worldly pleasure into 147, 148
spiritual practice 40, 50, 52, 62, 151
Spiritual Teacher 38, 138, 205, 207
spontaneous great bliss 163, 184, 203. *See also* great bliss
Stages of the Path to Enlightenment 10
stealing 39, 75, 122
subtle body 187, 200
subtle minds 171, 176
  black near-attainment 172, 173, 174, 175
    of reverse order 176
  red increase 172, 174, 175
    of reverse order 176
  white appearance 171, 172, 174, 175
    of reverse order 176
suffering 4, 6, 8, 9. *See also* future lives, suffering of; human beings, suffering of
  changing 81, 93
  conceptions of eight extremes, root of 120
  developing fear of 56
  from non-virtuous actions 38
  from self-cherishing 73
  future, prevention of 215
  human, basis of 45
  liberation from 6, 9, 36
  of ageing 8, 37, 47–50, 61
  of birth 43–45
  of death 8, 23, 37, 50–51
  of others 76, 79
  of rebirth 8, 53, 61, 79
  of sickness 8, 23, 37, 45–47, 61
  of this life 42
  other types of 52–56
  permanent liberation from 61–62, 199
  protection from 3
  root of 5
Sukhavati. *See* Pure Land
Superior being 124, 175
superior seeing 86, 137
suppleness 184, 198, 227
Sutra 1–142, 145, 147, 184, 188, 240
  as basic foundation 183
  Buddha nature in 185
  gross body is the real body, according to 188
  types of bliss 181
Sutra and Tantra 4, 10, 16, 20, 87
  no contradiction between 147
  union of 146
Sutra of the Four Noble Truths 41, 56, 58, 61

T

taking
  in conjunction with six perfections 87–92
  meditations on 89–90
taking and giving 83
  benefits of 87
  in conjunction with six perfections 87–95
  in Highest Yoga Tantra 245

Tantra 143–248. *See also*
  completion stage; generation
  stage; Mahamudra
 as Buddha's ultimate
  intention 183
 definition of 147
 divisions of 237
 four classes of 148
 preciousness of 145–151
 principal objects abandoned
  in 149–151
 synonyms of 145
 uncommon attainment of 16
Tantric commitment objects
  274
Tantric Grounds and Paths 272,
  290
Tantric practitioner 153, 189
Tantric vows 15
Temples 37
ten grounds 15
Theravada 3
The Yoga of Buddha Heruka 207,
  209, 273–290
things that we normally see
  57, 132, 133, 141, 148. *See
  also* inherent existence
three higher realms 8
three higher trainings 15–16,
  58–61, 181. *See also*
  concentration; moral
  discipline; wisdom
 meditation on 61
Three Jewels 37
three lower realms 8, 27, 32. *See
  also* lower rebirth; rebirth
Togden Jampel Gyatso 191

*Training the Mind in Seven
  Points* 109, 133
tranquil abiding 16, 85, 137,
  181, 184, 227
transference of consciousness
  30, 199
transmission 208
Trisong Detsen 16
true existence 98, 100, 105,
  107, 108, 117, 122. *See also*
  inherent existence
true-grasping ignorance 114.
  See also self-grasping
true nature. *See* ultimate
  nature; ultimate truth
 of body 105, 106
 of phenomena 107, 116
truth 107. *See also* conventional
  truth; ultimate truth; union
  of two truths
 synonyms of 123
Truth Body 85, 154, 173, 194,
  245
 cause of 187
 Heruka imputed upon 222
 Nature 149, 222
 Wisdom 149, 222
tummo 161, 183, 190, 198, 199
Tushita. *See* Pure Land
twenty-four places 264
 inner places 265, 266
 of Heruka 201
 of our body 201
 outer places 266
two abandonments. *See* central
  channel

U

ultimate bodhichitta 125, 138, 188
  definition of 97
  levels of 125
  simple training in 135–139
  training in 97–139
ultimate example clear light 163, 175. *See also* example clear light
  meaning of 179
ultimate nature 106, 107, 121, 128. *See also* ultimate truth
  of I 114
  of mind 109
ultimate search 101, 102
ultimate truth 97, 229. *See also* emptiness; ultimate nature; union of the two truths
  conventional truth and 121–127
  definition of 124
  solving daily problems of ignorance 5
  synonyms of 123
uncontaminated mind
  definition of 124
unfindability 107, 134
  of body 105
  of I 113, 114
  of mind 109
union of great bliss and emptiness 180, 185, 186, 188, 194. *See also* Mahamudra; meaning clear light
  as the actual inconceivability 247

union of meaning clear light and pure illusory body 163, 180
Union of No More Learning 187, 196
union of our very subtle wind and very subtle mind 164, 168
union of spontaneous great bliss and emptiness 265
union of Sutra and Tantra 146–147
  no pure practice of 17
union of the indestructible wind and mind 186
union of the two truths 127–132
  realization of 222
universal compassion 28, 69, 76, 90, 147. *See also* compassion
  quick path to enlightenment 71
  solving problems of anger 5
  training in 79–80
unmistaken awareness 124
unproduced space 118, 131

V

Vairochana 269
vajra body 185, 187, 188
Vajradhara 190, 192, 218, 243
Vajradharma 224, 243
vajra-like concentration 150
Vajra Master 182
vajra recitation 272
Vajrasattva 217, 243
Vajravarahi 193, 200, 201, 202, 203

Vajrayana 145. *See also* Tantra
Vajrayana path 231
Vajrayogini 194, 195, 197, 198,
  200, 236
  body mandala of 246
  instructions of 237–247
  mandala of 244
valid mind 122, 123, 134
very subtle body 93, 185, 187,
  221. *See also* body,
  continuously residing
  manifesting at sleep and
  death 186
very subtle mind 39, 99, 164,
  185, 221, 229. *See also* mind,
  continuously residing
  and emptiness 173
  imprint on 39
  manifesting at sleep and
  death 186, 238
  manifesting during sleep
  240
  mounted upon very subtle
  wind 173
  perceiving emptiness 238
  realization of clear light 239
  realizing two truths 230
very subtle speech 165, 185
  manifesting at sleep and
  death 186
very subtle wind. *See* winds,
  very subtle
Vidyakokila 12
Vinaya 17
virtue/non-virtue 32
virtuous actions 38, 39, 40, 49,
  51, 75

dedication of 220
rejoicing in 217

W

war 217
Wheel of Dharma 3, 219, 386
white appearance. *See* subtle
  minds, white appearance
wind/s 162–164
  called 'life-force' 267
  definition of 267
  different elements, of the
  169–171
  dissolving at death 175–176,
  186
  downward-voiding 163, 183,
  184, 268, 272
  entering, abiding and
  dissolving 159, 163, 166,
  190, 238
  degree of dissolution 179
  into indestructible drop 176
  signs of 168–176, 186
  through body mandala of
  Vajrayogini 246
  equally-abiding 163, 268,
  269, 272
  explanation of inner 267–272
  five branch 163, 269, 271–272
  chart of 271
  function of 267
  gross 169, 174, 272
  impure 163, 265
  life-supporting 163, 268, 271
  three levels of 272
  mounted by mind of black
  near-attainment 172, 173,
  174

mounted by mind of red
   increase 172, 174
mounted by mind of white
   appearance 171, 172, 174
mounts for minds 162, 267
   of self-grasping 163, 182
pervading 163, 268, 269, 272
root
   chart of 270
   six characteristics 268
seven, permanent cessation
   of 176
subtle 169, 174, 267
upward-moving 163, 268,
   269, 272
very subtle 164, 173, 186
wisdom 4, 67, 153, 155, 157.
   See also three higher trainings
   cause of Truth Body 85
   increasing 133
   inner light of 26, 80
   manifestation of 237
   nature and function of 59
   of meditative equipoise 125
   perfection of 84, 86–87, 88, 95
   possessed by Buddhas 230
   realizing emptiness, solving
      problems of ignorance 5
   uncontaminated 125
wisdom being/s 231, 233
   inviting 211–212
Wisdom Dharma Protector 11,
   144
wishfulfilling jewel 21, 82, 93
wishing love 66, 94, 95
   eight benefits of 78
   training in 77–78
world 51, 153, 158, 266

as karmic appearance
   116–117
conventional 133
created by mind 117, 145,
   158
dream 30, 99, 134, 145
impure 8
material development in 25
modern 4
waking 99, 117, 133, 134
worldly
   intelligence 60
   people 107
   pleasure 31, 54
   transforming 147, 148–149
wrathful actions 231
wrong awarenesses 57, 115,
   118
wrong objects 6
wrong views 39

Y

Yamantaka 195
Yeshe Ö 17, 18, 19
yoga, meaning of 238
yoga of being blessed by
   Heroes and Heroines 246
yoga of daily actions 247
yoga of equalizing samsara
   and nirvana 130
yoga of experiencing nectar
   242
yoga of immeasurables 243
yoga of inconceivability 247
yoga of purifying migrators
   245–246
yoga of rising 241, 242

yoga of self-generation 245
yoga of sleeping 238, 240–241,
    242
yoga of the Guru 243–245
yoga of verbal and mental
    recitation 246
yogas of the channel, drop and
    wind 165, 189

Yogi 142
Yogini/s 142
  of the great bliss wheel
    201–202

Z

Zen 3

Further Reading

———————— ❧ ————————

If you have enjoyed reading this book and would like to find out more about Buddhist thought and practice, here are some other books by Geshe Kelsang Gyatso that you might like to read. They are all available from Tharpa Publications.

INTRODUCTION TO BUDDHISM
An explanation of the Buddhist way of life

An ideal guide for everyone interested in Buddhism and meditation. This book presents the central principles behind the Buddhist way of life, such as meditation and karma, as tools for developing qualities such as inner peace, love and patience.

'A brilliantly clear and concise introduction to this vast subject. Very highly recommended.' *Yoga & Health Magazine*

TRANSFORM YOUR LIFE
A blissful journey

By following the practical advice given in this book, we can transform our mind and our life, fulfil our human potential, and find everlasting peace and happiness.

'We all enjoy limitless possibility for happiness and fulfilment; this book can help us attain it ... a work of deep spiritual insight.' *The Napra Review*

THE NEW MEDITATION HANDBOOK
A practical guide to Buddhist meditation

This popular and practical manual allows us to discover for ourselves the inner peace and lightness of mind that comes from meditation. The author explains twenty-one step-by-step meditations that lead to increasingly beneficial states of mind, and that together form the entire Buddhist path to enlightenment.

'This manual provides a succinct and inspiring overview of the many ways in which Buddhism can be applied to the situations and activities of daily life.' *Spirituality and Health*

HOW TO SOLVE OUR HUMAN PROBLEMS
The Four Noble Truths

This book shows how Buddha's popular teaching on the Four Noble Truths can help us to solve basic human problems such as dissatisfaction and anger, and provides a profound illumination of our human experience and our potential for deep inner freedom.

'This book offers peace of mind in these troubled times.' *Publishing News*

'Geshe Kelsang Gyatso has a unique gift for addressing everyday difficulties.' *Booklist*

MAHAMUDRA TANTRA
The supreme heart jewel nectar

Tantra is very popular, but very few understand its real meaning. This book explains how we can attain the sublime union of bliss and emptiness, known as Mahamudra, which is the very essence of Buddhist Tantric meditation.

'This book renders everything so clearly that I would propose this book as both an excellent introduction to Buddhist practice and for those seeking to complete the training.' *Amazon Reviewer, Madrid, Spain*

To order any of our publications, or to request a catalogue, please visit www.tharpa.com or contact your nearest Tharpa office listed on page 391.